KEY CONCEPTS IN CRIME FICTION

Palgrave Key Concepts

Palgrave Key Concepts provide an accessible and comprehensive range of subject glossaries at undergraduate level. They are the ideal companion to a standard textbook making them invaluable reading to students throughout their course of study and especially useful as a revision aid.

Key Concepts in Accounting and Finance
Key Concepts in Bilingualism
Key Concepts in Business and Management Research Methods
Key Concepts in Business Practice
Key Concepts in Criminology and Criminal Justice
Key Concepts in Cultural Studies
Key Concepts in Drama and Performance (second edition)
Key Concepts in e-Commerce
Key Concepts in Human Resource Management
Key Concepts in Information and Communication Technology
Key Concepts in Innovation
Key Concepts in International Business
Key Concepts in Language and Linguistics (second edition)
Key Concepts in Law (second edition)
Key Concepts in Leisure
Key Concepts in Management
Key Concepts in Marketing
Key Concepts in Operations Management
Key Concepts in Philosophy
Key Concepts in Politics
Key Concepts in Public Relations
Key Concepts in Psychology
Key Concepts in Second Language Acquisition
Key Concepts in Social Research Methods
Key Concepts in Sociology
Key Concepts in Strategic Management
Key Concepts in Tourism

Palgrave Key Concepts: Literature

General Editor: Martin Coyle

Key Concepts in Contemporary Literature
Key Concepts in Creative Writing
Key Concepts in Crime Fiction
Key Concepts in Medieval Literature
Key Concepts in Modernist Literature
Key Concepts in Postcolonial Literature
Key Concepts in Renaissance Literature
Key Concepts in Romantic Literature
Key Concepts in Victorian Literature
Literary Terms and Criticism (third edition)

Further titles are in preparation

Key Concepts in Crime Fiction

Heather Worthington

palgrave
macmillan

First published 2011 by
PALGRAVE MACMILLAN

Palgrave Macmillan in the UK is an imprint of Macmillan Publishers Limited, registered in England, company number 785998, of 4 Crinan Street, London N1 9XW.

Palgrave® and Macmillan® are registered trademarks in the United States, the United Kingdom, Europe and other countries.

ISBN 978–0–230–55125–1

This book is printed on paper suitable for recycling and made from fully managed and sustained forest sources. Logging, pulping and manufacturing processes are expected to conform to the environmental regulations of the country of origin.

A catalogue record for this book is available from the British Library.

A catalog record for this book is available from the Library of Congress.

Printed and bound by CPI Group (UK) Ltd, Croydon, CR0 4YY

To David, who made it all possible

Contents

General Editor's Preface

The purpose of Palgrave Key Concepts in Literature is to provide students with key critical and historical ideas about the texts they are studying as part of their literature courses. These ideas include information about the historical and cultural contexts of literature as well as the theoretical approaches current in the subject today. Behind the series lies a recognition of the need nowadays for students to be familiar with a range of concepts and contextual material to inform their reading and writing about literature.

The series is also based on a recognition of the changes that have transformed degree courses in Literature in recent years. Central to these changes has been the impact of critical theory together with a renewed interest in the way in which texts intersect with their immediate context and historical circumstances. The result has been an opening up of new ways of reading texts and a new understanding of what the study of literature involves together with the introduction of a wide set of new critical issues that demand our attention. An important aim of Palgrave Key Concepts in Literature is to provide brief, accessible introductions to these new ways of reading and new issues.

Each volume in Palgrave Key Concepts in Literature follows the same structure. An initial overview essay is followed by three sections – *Contexts, Texts*, and *Criticism* – each containing a sequence of brief alphabetically arranged entries on a sequence of topics. 'Contexts' essays provide an impression of the historical, social and cultural environment in which literary texts were produced. 'Texts' essays, as might be expected, focus more directly on the works themselves. 'Criticism' essays then outline the manner in which changes and developments in criticism have affected the ways in which we discuss the texts featured in the volume. The informing intention throughout is to help the reader create something new in the process of combining context, text and criticism.

Martin Coyle

General Introduction

Crime fiction, in the early twenty-first century, exceeds all other genres of fiction in popularity, even romance. More crime fiction is bought for and borrowed from libraries than any other genre of fiction. Best-seller lists in newspapers and magazines invariably include crime fiction titles; bookshops have dedicated crime fiction sections; television and film offer many and varied interpretations of the genre. The texts are read across the social scale, appealing to women and to a lesser degree men, to the young and to the old as well as the merely middle-aged. There is a widespread, even global, general acknowledgement and acceptance of the genre and of what its narratives comprise: a crime, a criminal, a victim and a detective. But it is precisely its popularity that has, in the past, barred crime fiction from serious literary consideration.

Academic study of the genre is a relatively recent addition to undergraduate courses, and students often approach crime fiction with no real concept of its importance or relevance to the study of literature and culture. After all, they reason, it is popular literature, pulp fiction, contemporary, ephemeral, disposable, accessible reading, undemanding, non-canonical, non-academic: an easy option. Nothing could be further from the truth; it is not by chance that poststructuralist critics such as Slavoj Zizek, Jacques Derrida, Barbara Johnson and Catherine Belsey have turned to crime fiction to illustrate, support and explicate their theoretical readings of the body—corpus?—of literature. Central to fictions of crime is the desire to discover that which is concealed, hear that which is unspoken, to decipher the codes. The very process of literary analysis is closely aligned to the work of the detective in fiction.

Crime fiction is at once deeply conservative in its formulaic conventions and yet potentially radical in its diversity. What seems superficially simple is, in fact, complex. The genre offers new and exciting insights into the cultures that produce it; its very status as popular and accessible literature means that it responds quickly to change, that it can incorporate cultural and social shifts almost immediately into its texts. We see clearly, in crime fiction, the anxieties, the morals and values of the contemporary society. And crime fiction can truly claim to be the only fiction that deals with fact. This is apparent on two levels: within the fiction, in order to discover 'whodunnit', the detective must necessarily ascertain the facts of the case; equally, because what constitutes crime is inscribed in the legislature of the nation in which the crime takes place, and because the procedures that the investigation and investigators must follow and the court proceedings that may result from that investigation are themselves factual, the crime fiction narrative must also know the legal, procedural, juridical facts. For these reasons, the genre, in the guise of entertainment, offers the reader unrivalled access to the legal, moral and social values of the past and the present.

Further, crime is the deviant action of the marginalised individual that defines the normative centre of society, and fictions of crime bring clearly into view the structures of power in society and the ideologies that promulgate and support those structures. As Nathaniel Hawthorne pointed out in *The Scarlet Letter* (1850), in early American settlements or other colonies, the first public building to be erected after designating a burial ground was usually a prison. Crime, like death, is always with us, and crime fiction is a useful tool in examining culture past and present. There is a general consensus among literary critics that it was in the nineteenth and twentieth centuries that crime fiction developed into a recognisable literary genre, but its origins are much contested and discussed.

Crime, after all, has appeared in narratives oral and written for as long as there have been communities of people co-existing together: co-existence requires regulation as the condition of its possibility, whether imposed or mutually agreed regulation. There has to be a system of ordering society to prevent a slide into chaos and anarchy. And in creating rules or regulations or laws, society implicitly creates the criminal in the individual who refuses or fails to comply with the system of governance. In very basic terms, it could be argued that, as Freud suggested, civilisation creates its own discontents; discontents frequently figured as criminal by the 'civilised' society that produces them. Crime, criminals and criminality, then, are evidence of deviance from the cultural and social norm; as such, they offer a useful way into reading the changes in cultures and societies over time. But what such study demonstrates is that crime is temporally and culturally conditional; consequently, the definition of what constitutes crime is constantly shifting.

Similarly, what constitutes crime fiction is equally difficult to define. I have suggested that the popular concept of crime fiction is a narrative that features a crime, a criminal, a victim and a detective. But this is not necessarily always the case. There are stories about crime that feature no detective; there are detective stories that feature no crime as such; there are even tales that focus on the elucidation of a mystery where there is no crime, no detective and no victim, or where the position of the characters as criminal, detective or victim changes according to the play of the narrative and the demands of the plot, as in Edgar Allan Poe's 'The Purloined Letter' (1845).

The game of defining the constituent texts and textual constituents of the crime fiction genre has been played by many critics over time. The apparently simplest description—a narrative which features a crime—seems rather to complicate than to simplify the task of definition. The Bible story of Cain and Abel has a crime, a victim and a perpetrator of crime who is subsequently discovered and punished; the story of Oedipus can also be read as a crime narrative. Dorothy L. Sayers has the Jewish apocryphal scriptural tales of 'The History of Bel' and 'Susannah and the Elders' as fictions of crime, along with extracts from the *Aeneid* and Herodotus. Under this umbrella definition we can also place folk and fairy tales: 'Little Red Riding Hood' is a narrative of social and implicitly moral transgression that results in death at the hands, or rather the teeth, of the wolf. In later versions, the wolf in turn is punished for his crime and Red Riding Hood survives. But tales such as these seem a long way from the genre as we recognise it today.

This, then, is one of the first problems the student of crime fiction—or the writer of a text about crime fiction—encounters. For the purposes of this text, I propose to use the term 'crime fiction' as a general signifier for this diverse range of texts, but to focus on the numerous sub-genres that have contributed, and are still contributing, to the genre as we know it today. Crime fiction, or criminography, here will, then, refer to all literary material, fiction or fact, that has crime, or the appearances of crime, at its centre and as its *raison d'être*. Such a definition permits me to reject the biblical stories or the classics or folk and fairy tales or indeed the works of Chaucer and the plays of Shakespeare, where the crime is of secondary interest, and to concentrate on narratives that concern themselves with crime in the modern sense. This further sets a temporal limit on the texts, themes and concepts to be discussed; broadly, the literature will be drawn from the nineteenth and twentieth centuries, with brief excursions into the eighteenth century in search of the emerging patterns of the genre and into the twenty-first century to locate the latest variations and experimentations.

Early crime narratives from the eighteenth century, the broadsides, the *Accounts* of the Ordinaries of Newgate and the collected editions of the *Newgate Calendars* all focused on the criminal, his or her life, crimes and execution and their formats—single sheet, pamphlet and five-volume edition—were geared to the income level of the intended audience (see Texts: Early Criminography). These early crime narratives were largely factual in content but written with profit in mind and so enlivened with personal details of the criminal and with revelatory glimpses into the life of crime they led. Some broadsides were clearly apocryphal, but even these often had their origins in something approaching reality. Importantly, William Godwin drew on precisely this kind of criminographic material in his 1793 novel *Caleb Williams, or; Things as They Are*, a narrative which used crime and the law in a philosophical critique of the contemporary social and political systems. This text has been discussed as an early example of detective fiction and as a crime novel, but its function as social commentary is clear evidence of how crime and criminality articulate the values of the society by which they are produced.

It was in this early criminography that what we know as crime fiction first began to take on a recognisable shape. Its production and proliferation in the eighteenth and early nineteenth century were in part a response to what was perceived to be a sharp rise in crime in Britain, a rise supported by, or more likely the result of, the enormous number of capital offences that came onto the statute books in this period. One of the consequences of this perceived rise, perhaps triggered by an awareness of the waste of human life and the labour demands of the burgeoning capitalist commodity culture, was the beginning of the move away from the focus on the punishment of the crime via the body of the criminal to the possibility of the recuperation of the criminal individual into an obedient and productive subject (as discussed by Michel Foucault in *Discipline and Punish*, 1977). A second consequence, and a vital factor in the creation of the crime fiction genre, was the inauguration, in London, of a State-funded police force in 1829.

But the New Metropolitan Police, as they were called, took some time to enter the world of literature. Crime, though, found a new mode of literary expression in the contemporary periodicals, and this can clearly be seen in *Blackwood's Edinburgh Magazine*, or 'Maga' as it became known. The fictional tales in *Blackwood's* dealt with the sensational, literally; they were narratives of terror and tragedy calculated to arouse physical and emotional responses in the reader, and a favourite topic was crime. The focus was still very much the criminal and his/her actions, but there is evidence of a questioning of the nature of crime, of the psychology or sociology that drives the individual to deviate from the norm. The periodical criminography in the early nineteenth century was often concerned with the reliability of circumstantial evidence, suggesting unease about the fairness and justice of the penal system. Where the ultimate criminal deterrent is death, it behoves the system to provide reliable evidence of guilt.

But it was not just narratives concerned directly with crime that contributed to the formation of the genre. It was in *Blackwood's* that the longest-running and the best example of the anecdotes of a professional man was published, with Samuel Warren's 'Passages from the Diary of a Late Physician' (1830-7). This short-lived sub-genre of fiction was instrumental in the later development of detective fiction. In Warren's 'Passages', the medical man recounts his encounters with a series of patients; nominally, he investigates illness, but the illness is more often the symptom of moral misdemeanour than physical disease. Actual crime plays a part in some of his cases, but the importance of the stories lies in the establishment of the case structure familiar to the modern reader of crime fiction and in the professional investigative figure who links the cases together.

Warren's 'Physician's' stories were followed by a spate of similar fictional professional anecdotes, published in a variety of journals and featuring a number of professions, circa 1830-50. The focus of the narratives shifted from the medical to the legal as the 'Experiences of a Barrister' appeared serially in 1849, followed by the 'Confessions of an Attorney' and, almost simultaneously, the 'Recollections of a Police Officer' (1849). While not crime fiction in the modern sense, these narratives brought together the case, the investigation, the professional dealing with, at least in the legal and police stories, crime and criminals. From these small and varied beginnings, then, developed the genre we know as crime fiction. But crime fiction has never been a fixed or stable form, and there would be many more developments and variations on the theme over the course of the nineteenth and twentieth centuries as the narratives responded to the changes in society and in culture, as well as in printing technology and publishing and in the audience for and the reception of printed material.

Nonetheless, by the 1860s, crime narratives had a form recognisable to the modern eye. With the Metropolitan police fully established and accepted by this time, the decade saw the proliferation of police stories (see Contexts: Police and Policing and Texts: The Police Procedural). Significantly, many of these narratives appeared in book form rather than in the periodicals, but they were not yet the full-fledged crime fiction novel. Rather, these early texts were collections of cases, a series of short stories connected by their protagonist and his/her profession. But crime also featured in the novels of the first half of the nineteenth century. The so-called 'Newgate Novels' of the 1830s, such as Edward Bulwer Lytton's *Paul Clifford* (1830) and *Eugene Aram* (1832) or William Harrison Ainsworth's *Rookwood* (1834) and *Jack Sheppard* (1839) took criminals real and imagined and made them the heroes of their narratives, and this too fed into the development of the genre. Dickens by contrast was fascinated by the criminal and equally by the police and their activities.

He had written on the real police in his 'Detective Police' anecdotes in the 1850s; *Bleak House* (1853) was concerned with crime, as had been *Oliver Twist* (1837) and *Martin Chuzzlewit* (1843–4). By the 1860s, crime was, if not central to many of the novels being published, frequently present, if only peripherally so: the presence of crime in fiction was an essential part of what became known as sensation fiction, a genre which consisted of novels that, as the name suggests, aroused physical and emotional sensations in their readers.

Sensation novels such as Wilkie Collins's *The Woman in White* (1860), Mrs Henry Wood's *East Lynne* (1861), Mary E. Braddon's *Lady Audley's Secret* (1862), all incorporated crime into their tales of love and intrigue. But this is still not crime fiction; the short stories circulating in the periodicals, the use of crime in fiction, these were commonplace in this period. Then, in 1868, Wilkie Collins's *The Moonstone* began its serialisation. T. S. Eliot claimed this text to be 'the first and the greatest of English detective novels' as well as the longest, and it can fairly be considered as crime fiction in a very modern sense, featuring a crime, a country-house setting, a number of detectives, private and police, and the presentation of clues to the reader. In Britain, then, from the 1860s , crime featured in short stories in the periodicals and in novels, and became a popular item on the nation's literary menu. But the development of the genre was not solely within the realm of the British. Writers elsewhere had been playing with crime in their narratives, and this too had an influence on the nascent genre in England.

In France, ex-thief and police informer Eugène Françoise Vidocq rose through the ranks of the police to become head of the *brigade de sûreté*, in which capacity he continued to work until 1827. On his retirement, he published his autobiography, first in France, and subsequently in England. His *Mémoires* cannot be ignored: they are an important element in the development of the crime fiction genre and influenced other writers concerned with crime, most clearly, perhaps, Edgar Allan Poe and Arthur Conan Doyle. Poe is, of course, American, but he chose to set his stories concerned with crime in the Paris of Vidocq, that is, the Paris of the early nineteenth century. Poe wrote just three narratives featuring his proto-detective, the Chevalier C. Auguste Dupin: 'The Murders in the Rue Morgue' (1841), 'The Mystery of Marie Rogêt' (1842) and 'The Purloined Letter' (1845). In these short stories, Dupin undertakes to find the solution to a mystery rather than of a crime, but many of the methods he appears to use and his characterisation find their way into later crime fiction, specifically in the depiction of Doyle's Sherlock Holmes.

And the French influence does not end there. In the 1860s, Emile Gaboriau produced a series of novels featuring a private and a police detective, starting with *L'Affaire Lerouge* (1865), followed by *Le Crime d'Orcival* (1867), *Le Dossier no. 113* (1867) and *Monsieur Lecoq* (1869). These texts rapidly came into circulation in Britain and America as well as France, although they were not available in translation in Britain until the 1880s (earlier in America). Their influence, largely unremembered though the texts are now, like that of Vidocq and of Poe, cannot be ignored. Nor can, or should, nineteenth-century American criminography other than that of Poe be disregarded. There are strong connections and parallels between the development of the crime fiction genre in the United Stares and in Britain which continue to this day (see Texts: American Crime Fiction). Charles Brockden Brown has been considered an early American exponent of proto-detective fiction with *Edgar Huntley* (1799) and *Arthur Mervyn* (1799/1800), while James Fenimore Cooper's pioneer novels introduced the skilled, independent tracker-hero who would develop into the hard-boiled detective hero of 1930s American crime fiction.

America also had its periodicals which, like their British counter-parts, had a considerable output of criminal material. Edgar Allan Poe published his many short stories, criminal and Gothic, in periodicals, and was, for a time, the editor of William Burton's *Gentleman's Magazine* (Burton himself was of British origin). In 1838, this magazine published a series of professional anecdotes entitled 'The Diary of a Philadelphia Lawyer', paralleling 'Passages from the Diary of a Late Physician' and pre-dating the British legal anecdotes such as 'Experiences of a Barrister'. Louisa May Alcott and Harriet Prescott Spofford both wrote sensational crime–inflected stories for the periodicals in the late 1850s and 1860s. In terms of female authorship of early crime fiction, the Americans seem to have taken the lead. Anna Katharine Green's *The Leavenworth Case* (1878) has long been considered the first full-length detective novel written by a woman, and her later spinster-detective, Miss Amelia Butterworth, can be seen as the prototype for the subsequent elderly spinster-detectives of Golden-Age crime fiction such as Agatha Christie's Miss Marple. More recently, *The Dead Letter* (published in 1866 in book form; originally appeared in *Beadle's Monthly* from 1865) by Seeley Regester, the pseudonym of Metta Victoria Fuller Victor, has claimed the title of the first female-authored detective novel. Green, however, published under her own name, which suggests that women writing crime had become acceptable by the 1870s (see Texts: Feminist Crime Fiction; American Crime Fiction).

By the 1870s, fictions of crime were, then, on both sides of the Atlantic and in Europe, beginning to take on a recognisable appearance. The next major stage in the development of the genre was the creation of Sherlock

Holmes, the archetypal detective and the creation that has most strongly influenced subsequent crime fiction and its authors from Agatha Christie to P. D. James, Raymond Chandler to Thomas Harris. Doyle's Sherlock Holmes and his cases were both an end and a beginning: Doyle's genius was to take the best from what had come before and refine it into a cohesive and compelling form, and so successful was his format that it superseded its predecessors and shaped its successors (see Contexts: Detectives and Detection; Evidence). What Doyle's narratives established was a recognisable, fully formed detective figure whose profession was the detection of crime. They also established a strong narrative form and brought together a number of themes that would shape future crime fiction: the crime, followed by the pursuit and capture of the criminal, culminating in the retrospective explanation; the humble assistant who functions to enhance the brilliance of the detective and to narrate his adventures; the relationship between criminal and detective. Perhaps most important of all was the character of Holmes himself; cultured but not pretentious, intellectual but also a man of action, arrogant and intimidating but moral and sympathetic, his superiority ameliorated by his eccentricity. The allure of the character was used to maximum advantage by the serial form in which the narratives were published. Each Sherlock Holmes case was a reminder of earlier stories and a promise of future tales.

While Doyle's creation is widely thought of a nineteenth-century or Victorian figure, Holmes's cases continued to appear in the *Strand Magazine* and in collected form up until 1927. Simultaneously, the early twentieth century saw a multitude of crime and detective fiction published, initially largely in the periodicals and then increasingly in novel form. Where the nineteenth century had seen the consolidation of the genre, the twentieth would see its diversification. In the early 1900s, the short story was particularly popular, and writers continued to draw heavily on the Holmes pattern of detection and on the series concept, pursuing a single detective figure through a number of cases. Intellect, rationality and science were key concepts in the depiction and detective methods of many of these serial detectives, masculine attributes that were calculated to appeal to the largely masculine, white-collar, suburban and commuting readers of the periodicals in which the narratives appeared.

Not all the protagonists of these short stories aspired to the genius of Sherlock Holmes; Arthur Morrison's Martin Hewitt was an ordinary and unassuming detective, while G. K. Chesterton's Father Brown appears to reject scientific detection in favour of a kind of psychological and intuitive reading of character and motive—actually an illusory shield for inductive reasoning. Jacques Futrelle's super-intellectual detective,

Professor Augustus S. F. X. Van Dusen, or 'The Thinking Machine', was an American challenger to Holmes. Dr John Thorndyke, the creation of R. Austin Freeman, drew on the scientific aspects of Holmes in his forensic approach to detection. But the field was not entirely populated by men: female detectives also featured in the pages of the periodicals, although to a far lesser extent than their masculine counterparts. Grant Allen wrote two different female detectives, Miss Caley and Miss Wade, whose stories appeared in the *Strand Magazine*; L. T. Meade—a female author—and Robert Eustace collaborated in the creation of Florence Cusack, another lady investigator. Whether featuring male or female detectives, these short stories all bore the imprint of Doyle's Holmesian fiction in one way or another.

In tandem with the proliferation of short stories in the early years of the twentieth century was an increase in the number of detective novels written and published. Many of their detectives, and indeed, the plotting and structure of their narratives, showed the influence of Sherlock Holmes, but the pattern was becoming diffuse as writers of criminography experimented with or challenged the archetype. But changes to and developments within the genre notwithstanding, detective fiction continued to be widely read. There have been many suggestions as to why the genre should have enjoyed such widespread popularity; the most convincing for me is that detective fiction offered, and indeed still offers, the illusion of security and safety and continuity in what was becoming a disordered, insecure and disturbing world as the Victorian era drew to its end and the Edwardian period commenced. A significant turning point in the evolution of crime fiction was World War I (1914–18). The enormous social, technical and economic changes resulting from that conflict were instrumental in changing British society and its reading habits.

There were two important factors here: the emancipation of women that occurred during the war created a new and demanding audience for novels, which was catered for by the increasing number of circulating libraries such as those associated with Boots the Chemist or W. H. Smith, the book and newspaper wholesaler. This new audience had more economic power as working women, or more leisure time as non-working middle-class wives, and the books they demanded were those that would represent their own worldview and society to themselves. Detective fiction, with its implicit promise of the preservation of the social status quo, was ideal for this audience, and crime fiction vied for space with romances and light novels on the library and bookshop shelves. The second significant factor in changing patterns of reading was the alteration in the format of the material resulting from the decline in popularity of the magazine and periodical. Urban living and working patterns and new modes of transport meant that readers no longer had the time or the opportunity to read short stories as they travelled to work; many now went by car; railway journeys became shorter and quicker. Newspapers took over from the periodicals in providing entertainment for men going to and from work, and in their leisure time men as well as women looked to books to provide their fictional reading material.

This move from the short story to the novel form marks the beginning of what has become known as the 'Golden-Age' of detective fiction, commencing broadly circa 1913 and continuing on into the 1940s. While this period saw the inauguration and rise in popularity of what have become known as 'clue-puzzle' mysteries, there were many variations of the theme and other sub-genres of crime fiction were published and widely read in these years, including the psychothriller and the police procedural. According to Julian Symons in *Bloody Murder: from the Detective Story to the Crime Novel* (1972), based on reviews of detective novels appearing between 1914 and 1939, 'the number of crime stories published had multiplied by five in 1926 and by ten in 1939'. Crime fiction in the sense in which we know it today had come firmly into being. While there were many male authors writing crime fiction in this period, in keeping with its new, predominantly female audience, a new generation of female writers appeared. And perhaps the best-known contributor to the genre in this 'Golden' era was Agatha Christie.

Christie's first novel, *The Mysterious Affair at Styles*, appeared in 1920, in the early days of the Golden-Age. It clearly showed the influence of Doyle's Sherlock Holmes stories in its introduction of Hercule Poirot and his assistant in detection, Hastings. The relationship between the two characters mimics faithfully that of Holmes and Watson, though Christie subsequently broke the Poirot–Hastings alliance, sending Hastings off to Argentina and providing Poirot with a faithful valet/secretary as assistant, a master–servant partnership seen in various forms in other crime fiction of the period: Dorothy L. Sayers's protagonist Lord Peter Wimsey has his valet, Bunter; Margery Allingham's Albert Campion his manservant, Lugg; Gladys Mitchell's Mrs Lestrange Bradley her chauffeur, George Cuddleup. Christie firmly established the 'clue-puzzle' format in which the reader of the narrative is provided with all the clues and information that the detective is afforded. The focus is firmly on plot rather than character, and a common complaint amongst critics of Christie's work is the thinness of her characterisation.

But where many of her (masculine) competitors' popularity has waned over time, Christie's books still sell in their millions. I mention above a number of Golden-Age authors, and it is with intent that I offer Sayers,

Allingham and Mitchell. I could also have included Patricia Wentworth with her spinster-detective Miss Silver and Ngaio Marsh with her patrician police detective Roderick Alleyn. Women writers all, their books also have withstood the test of time and, with the exception perhaps of Patricia Wentworth, are still to be found on library shelves and in book-shops. As Jessica Mann observes in *Deadlier than the Male* (1981), these 'respectable English women are so good at murder'. This preponderance and success of women writers of crime fiction marked the first major break away from what had been a genre largely dominated by men, a break that would in part enable the later appearance and triumphs of not only female writers, but also female detectives.

In America, with Anna Katharine Green as an inspiration, women such as Carolyn Wells and Mary Roberts Rinehart had already ventured into crime fiction with some measure of success, and their work also has survived into the present. The Golden Age was not confined to Britain, then, and was also an American phenomenon, although its focus was certainly British. American authors such as S. S. Van Dine (pseudonym of Willard Huntington Wright), Ellery Queen (actually cousins Frederic Dannay and Manfred B. Lee) and Rex Stout all wrote books that strictly—or sometimes loosely—conformed to the Golden-Age model. These rather mannered narratives were a largely East coast product, although Ellery Queen moved to West coast Hollywood, at least in character. But there was a parallel development in the crime fiction genre in America, one that responded to the frontiersman aspects of the far west. This was what would become known as 'hard-boiled' detective fiction, a sub-genre featuring hard men who faced real and graphic violence in their work, dealing with organised crime and with the crime that proliferated on the West coast in the wake of the oil boom and in tandem with prohibition. The best-known proponents of this genre were Dashiell Hammett, a one-time real Pinkerton detective, whose short stories and novels appeared from 1922 onwards, and Raymond Chandler, who took the gritty material of Hammett and transformed it into a more stylish but still gripping version with his laconic, witty and streetwise detective, Philip Marlowe, who first appeared in *The Big Sleep* (1939). American crime fiction and its hard-boiled sub-genre continued to develop over the twentieth and into the twenty-first century and are discussed further in the 'Texts' section of this volume.

A common, and increasingly important, element in these novels, whether American or British, was the presence of the police. The Holmesian tradition of the bumbling British policeman as foil for the brilliant private detective gradually gave way to a more sympathetic depiction of the police. And in the 1940s, the sub-genre of crime fiction known as the police procedural came into being. George N. Dove suggests in *The Police Procedural* (1982) that the sub-genre came into being in 1945 with the publication of *V as in Victim*, by Lawrence Treat. The police procedural demonstrates clearly how crime fiction responds to cultural change and how immediately and realistically it can re-present contemporary society to itself and to its descendants. Police detectives in fiction now abound and in European crime fiction particularly the protagonist is most likely to be a police officer. The police procedural is still around, if in a mutated form where the emphasis is on the individual maverick police detective rather than on the procedures of the police. Because of their basis in reality, in their dealings with the real fears of society, and because the police, by virtue of their status as employees of the State, are strongly linked to the politics of the day, police procedurals are particularly sensitive to cultural issues such as race and gender and are strongly indicative of national attitudes to and conceptions of criminality and crime.

An early foray into representing race in crime fiction used the police procedural format in that the two protagonists of African-American writer Chester Himes' series of detective novels, set in Harlem, were black police officers. 'Coffin Ed Johnson' and 'Grave Digger Jones' first appeared in *La Reine des Pommes* in 1958 in France, then in America—and in English—as *For the Love of Imabelle* (1959), followed by a further nine books until the series ended in 1970. Race continues to be addressed in crime fiction from the 1960s onwards, initially more usually in America, but today crime fiction is utilised as a locus for the exploration of racial issues and tensions across the globe.

Black women writers have found also crime fiction a useful forum for expressing not only perspectives on racial issues, but also on issues of gender and sexuality; from Dolores Komo's *Clio Browne, Private Detective* (1988) onwards there have been a number of black female detectives, both private and police. Often the protagonists have been not only black, but also lesbian, for example Nikki Baker's Virginia Kelly (four novels, 1991–6). But while the introduction of the modern black female detective, lesbian or heterosexual, was delayed until the late 1980s (Pauline Hopkins' *Talma Gordon*, 1900, is concerned with crime and Hopkins has been designated the 'mother of African-American detective fiction'), crime fiction had for a long time prior to that decade been the site of feminist writing. In a small way the Golden-Age writers such as Christie, with her feminised Poirot and later elderly spinster-detective Miss Marple, and Gladys Mitchell with her fiercely independent Mrs Lestrange Bradley, or even Dorothy L. Sayers with Peter Wimsey's love interest, Harriet Vane, had quietly been promoting proto-feminist values.

In the 1960s, 'Amanda Cross' (pseudonym of feminist theorist and literary critic Carolyn Heilbrun) made an early move towards feminist crime fiction with her creation of Kate Fansler, an intellectual English Literature Professor in New York, who acts as a private detective rather in the clue-puzzle mode. P. D. James made another tentative move towards this sub-genre with Cordelia Gray, a professional female private investigator in *An Unsuitable Job for a Woman* (1972). In line with the early development of the feminist movement itself, it was in America that feminist crime fiction really came into being, and it did so in what has been described as an appropriation of the very masculine genre of hard-boiled detective fiction. Marcia Muller made the first foray into this new territory in *Edwin of the Iron Shoes* (1977). This text depicted Sharon McCone, a single professional woman more than holding her own in the world of private investigation, and set in place many of the patterns seen in later feminist crime fiction: the substitute and/or extended support system of family and female friends, the romantic entanglement, firm sexual identity, empathy with the victim, a strong liberal message, the fight against urban corruption and racial and gender discrimination. Muller's feminist message is relatively low key and implicit, and her text's relationship to the hard-boiled tradition is clear but limited.

With Sara Paretsky's detective protagonist, V. I Warshawski, there are no such limits. Starting with *Indemnity Only* (1982), Paretsky firmly took the Chandleresque model and used it to transmit a liberal feminist message to her readers. The use of the hard-boiled paradigm is made clear in her protagonist's passing references to Philip Marlowe. While Paretsky's early texts can now feel somewhat laboured in their feminism, her work demonstrates the facility with which crime fiction responds to cultural moments and changing anxieties. Her most recent books have moved away from urban corruption and racial/sexual discrimination to consider a wider world perspective and the new threat posed, post 9-11, by terrorism. Sue Grafton perhaps offers a less political and more user-friendly approach to feminist crime fiction with her female private eye, Kinsey Milhone, in an alphabetically titled series (*A is for Alibi*, 1982; the most recent is *U is for Undertow*, 2009; *V is for ?* is promised for late 2011). These texts have provided a platform from which diverse other women detectives have sprung, both private and police.

While Muller, Paretsky and Grafton drew on the hard-boiled tradition in creating their female detectives, their heroines were resolutely heterosexual. Another strand of feminist crime fiction that developed in tandem with the rise of feminism was lesbian detective fiction, exemplified in the novels of Barbara Wilson featuring Pam Nilsen, in Mary Wings' Emma Victor narratives and, in Britain, the Lindsay Gordon novels of Val

McDermid and Stella Duffy's Saz Martin series. That lesbian crime fiction has developed and diversified so rapidly over the last twenty years illustrates crime fiction's ability to respond to and represent changing cultural modes. By contrast, gay crime fiction seems not to have developed so strongly and has always been something of a niche market, as discussed further in the Contexts section of this volume. In terms of gender politics, crime fiction has proven an excellent vehicle for exploring sexual identity and carrying feminist messages to a wide and potentially resistant audience; cloaking the politics in the mantle of popular-genre fiction has made its message more palatable—or even invisible, to be unknowingly internalised by the reader who identifies with the female protagonists of the texts.

The concept of the woman writer as good at crime has continued and been strengthened over the twentieth century. A glance at the best-seller lists in any magazine will show a preponderance of crime fiction titles in the top ten, of which the majority will often be written by women. There are clearly social, cultural and political reasons for this female ownership of the crime fiction market, but perhaps the most important is that women are more likely to experience anxiety and to feel vulnerable in what is still a predominantly patriarchal world. As women have gone out into the world, so to speak, so they have become exposed to potential threats, particularly the threat of physical violence; women demanding equal rights with men have, historically, been met with masculine, often violent, resistance. In the early 1900s, the suffragettes suffered physically at the hands of men, and in the 1970s the feminist movement aroused a violent response in men, particularly in the United States. Historically, women have always been considered to be sexually vulnerable to men. In crime fiction, the threats are combined: the murderer who brings together sexual vulnerability and overt and brutal violence is the serial killer.

This criminal is the main threat in modern crime fiction; in Sherlock Holmes's time, the motive for murder tended to be a perfectly rational and comprehensible desire for money, usually associated with property and inheritance. Money and/or property continued to be the motive in many of the Golden-Age mysteries. But over the twentieth century, the threat to property has become more personal, and what is now at stake in many crime fiction novels is the ultimate property, that is, the self. The life of the individual is, in our solipsistic Western society, our most precious possession. And the crime that has become the most terrifying, that arouses the greatest anxiety, is the crime which we cannot understand, the criminal whose motivation is incomprehensible to us: the serial killer. Serial killers are frequently motivated to kill by sexual desire, but it is a sexual desire that to the man or woman in the street is incomprehensible. Equally frightening is that the serial killer is undifferentiated from the crowd; he has no distinguishing features by which we might identify him. The serial killer is very much a product of and a threat in our alienated and urbanised society.

Crime fiction responded to this fear of the serial killer, and in some ways fostered that fear in representing it to the reading public. The seminal serial killer text, the novel that, like Doyle's *A Study in Scarlet*, brought together a number of themes and tropes in crime fiction in order to create a new sub-genre, was Thomas Harris's *The Silence of the Lambs* (1988). There had been other texts that had serial killers at their centres, including Harris's own *Red Dragon* (1981). But while the killer in *Red Dragon* brutally murdered whole families, the violence was a sub-text to the psychological investigation of his motives and the fictional detective processes used to track him down. In *The Silence of the Lambs*, violence had become a central theme: there are two serial killers, Jame Gumb, whose motives are psycho-sexual, and Hannibal Lecter, whose motives are incomprehensible. Hannibal the cannibal, with his taste for human flesh, is the dark doppelganger of Sherlock Holmes, super-intellectual, cold, rational, 'other', super-human, but with none of Holmes's mitigating characteristics and with no comfortable Watson figure to explain his motives and actions to the reader.

The threat the serial killer poses has not lessened, but his, and sometimes now her, motivation has become the puzzle that writers of crime fiction pose and seek to solve. The late twentieth-century focus in crime fiction on the individual and on the violence done to the individual has insisted on a new emphasis on the body. Where in Golden-Age mysteries the body of the victim was the excuse for the detective's activities, and was usually swiftly removed from the scene of the crime and the pages of the text, recent crime fiction has made the body of the victim central to the investigation. No longer satisfied by the reading of the exterior of the body, the location of the stab wound, the marks left by the noose, now we are invited to view the interior of the body, to make the body signify in new ways. The late twentieth and early twenty-first centuries have seen the rise of the forensic pathologist as detective: Patricia Cornwell's medical examiner protagonist Kay Scarpetta; Kathy Reichs's forensic anthropologist Tempe Brennan; Jeffrey Deaver's paraplegic detective, Lincoln Rhyme; Nigel McCrery's Samantha Ryan of *Silent Witness* fame; Sharyn McCrumb's Elizabeth MacPherson.

A parallel development has been the rise of the psychologist, of the investigator who looks into the mind of the killer rather than the body. Part of Hannibal Lecter's skill in understanding Jame Gumb and a major factor in his fascination for the reader is his role as a psychiatrist; Jonathan Kellerman's child psychologist protagonist Alex Delaware brings his professional skill to the assistance of his homicide cop friend in tracking down killers. The term 'serial killer' came into being in the mid-1970s, coined by an FBI criminal profiler, and the criminal profiler, who brings together psychology and criminology, now also makes an increasingly frequent appearance in crime fiction. Val McDermid's 1995 novel, *The Mermaids Singing*, introduces criminal profiler Dr Tony Hill, who has since appeared in a further five novels, the most recent in 2009. *The Mermaids Singing* is another seminal text in the development of the crime fiction genre. It brings together the investigation into the mind of the murderer; explicit violence and the opening of the body to the gaze; the police procedural; gender politics, and it plays with the possibility of a female sexual serial killer. In keeping with the mood of the late twentieth century, it has a postmodern air. The text has two distinct narratives and narrator positions, one ungendered. It pays homage to Thomas de Quincey's essay 'On Murder Considered as One of the Fine Arts' (1827) and to Harris's *The Silence of the Lambs* and is overtly intertextual; it plays with the concept of reality and is implicitly concerned with the cultural constructions of gender and sexuality.

Contemporary crime fiction more openly addresses the anxieties and concerns of its readers, unlike its predecessors, where the real threats were concealed beneath the crime, and real anxieties encrypted in the criminal narrative rather than directly discussed. Yet the importance and significance of crime fiction as a suitable case for academic investigation remains: it is still the genre which most clearly and immediately represents society back to itself. Its structural conservatism lends itself to postmodern playfulness; its essential plot—crime, criminal, detective— allows for endless variation; the concept of crime and its place in every culture ensures cultural, sexual and racial diversity. For many years crime fiction has been Western and mainly white, it has been written in English and set more often than not in Britain or America. Australia has its own rich history of crime fiction and the development of the genre in Australia to some extent parallels that of British and American crime fiction, but Australia's status as an ex-colony, historically as a destination for convicts, and with its colonisers' uneasy relationship with the indigenous Aborigines, has made for some interesting and innovative criminographical variations.

Now there is a literary Diaspora of criminography, as Anglophone writers set their fictions in Italy, in France, in Africa, in Morocco, in Japan, and as an increasing number of non-Anglophone authors, Russian, Spanish, French, Italian, Latin-American, Japanese, South

African, Indian, Scandinavian, write crime fiction that is subsequently translated into English. Crime fiction has diversified as a genre; now it begins to diversify across cultures in the wake of globalisation. As ever, crime and its fictions respond to and represent the world and, in the pages that follow, the contexts for, the themes of and the critical approaches to this popular yet complex genre are explored. Inevitably there are elements of cross-over in the different sections as often it is impossible to separate completely text from context and as context is frequently best demonstrated in texts. Equally inevitably, given the time span covered here, it has proved impossible to include all the many and varied aspects of crime fiction, particularly the more recent developments consequent precisely on the Diaspora mentioned above. I have elected therefore to focus on what I consider to be the key elements in order to fulfil the remit of the Key Concepts series; the 'Further Reading' coda to each entry will, I hope, direct the reader to the rich supply of critical material that the genre of crime fiction has generated.

1 Contexts: History, Politics, Culture

Introduction

Crime fiction is a popular genre, produced and consumed quickly. Consequently, it can be and often is very responsive to the context in which it appears, affording important insights into its cultural, political and historical moment. But equally, both its status as popular fiction and its responsiveness create problems when it comes to locating crime fiction in particular contexts; popularity does not necessarily ensure literary longevity, meaning that the texts which survive the test of time are not always fully culturally, historically or politically representative, and the events to which criminography responds often lose their relevance once a particular moment has passed. As the General Introduction suggests, this text discusses crime narratives produced from circa 1700 to the present day, a period of over 300 years in which there have been enormous changes in society, particularly in terms of the growth of population, urbanisation, industrialisation; there have been unimaginable technological advances and scientific discoveries which have contributed to globalisation and the creation of a diverse and multicultural world. These changes have taken place against a historical backdrop of colonialism, revolution, national and international politics, two World Wars, the Cold War and in a concomitant rapidly evolving cultural context.

While crime fiction may not directly represent these major and cataclysmic contextual developments, it has been and is shaped and influenced by them. The following section will, then, take a broad approach to the contexts in which crime fiction is produced between the eighteenth and the twenty-first century, considering major cultural, historical and political changes in the period. The massive growth of cities and consequent urbanisation of populations; the perceptions and constructions of gender; changing attitudes to sexuality; the implications of a culturally and racially diverse world; conceptions of what constitutes criminality; all these have an effect on how societies perceive and construct crime

1

and the criminal, and this is visible in their literary representations. These topics afford a general context in which I locate more specific issues that circulate around, contribute to the construction of and are consequent upon crime: the context of the law; of evidence; of police and policing; and of detectives and detection.

The section is not intended to be encyclopaedic in its contents but to give the reader a contextual framework for and a sense of the historical background to and development of crime fiction. For those readers who wish to place major or canonical crime fiction texts in their historical moment, a Chronology is appended to this volume. The Contexts entries are intended to enable the reader to learn about and understand the origins and development of and the events that shaped crime and its fictional representation, and to encourage further exploration of the subject and the genre. To this end, each entry is supplemented by a 'See Also' sub-section, which directs the reader to other entries in the volume that are related to or which build upon the contextual material. A second sub-section, 'Further Reading', suggests sources for those wishing to take their research beyond this volume. Both sub-sections are aimed at encouraging readers of the text to enrich their understanding as well as their knowledge of crime fiction and to read critically and theoretically across the genre. The 'Further Reading' gives the reader access to the rich, varied and ever-expanding mass of critical and cultural material on crime, its literature and its response to and representation of the world in and by which it is produced.

Cities and urbanisation

Real-life crime has generally been considered to be a product of the city, a consequence of urbanisation and the concomitant proximity of rich and poor within the confines of urban spaces. The physicality of the city, the very denseness of the mass of buildings, the miles of roads and streets, the urban sprawl, the huge populations and the anonymity conferred on the individual by the crowd, all lend themselves to the construction of the criminal and the creation of crime. While to say that crime is solely to be found in the city is clearly a gross oversimplification, as crimes are also committed in the country, in villages and small towns and in the rural community, the perception of crime as an urban problem is still prevalent in many societies. Crime reportage in the West seems to confirm this concept, as does the statistically proven incidence of crime within cities like London or Glasgow, Los Angeles or New York. But this is not a twentieth or twenty-first-century perception: history shows that the increase in crime and the growth of the city have always been inextricably linked.

The growth of cities was consequent, in the Western world, on the rise of industry and the increase in trans-national mercantilism, particularly from the 1800s and onwards. Factories, ports and mills required large numbers of employees and so were located where possible in areas of high population, while the employment they offered attracted more people to those areas. This migration of the population from rural to urban was a secondary effect of industrialisation and the growth of cities contributed to the erosion of rural communities whose small size meant that individuals were known to each other. In small villages or parishes within towns criminality was visible; the criminal was either literally observed in the act of crime or his/her criminality was evident in unusual behaviour or strange demeanour. In contrast, the city environment made individuals strangers to each other and thus crime and criminality became more difficult to detect.

This contrast between the rural and the urban is apparent in Henry Fielding's *Tom Jones* (1749), where the country may contain thieves but there is nonetheless a sense of moral values, while the city is the site of corruption rather than the repository of civic values. Fielding, a magistrate, was deeply interested in questions of crime, and in 1749 recruited what came to be known as the Bow Street Runners, initially just seven men. They were based at Bow Street Magistrate's Office in London, and they functioned as a quasi-detective force in the metropolis. The continued association of crime with the city, in fact as well as in fiction, meant that Britain's first official State-funded uniformed police force, inaugurated in 1829 eighty years after Fielding's privately funded Bow Street force, operated in London. The Metropolitan Police, as they were called, drawing attention to their location in the city, were intended to prevent, rather than detect, crime; an official detective force followed in 1842.

Apparently increasing rates of crime meant that by the mid-nineteenth century there was a perception of an actual criminal class, a perception fostered by the sprawling slums, or rookeries, as they were known, in cities such as London. From 1850–3, Charles Dickens wrote a series of articles based on his journalistic collaboration with the Metropolitan Police Detectives. In 'On Duty with Inspector Field' (1851), Dickens recounts a visit to the criminal underworld of London, to the rookery of St Giles with its 'Rats' Castle', the haunt of known thieves, and a visit to the 'Thieves' Kitchen and Seminary' of Holborn Hill and Rotten Gray's Inn Lane. In the earlier *Oliver Twist* (1838), Fagin teaches young boys and girls the art of thieving in just such a 'Seminary'. That the rookeries of the city were in part inhabited by criminals there is no doubt, but many of those living in the rookeries were condemned to the slums by poverty and unemployment, circumstances that led to them being classified as actually or potentially criminal. In reality, it was probably less an actual increase in crime in this period than an increase in the number and kind of activities that became classed as criminal so constructing the individual as criminal, as Clive Emsley observes in *Crime and Society in England 1750–1900*.

Fiction, including crime fiction, has always taken its inspiration and content from the lived reality in which it is produced, responding to cultural and social patterns, changes, anxieties. The reality of and problems inherent in and consequent upon city living discussed above thus find their way into literature. Fiction by nineteenth-century socially aware/reformist authors such as Dickens (many of Dickens's novels feature city life, poverty and crime in some form or another), or Disraeli (*Coningsby* [1844], *Sybil* [1845]) and Elizabeth Gaskell (*Mary Barton* [1848], *North and South* [1855]), while not necessarily directly concerned with crime, drew on the reality of life in the urban slums and demonstrated how easily, for the poor, the line between honesty and criminality could be crossed. City living, then, did not just provide the location and opportunity for crime but was perceived actively to foster criminality.

With social reform in Britain and elsewhere came the clearing of the rookeries and attempts to obliterate city slums, but new building programmes contributed to urban sprawl, and new housing or high-rise living afforded no real solution to poverty and deprivation or the crime with which they are associated. Patterns of crime in the cities of the twentieth century changed from those in the 1800s; petty crime consequent upon poor social circumstances remained, but there was also organised crime, often focused around drugs and prostitution. In Britain the infamous Kray Brothers (1950s and 60s) epitomised this new, city-bred criminality, while in the United States the early twentieth century saw a proliferation of gangsters in the wake of the Great Depression of the 1930s, Prohibition and the establishment and rise of the Mafia.

In crime fiction, representations of this kind of criminality can be seen in the sub-genre known variously as the crime novel, the thriller, the *noir* thriller (after Marcel Duhamel's '*série noir*' books, which were translations of the thrillers of American and British writers such as Chandler or Cheyney as well as original French texts in the same style); texts in which the focus is on the criminal and his/her actions and motives rather than on the detection of the crime. Graham Greene's *Brighton Rock* (1938) offers an early introduction into the world of the British gangster; Ted Lewis's *Jack's Return Home* (1970) introduced the reader to the London criminal underworld and to Jack Carter, played by Michael Caine in the 1971 film version of the novel, *Get Carter* (Dir. Mike Hodges).

Victor Headley's *Yardie* (1992) looks at the Jamaican infiltration into drug-smuggling in London; Karline Smith's 1990s Moss Side series examines gang warfare in Manchester and Jake Arnott has explored the gangster theme in *The Long Firm* (1999) and its sequels. In America, the first 'crime novel' or gangster story is generally considered to be William Riley Burnett's *Little Caesar* (1929); Dashiell Hammett's protagonist 'Continental Op' and Raymond Chandler's private detective Philip Marlowe both come into contact with gangsters of various kinds; and of course Mario Puzo's *The Godfather* (1969) epitomises the Mafia novel.

Crime also flourished in post-war Europe and crime and the city continued to be closely linked, but as the century progressed the stakes were higher and there was an escalation in violence as the financial rewards of crime increased. The rebuilding of European cities after World War II and the rapid growth of cities in America resulting from economic expansion and high levels of immigration created opportunities for corruption in the building and associated trades; cities are the preferred location for financial and fiscal institutions and the opportunities they afford for fraud; political corruption is often associated with the cities where the game of politics is played out. In the twentieth century criminality is no longer seen to be the province of the poor and deprived, but increasingly a cross-class concern.

Crime and violence have always been partners, but this is increasingly so in the late twentieth and early twenty-first centuries, and the city is still the site of the most extreme violence, from muggings to gang wars to terrorism. Where the threat of crime had in the nineteenth century more ordinarily been to property, with violence as an unfortunate occasional accompaniment to robbery, in the twentieth century the threat is perceived to be to the individual and particularly focused on the body. Perhaps the greatest criminal threat to the individual that the city engendered is what we now call the serial killer. The anonymity of city living means that it is impossible to know the people who fill the crowded streets: the criminal is not marked in any way. When a killer strikes in the city, not once but a number of times, the whole population feels vulnerable to the stranger who attacks for no comprehensible reason. While the term 'serial killer' was coined only in the 1970s, there have been multiple murderers in the past.

In 1811, two entire families and their servants were massacred with no apparent motive in what became known as the 'Ratcliffe Highway Murders' after their London location; again in London in 1888 the murderer known only as 'Jack the Ripper' savagely slaughtered at least five women in the Whitechapel area; in the twentieth century there have been many more serial killings and killers, in Britain and America and Europe. While

not all these serial killers operate in the city, it is a peculiarly urban phe-
nomena fostered by the paradoxical proximity and alienation that city
living enforces. In twenty-first century, the threat of terrorist attack, again
a crime focused on the city, is to some extent displacing the fear of the
serial killer, at least in real life, and crime fiction is beginning to incorporate the terrorist theme into its texts. Sara Paretsky's *Black List* (2003)
questions the United States' political stance and attitude to the terrorist
threat in the wake of 9-11; Val McDermid's *Beneath the Bleeding* (2007)
incorporates a supposed terrorist attack into its serial-killer plot.

As crime fiction developed as a genre it represented the perceived realities of crime and its connection with city living: Edgar Allan Poe's short
stories featuring the Chevalier C. Auguste Dupin (1841–5) are set in Paris;
Dickens's detective police anecdotes (1850–3) and the novels *Oliver Twist*
(1838) and *Bleak House* (1853) are set mainly in London; James McLevy's
Curiosities of Crime in Edinburgh (1861) openly states its location in
the title; Sherlock Holmes's adventures often take place in London.
In America, the city was, and is, the preferred territory of the professional
detective, or private eye, from Anna Katharine Green's Ebenezer Gryce in
her 1878 novel *The Leavenworth Case* (New York), to Raymond Chandler's
hard-boiled investigator Philip Marlowe and Walter Mosely's unwilling
amateur detective Easy Rawlings (Los Angeles), or Sara Paretsky's feminist detective V. I. Warshawski (Chicago). Serial killers operate in cities
fictional and real on both sides of the Atlantic and elsewhere but, with the
exception of Thomas Harris's Hannibal Lecter (*Red Dragon* (1981), *The
Silence of the Lambs* (1989), *Hannibal* (1999) and *Hannibal Rising* (2006)),
are rarely the central protagonist of a series. Rather, serial detectives deal
with a series of serial killers, as in Patricia Cornwell's novels featuring
forensic detective-heroine Kay Scarpetta, located in Richmond, Virginia,
US; or in Britain Val Mc Dermid's detective team of Tony Hill and Carol
Jordan who operate mainly in and around the imagined northern city of
Bradfield.

While the city remains the preferred location for much crime fiction,
especially in America, in Britain, from the 1920s and 30s on, there has
been a tendency to locate crime in small communities, either rural or
within yet separated from the city (in early twentieth-century America,
Carolyn Wells and Mary Roberts Rinehart also located their crime narratives away from the city and the modern-day primarily US-authored
'cozies' often follow that pattern). This trend is especially apparent during what has come to be known as the 'Golden Age' of the genre which
had its heyday between the two World Wars. The removal of the crime
narrative from the city was perhaps in part the result of the physical effect
of the war on the fabric of cities and society; the economic depression

or 'Great Slump' which affected the United Kingdom in the 1930s, and attributable also to the escapist aspects of fiction. In America, while the global war had little or no physical effect, the Great Depression saw a migration of rural workers to the cities, where poverty and desperation made crime seem an attractive alternative lifestyle choice. The city, then, in America in fact and fiction, continued to be the location for crime and criminality.

The city, further, lends itself to certain kinds of crime narrative. The private detective, or 'private eye', especially the hard-boiled version typified by Chandler's Philip Marlowe, is very much the product of the city, modelled on the nineteenth-century French construction, the *flâneur*, that is, the leisurely and keenly observant wanderer through city streets. Walter Benjamin makes a direct link between the *flâneur* and the detective in *Charles Baudelaire: A Lyric Poet in the Era of High Capitalism* (1983), and indeed, the very words 'private eye' or 'PI', that is, the private investigator, allude specifically to the powers of observation essential to detective work. The city is considered to be the breeding ground of criminals and the site of crimes; consequently the private detective finds most of his—or increasingly her—employment there. The city, then, not only creates the criminal in fiction and fact but also provides the solution to the problem of crime, at least in fiction, in the figure of the detective.

And it is not just the private detective that the city encourages. Where crime is rife, and costing the State money, a State-funded police force will, sooner or later, begin to operate. In London this was in 1829 with the introduction of the Metropolitan Police, while other cities gradually drew on this as an example and instituted their own forces in turn; France had a policing system much earlier with a sovereign-controlled policing force created by Louis XIV in 1667, which was replaced in the wake of the French Revolution by the State-controlled Prefecture of Police in 1800; in America the process was made complex by the autonomous State system, but State-funded police forces were introduced in individual cities and states in the years between 1838 and 1854, again drawing on the British model. In crime fiction the relationship of the police detective and the city came into sharp focus in the police procedural, in which teams of detectives worked together, usually in a city, to track down criminals.

The first police procedurals in the modern sense came out in America in the 1940s and 50s and quickly spread to Britain and Europe: Ed McBain's 87th Precinct series is perhaps the longest-running and best-known example. While the somewhat plodding nature of the genre limited its popularity and did not lend itself to longevity, there are still city-based procedurals appearing; Jim Tucker, writing as 'David Craig', has a police team working in Cardiff in *Bay City* (2000). Interestingly, perhaps following in the steps of the novels by Georges Simenon featuring his police chief Maigret, many of which are set in and around Paris, there are many police detective narratives set in European cities: Maj Sjöwall and Per Wahlöö's Martin Beck series is set in Stockholm; Henning Mankell's Inspector Wallander works in the Swedish city of Ystad; Arnaldur Indridason's Detective Erlunder operates in Reykjavik; Fred Vargas's peripatetic Commissaire Jean-Baptiste Adamsberg is based in Paris and Donna Leon's Commissario Brunetti is located in Venice. The police detective in the city is a recurring figure, and the city in which detectives such as Ian Rankin's Inspector Rebus (Edinburgh), John Harvey's Resnick (Nottingham) or Colin Dexter's Morse (Oxford) work becomes, like Philip Marlowe's Los Angeles, a character within the narrative.

The city and urbanisation are, then, inextricably connected with crime and consequently the genre of crime fiction. The city in much criminography has come to be an important factor in the narrative, enabling the exploration of matters other than crime: social, cultural, sexual and racial tensions, for example, can be explored within crime fiction set in the city as it is in cities where these tensions are most apparent. The majority of the world's population lives in cities and a city setting in fiction provides the audience with a point of entry and a feeling of familiarity. Equally, the city setting draws on reality to examine in fictional form the anxieties of the contemporary society concerning crime.

See also   *Contexts*: Crime and Criminality, Detectives and Detection, Police and Policing, Race, Colour and Creed; *Texts*: the American Crime Novel, Early Criminography, Feminist Crime Fiction, Hard-boiled Crime Fiction, the Police Procedural; *Criticism*: Postcolonialism, Postmodernism.

Further reading

Arvas, Paula and Andrew Nestingen (eds), *Scandinavian Crime Fiction* (Cardiff: University of Wales Press, 2011).

Earwaker, Julian and Kathleen Becker, *Scene of the Crime: A Guide to the Landscapes of British Detective Fiction* (London: Aurum Press, 2002).

Emsley, Clive, *Crime and Society in England 1750–1900*, 3rd ed. (London: Longman Group, 2005).

Fine, David (ed.), *Los Angeles in Fiction*, rev. ed. (Alburquerque: University of New Mexico Press, 1995).

Geherin, David, *Scene of the Crime: The Importance of Place in Crime and Mystery Fiction* (Jefferson N. C.: McFarland & Co., 2008).

Willett, Ralph, *The Naked City: Urban Crime Fiction in the USA* (Manchester: Manchester University Press, 1996).

Crime and criminality

It is crime that constructs criminality, the transgressive act which defines the criminal. However, defining 'what is crime' is much more problematic. Crime, and thus criminality, is culturally, socially, temporally—even geographically—specific. Consequently, this entry will consider crime and criminality in the Western world, focusing mainly on Britain. In the Western world, not only is crime culturally constructed and indicative but also, to complicate things further, is often bound up with religion. One function of religion is to provide codes of behaviour for its followers; religion can act as a kind of social lubricant, enabling individuals to live in harmony with others. In Christianity the guidelines for communal and Christian living are enshrined in the Ten Commandments given to Moses, as described in the Bible. Such codes are, in effect, rules; so breaking the rules is, in religious terms, a sin. While the overt function of codes of behaviour such as these is to enable individuals to co-exist, the acts that are forbidden also reveal the anxieties of the society and culture in which they are produced. The representation of crime and criminality in fiction reiterates this duality; crime fiction expresses not only the fear of the criminal and his/her act but the social anxieties aroused by deviance from the norm.

The confusion between 'sin' and 'crime' has contributed to the difficulty of defining what exactly constitutes crime but, broadly, from eighteenth century onwards in the West the decline of religion and the rise of secularism meant that 'crime' came to encompass much that had previously been considered 'sin'. In the period when crime and sin were still to some extent interchangeable, the notion of sin had been in part used as a form of social control. Those empowered by their social position—landowners, for example—extended the basic precepts laid down by religion into 'godly', or good, behaviour, and their opposite, 'ungodly' behaviour. Ungodly acts included drunkenness, immorality, idleness, petty theft, poaching, deeds which would later (with the exception perhaps of idleness), in various ways, become classified as crimes.

There is then, for a long time, some slippage between sin and crime, and criminal acts were often perceived to be worse when they included an element of sinfulness. Equally, the criminal was frequently seen to be innately sinful, leading naturally to criminal behaviour. This is particularly apparent in Britain in the very popular stories of criminal lives found in the eighteenth-century *Accounts* of the Ordinaries, or Chaplains, of Newgate Gaol and other prisons and, from the late 1700s and early 1800s, the *Newgate Calendars*. The *Accounts* were exactly that; criminals' life stories as told to the prison Chaplain, who wrote them down and had multiple copies printed in pamphlet form. These were then sold to the public, raising money which helped the criminal to pay for his/her stay in prison and for burial after execution. The *Newgate Calendars* were collections of these *Accounts* and similar material taken from other sources and were published in book form.

These criminal lives often began with the protagonist deviating from normal behaviour in youth, sometimes by turning against their parents in direct contradiction to the biblical Commandment that requires the individual to honour his/her parents; sometimes as the consequence of being orphans; sometimes by disobeying the employer who stood in *loco parentis*. There would frequently be a move from the country to the city, and a gradual slide into dissipation, sinfulness and finally crime. A classic example is the Ordinary's *Account* of Mary Young, alias Jenny Diver, who was executed in 1741. The crimes for which she was indicted were all forms of theft; Mary Young is described as 'the artfullest Pick-pocket in the world'. The *Account* relates the tale of Mary's beginnings, her move to London and her descent into crime. But it also focuses on aspects of her career as a thief which are sinful as well as illegal. She steals while in a churchyard, on a Saint's Day; she abuses the sacred state of motherhood when she fakes pregnancy to enlist the sympathy of and deceive those she goes on to rob; she is shown to live in sin, that is with a man but unmarried; she uses her sexuality to deceive men. Sinfulness, especially sexual sin, is deliberately invoked both to make Mary's crimes more shocking and so deserving of the death sentence, but also to entertain the reader, and in these embroidered accounts of real crime and criminality is arguably where crime fiction, as we understand it, can be said to have its origins.

Religious rules were gradually superseded by secular law. In Britain, the law dictates what is criminal: some law has its origins in religion, but much comes from unwritten social contract or from rules imposed by those in power in order to maintain that power. There is a long-standing association between poverty and deprivation and crime, and social and class issues are inextricably bound up in criminality. Research into historical records of crime reveals that the majority of 'criminals' were of the lower classes, and shows clear correlations between severe economic hardship caused by poor harvests, trade depressions, war or the plague, and an apparent rise in crime. Extreme poverty made honest people into criminals, creating what was seen as a criminal class. In the latter part of the nineteenth century there was a quasi-scientific school of thought articulated in the work of the Italian criminologist Cesare Lombroso (1835–1909) which considered that criminality was less a product of deprivation than an inherent and inherited trait that could be identified by visible physical signifiers such as low foreheads or receding chins. The concept of criminality as visible was comforting for those who perceived themselves as most likely to be the victims of crime.

The vast majority of crime was theft in one form or another: offences against property. Thus crime becomes seen as something that is very much a threat to the propertied classes who are of course the classes in power. Increasingly, towards the end of the 1700s, what had been seen as petty thefts or what Clive Emsley calls the 'fiddles, perks and pilferage' associated with the workplace became codified as felonies, often attracting the death penalty. By 1815, in Britain there were approximately 280 felonies for which the perpetrator could be hanged, including offences as minor as stealing goods worth five shillings (25 pence), poaching rabbits, cutting down a tree, damaging a horse and so on: the law in this period is known as 'The Bloody Code'. It is difficult not to see the creation of these new crimes as serving the interests of the wealthy property owner and the number and type of offences as a method of controlling that part of the population who were neither wealthy nor property owners.

Very broadly, over the late eighteenth and into the nineteenth century, there is a gradual transition from a concept of crime and criminality based on sin to notions of crime and criminality firmly based on concerns about property. Texts such as Dickens's *Oliver Twist* (1839) show clearly the contemporary fears of crime associated with property, both in the actions of Fagin as he teaches his motley collection of abandoned children how to steal handkerchiefs and in the plot of the novel, in which Oliver's half-brother, Monks, is inspired by hatred and greed to defraud Oliver of his rightful inheritance. Equally, the text reveals the close association of crime with poverty and social deprivation. The figures of Fagin, Bill Sikes and Nancy and the text's fascination with the criminal underworld of London and with the motivations of the criminal, speak back to the earlier factual Ordinaries' *Accounts* and the *Newgate Calendars*, and to texts such as Daniel Defoe's *Moll Flanders* (1722), a fictional autobiography of the heroine's life of crime, or Henry Fielding's political satire based loosely on the real life and times of the infamous Jonathan Wild ('The Life of Jonathan Wild the Great', in *Miscellanies*, Vol. III, 1743).

The real Jonathan Wild in some ways embodies the complexities of defining crime and criminality: known as 'the Thief-Taker General' Wild was both the organiser of crime and the catcher of criminals. He recruited and trained thieves, collected the goods they stole and then arranged, or facilitated, the return of the stolen goods to the rightful owner for a small fee. In order to project the right, legal image, to maintain his control over the thieves who worked for him, and to earn a little extra money, every now and then Wild would deliver a thief or two to justice, collecting the reward money. He was eventually successfully prosecuted and was hanged in 1725, but his ability to work both for and against the law demonstrates the lack of cohesion in and organisation of the legal system at the time and also shows how unclear was the distinction between the legal and illegal.

Crime and criminality was, in the eighteenth and early nineteenth centuries, a popular and financially rewarding topic for literature. The stories of criminal lives sold well across the social spectrum, as did the accounts of the public executions that ended many such criminal lives. The novel utilised the popularity of criminal biography and featured crime and criminality in its narratives, as in *Moll Flanders* and *Oliver Twist*. This use of the criminal was so successful that in the 1830s and 40s there was a sub-genre of fiction which became known as the 'Newgate Novel' because of its focus on and glamorisation of the criminal, often a real-life villain: William Harrison Ainsworth's *Rookwood* (1834) devoted a whole section of its narrative to the highwayman, Dick Turpin; the protagonist of *Jack Sheppard* (1839) was a fictionalised version of the real Jack Sheppard, a thief who briefly worked for Jonathan Wild and who was famous for his many escapes from Newgate Prison.

Oliver Twist was classed as one of these 'Newgate Novels' and was criticised on that account, as were Edward Bulwer Lytton's *Paul Clifford* (1830), *Eugene Aram* (1832) and *Lucretia* (1846) (the last two are based on actual crimes and criminals). What these texts made clear was both the ease with which real-life crime and criminality successfully translated into fiction and the public popularity and critical censure such texts aroused, as Keith Hollingworth demonstrates in *The Newgate Novel 1830–47* (1963). 'Newgate Novels' were considered to have the potential to incite criminality in susceptible readers as a consequence of their 'heroisation' of the criminal. But the vogue for this kind of fiction was not to last. In Britain, as a consequence of various reform bills passed between 1808 and 1834, the number of crimes attracting the death penalty under the Bloody Code was vastly reduced and the penal system became much more rational and organised. By 1861, there were only four capital offences, that is, crimes attracting the death penalty: murder, treason, arson in the Royal Dockyards and piracy with violence. What exactly constituted crime was clarified and the rationalisation and categorisation of crime and the consequent reduction in numbers of offences contributed to an apparent fall in the number of criminals.

These factors, in combination with increasing prosperity in the mid-nineteenth century and the introduction of a regulated and regulatory police force resulted in public attention shifting, certainly from the 1850s onwards, from the criminal to the detective in criminography. This shift is evident in Dickens's factual detective police anecdotes of 1850 featuring 'Inspector Wield', actually the real police detective Inspector Field, and Dickens's fictional Inspector Bucket in *Bleak House* (1852–3) or Wilkie Collins's Sergeant Cuff (based on the real-life Inspector Jonathan Whicher) in *The Moonstone* (1868): in fiction the criminal hero is rarely seen again until the later twentieth century, and even then relatively infrequently. The criminal is still important, though, and is often set in direct opposition to the detective in what becomes a battle between opponents of apparently equal intelligence and ingenuity.

In the twenty-first century we are accustomed to murder as the central crime in crime fiction, but in reality most crimes, now and in the past, are much more mundane and involve property. Where murder occurs, it is more usually as an unplanned adjunct to theft, or as a precursor to acquiring goods/property illegally, or is the consequence of domestic squabbles or drunkenness. In the nineteenth century murder as a consequence of other crimes was often the case in crime fiction as in reality. In Arthur Conan Doyle's Sherlock Holmes stories from the 1890s to 1926 this pattern is apparent, with the majority of criminal cases solved by Holmes being focused on property and inheritance; in the first series of *Adventures* only three out of the twelve stories feature violent crime. But the Sherlock Holmes tales also suggest the movement from the nineteenth to the twentieth century in terms of the kinds of crime and criminal featured; in the later stories the incidence of violence and murder increases. As the twentieth century progressed, fiction gradually began to locate murder at the centre of its crime narratives and the murderer becomes the most usual criminal.

In the so-called Golden Age of crime fiction (circa 1918–30), the 'clue-puzzle' mystery was the most prevalent form, epitomised by the texts of Agatha Christie. Not only do her narratives feature murder(s) but they often advertise the fact in their titles: *Murder on the Links* (1922), *The Murder of Roger Ackroyd* (1926), *Murder at the Vicarage* (1930), *Death on the Nile* (1937). Strangely, her later novels have rather more cryptic titles, although murder remains the central crime. And this concentration on murder in crime fiction, especially in detective fiction, remains to the present day: while the pattern of murder as a consequence or in the commission of another crime is still seen, texts from the latter part of the twentieth century often feature criminals for whom the act of murder is complete in itself, requiring no motive other than the satisfaction of the desire to kill. We are simultaneously fascinated and terrified by the psychopathic killer, the predator whose motives are incomprehensible.

The shift of focus in fiction from theft to murder, property to person, is perhaps in part a response to the fact that most real crime is mundane and ordinary whereas fiction seeks to excite and entertain. Furthermore, in a capitalist and solipsistic society where the individual is of the utmost importance, murder has become the ultimate crime against the ultimate property—the self. The sub-text of social anxieties present in the cultural construction of crime and criminality and in its fictional representations is now focused on the threat to the individual and on extremes of deviance from the norms of society. Much that had in the past been considered first sinful and then criminal, especially deviant sexuality, has now been decriminalised. Nonetheless, society is haunted by the spectre of paedophilia, as in Ruth Rendell's *Harm Done* (1999), Minette Walter's *Acid Row* (2001) or Belinda Bauer's *Blacklands* (2010) and by the threat of the predatory, often sexually motivated killers who feature in numerous fictions of crime by authors as diverse as Kathy Reichs (Canada), Mo Hayder, Denise Mina and Mark Billingham (Britain), Lisa Scoppetone, Jeffrey Deaver, Linda Fairstein (America) and Henning Mankell (Sweden), to name but a few. While the serial killer is found in British crime fiction, the phenomenon is more common in American texts as it is in reality.

The fear of terrorism too is now woven into the social fabric of the West, as demonstrated in Ian Rankin's *Naming of the Dead* (2006) or Val McDermid's *Beneath the Bleeding* (2007). While the topic is not always addressed directly it forms part of the backdrop of the fictions, as in Sara Paretsky's *Black List* (2003). In the late twentieth and early twenty-first centuries crime is associated with new levels of violence in fiction and in reality. The act of murder alone, it seems, is no longer sufficient: crime fiction must respond to the reality of a world in which graphic violence, real and imaginary, is visible in the press, on television and in film. The criminal is still constructed by the crime but, as the crime becomes increasingly extreme, the perpetrator is not simply criminal but monstrous and his or her motives are incomprehensible. In a return to earlier modes of criminography the criminal once again is, in some sub-genres of crime fiction, taking centre stage: Elizabeth George's *What Came Before He Shot Her* (2007) focuses entirely on the criminal and is the account of the motives and rationale for a young, mixed-race boy's murder of the wife of Inspector Lynley, George's serial detective hero. The murder itself is the climax of George's previous Lynley text, *With No One As Witness* (2006), which features a serial killer preying on mixed-race boys and which explores racial tensions aroused by and the criminalisation of the racial Other in inner-city London.

This is not to say that all crime fiction features serial killers, paedophiles, street/gang crime or terrorism. The genre still has space for many kinds of crimes and many types of criminal and it responds to society's concerns about crime. But as the definition of what constitutes a crime has become clearer in the light of contemporary awareness of cultural construction and difference, fiction seeks to complicate crime and criminality and to portray its excess. Criminality as the consequence of social deprivation is easy to understand; criminality as a side effect of uncontrolled passions is comprehensible, as are drug-fuelled crime, murder committed in self-defence, mercy killings—the list is long. Psychiatry, psychology and psychoanalysis allow us to understand the criminal as never before. But even as our understanding improves, as society becomes more tolerant of deviant behaviour, criminality continues to push the boundaries of that tolerance and understanding, and it is crime fiction that best represents criminal excess back to the culture in which it is created.

See also *Contexts*: Cities and Urbanisation, Gender and Sexuality, Law, Race and Ethnicity; *Texts*: American Crime Fiction, the Detective Novel, Early Criminography; *Criticism*: Feminism, Cultural Materialism.

Further reading

Ascari, Maurizio, *A Counter-History of Crime Fiction: Supernatural, Gothic, Sensational* (Basingstoke: Palgrave Macmillan, 2007).

Bell, Ian A., *Literature and Crime in Augustan England* (London and New York: Routledge, 1991).

Cameron, Deborah and Elizabeth Frazer, *The Lust to Kill: A Feminist Investigation of Sexual Murder* (Cambridge: Polity Press, 1987).

Emsley, Clive, *Crime and Society in England 1750–1900*, 3rd ed. (London: Longman Group, 2005).

Gillis, Stacy and Philippa Gates (eds), *The Devil Himself: Villainy in Detective Fiction and Film* (Westport, CO and London: Greenwood Press, 2002).

Simpson, Philip L., *Psycho Paths: Tracking the Serial Killer Through Contemporary American Film and Fiction* (Carbondale: South Illinois University Press, 2000).

Szuminskyj, Benjamin (ed.), *Dissecting Hannibal Lecter: Essays on the Novels of Thomas Harris* (Jefferson, N. Carolina and London: McFarland, 2008).

Wiener, Martin J., *Reconstructing Crime: Culture, Law and Policy in England, 1830–1914* (Cambridge: Cambridge University Press, 1990).

Detectives and detection

A brief glance at the *Oxford English Dictionary* reveals that the words 'detect' and 'detection' have been in circulation in English from the fifteenth century, usually in the sense of discovering or finding out, but not necessarily connected with crime or criminality. The word 'detective', in contrast, only has its first outing four centuries later in an 1843 edition of *Chambers's Journal*: 'men have been recently selected to form a body called the "detective police"'. And according to R. F. Stewart, in...*And Always a Detective*, the phrase 'detective fiction' as the descriptor of a literary genre does not appear until 1886, when the *Saturday Review* published an account of the development of the genre called precisely 'Detective Fiction'. To the modern reader, the terms are wholly familiar and inextricably connected. In the twenty-first century, the figure of the detective and the process of detection have become practically synonymous with crime fiction, and detective fiction is arguably the most popular sub-genre of the literary form.

Where criminality features in a text, it seems, there will, must, be a detective who solves the crime and tracks down the criminal. Even in those texts which focus on the criminal, or which depict the actions of gangs and gangsters, the detective, amateur or professional, private or police, will at the very least lurk in the margins of the narrative. Crime and criminality in fiction as in fact generate the need for a mechanism, a system, that will either prevent or limit criminal activity or, where crime has occurred, track the perpetrators and remove their threatening presence from society. Central to most attempts to control and contain crime is the need to demonstrate the apparent certainty that crime will be detected and the criminal punished. Such a demonstration serves both to warn potential criminals of the consequences of their unlawful acts, and also to reassure the public who are the potential victims of crime that the system works. Crime fiction is implicated in this system, frequently representing in the very structure of its narrative the containment of crime: a criminal act is carried out; the motive ascertained; the criminal discovered and delivered to justice. And the most common facilitator of this process and this narrative is the detective.

But as shown above, the modern understanding and use of the terms 'detection' and 'detective' in fiction are relatively recent. Historians of crime fiction argue that there have been detective figures and modes of detection in literature from the distant past—Dorothy L. Sayers refers to Bible stories from the Book of Daniel such as that of Susanna and the Elders or Daniel and the Priests of Bel as proto-detective stories; the classic tale of Oedipus has elements of crime and detection; Shakespeare's Elizabethan revenge play *Hamlet* has a crime at its centre and the detection of the criminal is essential to the process of revenge—the play's place in the history of detection is surely made clear in Agatha Christie's play *The Mousetrap*, whose title pays homage to *Hamlet*. But the detective figure whose *raison d'être* is the detection of crime is very much a nineteenth-century creation, in fact as well as in fiction.

Fact is an important element of crime fiction: crime narratives insist that they deal in fact; the genre itself speaks often of the 'facts of the case', and it is in fact that the detective proper and his profession of detection can be said to begin. In the early 1700s, Jonathan Wild, or the 'Thief-Taker General' as he was also known, set in place what was in essence a system for the detection of crime and the capture of criminals. Wild was himself a criminal and his system took advantage of the rewards offered for the capture of criminals and the return of stolen goods. His scheme was largely for his own benefit, with public benefit as a secondary aspect, and Wild was eventually hanged for his crimes. Wild was able to convince the population of London that his scheme was in their interests in part because of the increasing crime rate that occurred with urbanisation and the growth of cities. In a small community, no special figure is required to detect crimes and catch criminals as community members are known to one another and criminal behaviour witnessed or revealed in the perpetrator's aberrant behaviour. In a city environment crime becomes not only more tempting, as the rich rub shoulders with the poor, but also easier as the individual can disappear into the crowd.

Police detectives

In utilising the State system of rewards paid for the capture of criminals, Wild brought together the private and the public interests in crime, demonstrating that the private individual could, in a criminal context, serve the public and the State. From this point onwards, the development of the detective in fact and fiction follows two similar public/private separate paths: the individual, professional or amateur, in the private sector and the individual in the service of the State. In the latter case, the detective figure is clearly linked with the development of the police. In 1749, responding to the perceived increase in crime, Henry Fielding, a Bow Street Magistrate as well as a novelist, recruited seven men who were the foundation of what came to be called 'Bow Street Runners'. This was a tiny force, in London, dedicated to the detection of crime. In 1757, John Fielding, Henry's brother and successor, obtained State funding for this force, who otherwise obtained their income mostly from the reward monies still being paid for the capture of criminals. The Bow Street Runners had a clear detective function in their pursuit of the criminal after a crime had been committed and continued in that role if without that designation until 1839, ten years after the establishment of the New

Metropolitan Police in 1829 and three years before the inauguration of the Metropolitan Detective Police in 1842.

The Runners were tainted by the opportunities offered—and taken—for corruption that their work entailed. Much of their income was derived from reward money, and they also undertook private employment for a fee. Added to this was the fact that they worked in plain clothes and so were indistinguishable from the ordinary man in the street, a mode of working that was unpopular, suggesting a spy system similar to that seen in post-Revolutionary France. Possibly because of this unpopularity, the Runners do not feature much in the contemporary literature, except as marginal figures, and where they do appear, it tends to be a negative representation. *Oliver Twist* (1838) has Runners Blathers and Duff, whose very names suggest their character and incompetence. An anonymously authored text, *Richmond: Scenes in the Life of a Bow Street Runner* (1827) purports to be the memoirs of a Runner, but is clearly a fabrication, and its poor sales (it was quickly remaindered) suggest the unpopularity of the topic.

In contrast, the *Memoirs of Vidocq* (1828–9), the embellished and partly ghost-written autobiography of the real Eugène François Vidocq, Head of the *Sûrêté de Police* in France in the early nineteenth century, proved very popular in Britain as well as in France. Vidocq was a thief-turned-thief taker who, rather like Jonathan Wild, used his own experience of criminality in order to track down criminals. His 'police' career began when he turned informer, and he quickly rose to a position of authority because of his proven efficiency. Forced to retire in 1832 when faced with charges of corruption, he went on to form a private enquiry agency. Vidocq is often called the first 'detective', although the term was not in existence at the time: certainly, his actions and his *Memoirs* proved an inspiration to later crime writers. Edgar Allan Poe's investigative figure, C. Auguste Dupin and Emile Gaboriau's detective, M. Lecoq, owe something to Vidocq, as does Arthur Conan Doyle's Sherlock Holmes.

But Vidocq's 'detection' was more a case of spying, using disguises, informants and entrapment in the pursuit of criminals and while this might have been considered acceptable in the French system there was strong resistance to such methods from the general public in Britain. Nevertheless, perceived increases in crime, particularly in London, resulted in the introduction of a State-funded police force in 1829. But this was a uniformed, and therefore visible, force, intended to act as a preventive against crime rather than to detect the criminal after the act. When the preventive measures were seen to be insufficient, the public reluctantly accepted the necessity for a detective force, which was founded in 1842. As with the Bow Street Runners, the police, preventive and detective, initially had little place in fiction, although they were a strong presence in newspapers and magazines. However, in 1849 a pseudoautobiographical series, 'Recollections of a Police Officer' appeared in *Chambers's Edinburgh Journal*. Purporting to be the memoirs of 'Waters', a serving police officer, the fictional tales were the work of hack journalist William Russell. As a police officer, technically 'Waters' would have worked in uniform, but in carrying out what are clearly detective activities, he works in plain clothes, and the narrative itself contains anachronistic slips where 'Waters' refers to his fellow 'detective officers'. The police detective had arrived in fiction: a collected edition of the 'Waters' stories published in 1856 was re-titled as *Recollections of a Detective Police Officer* (emphasis added).

Although Charles Dickens is best known for his novels, he wrote a series of 'Detective Police Anecdotes' (1850–3) in *Household Words*. These were factual accounts of the work of the Metropolitan Police Detectives which proved popular with the public and so contributed to the popularisation of the police detective. Dickens's *Bleak House* (1853) returned the police detective to fiction with its depiction of Inspector Bucket who was loosely based on the real detective Inspector Field. The kind of detection carried out by both fictional and factual detectives was similar to that of Vidocq: much surveillance, following (inconspicuously) suspects; the use of informants; knowledge of the criminal world, and even disguise and infiltration of criminal gangs. As detection evolved into a science, in parallel with scientific developments in the period, it became rather more technical and forensic in its investigations, but these early detectives were ordinary men and relied more on knowledge and native cunning than intellect and science.

The 1860s saw a proliferation of detective stories, often in the form of memoirs or diaries claiming to be truthful accounts of police detection: *The Detective's Notebook* (1860) and *The Diary of an Ex-Detective* (1860) by 'Charles Martel' (Thomas Delf); James McLevy, a real detective, produced his quasi-factual *Curiosities of Crime in Edinburgh* and *The Sliding Scale of Life* (1861); *The Irish Police Officer* (1861) by Robert Curtis; *The Experiences of a Real Detective* (1862) by William Russell. There are even female detectives who, while not members of the police force, work with them: Andrew Forrester's *The Female Detective* (1864) featured a Mrs G___, who was followed later that year by a Mrs Paschal in William Hayward's *Experiences of a Lady Detective*. Once established, the police detective continued to appear in crime fiction, although his elevated status and popularity declines in the latter part of the nineteenth century, at least in Britain. Doyle's Sherlock Holmes shows his contempt for the police detective in *A Study in Scarlet* (1887), declaring that detectives

'Gregson [...] and Lestrade are the pick of a bad lot [...] conventional, shockingly so.'

By the beginning of the twentieth century the private detective, amateur or professional, had largely replaced the police detective in fiction, and it was not until the police procedural appeared in the late 1940s and early 1950s that the police detective returned to a central role. This is not to say that there were no police detective protagonists in the period, but they were few in number and, rather than the ordinary police officer drawn from the lower classes seen in the early detective police stories, the later police-detective heroes tended to be of superior rank and from a superior background, for example Ngaio Marsh's Inspector Alleyn, or more recently Elizabeth George's Inspector (Lord) Lynley or P. D. James's Inspector Dalgleish. Ruth Rendell's Inspector Wexford is cut from different cloth, as are R. D. Wingfield's Inspector Frost and Ian Rankin's Inspector Rebus who, as 'common men' are all more in the tradition of the Victorian police detectives or later fictional detectives from the 1920s and 30s such as Freeman Wills Crofts's Inspector French or George Simenon's Inspector Maigret.

The police detective, then, appears in the context of public anxieties concerning a perceived increase in crime in the wake of urbanisation and rising population figures. But, in nineteenth-century Britain at least, because the police were created specifically to deal with what was seen as the criminal class and policemen were recruited from the lower classes, there was a problem when it came to police detectives dealing with the middle and upper classes and this is very apparent in fiction. Successful investigations into crimes occurring in the higher social classes required a certain social mobility in the investigating officer, a requirement satisfied in the case of Russell's 'Waters' by making him a gentleman fallen on hard times. But in Wilkie Collins's *The Moonstone* (1868), Sergeant Cuff, a police detective loosely based on the real Sergeant Whicher of the Metropolitan Police Detectives, exemplifies the difficulties facing the proletarian police detective in an upper-class world. His enquiry into the disappearance of the diamond, the Moonstone of the novel's title, is rendered ineffectual by the class divide. Sergeant Cuff cannot function effectively within the aristocratic world of the Verinder family and comes to the wrong conclusions about the theft of the diamond. Yet once the diamond leaves the domestic and upper-class *milieu* and falls into criminal hands, Cuff is able to carry out his detective work successfully. The solution to the diamond's original disappearance is discovered by private individuals—amateurs in the art of detection. One of these 'detectives' is upper-middle-class Franklin Blake, the other important figure is Ezra Jennings, a doctor.

Private detectives: Professional

Doctors, or physicians, are significant contextual elements in the creation of the private detective. This second strand of detection took rather longer to come into being in a recognisable and recognised form, factual or fictional, and it too has two elements: professional and amateur. The private but professional detective can again be said to derive in some measure from Jonathan Wild, who worked in a private capacity, and much of the police work of Vidocq seems, retrospectively, to resemble the work of the professional private detective. The Bow Street Runners were available for hire by private individuals, and so could be considered private detectives and there were men, known as 'thief takers', who, for a fee, would track down debt defaulters or other criminals at the behest of private citizens. Before the Prosecution of Offences Act 1879 there was no public prosecutor to take criminal cases to court. People had to find their own lawyers or present the prosecution case themselves and finding evidence was, prior to the establishment of a police force, in the hands of the person wishing to prosecute. In this context, there were in effect professional investigative figures and these can be seen in fiction as well as fact.

But these figures were often not considered entirely respectable, open to corruption, tainted by the criminals with whom they necessarily associated, and certainly not members of the respectable middle classes. A classic example of such a figure is seen in William Godwin's *Caleb Williams* (1794), a text often considered to be an early proto-detective crime fiction. While the central 'detective' figure in this narrative is the protagonist, Caleb Williams, he is rather an amateur detective. But there is a secondary detecting figure, a minor character called Gines who is, like Jonathan Wild, a thief-turned-thief taker. He is a deeply unattractive figure who embodies the negative aspects of such investigators. He is also clearly of a low social class, and so lacks social mobility, as will his later police successor.

The ability to work across social strata is increasingly important in the nineteenth century when class divisions multiplied and became more complex. Where the essential class division had been between the aristocracy and everyone else, or the 'haves and have nots', the nineteenth century saw the rise and the consolidation of the middle classes. Important elements of this social stratum were professional men: doctors, lawyers, businessmen, bankers and so on. Concomitant with the proliferation of such professionals was an increase in bureaucracy, which in turn led to an increase in white-collar office workers and consequently white-collar crimes such as fraud, embezzlement, forgery. In this context, the need for a professional, but non-police, detective figure to deal with middle-class crime seems clear, but it was a slow process in reality. Factual articles discussing crime and its causes in the early nineteenth century often used the metaphor of crime as a disease of the social body and in fiction the basis of a professional investigator can be seen in the figure of the physician. The doctor, after all, looks for evidence of disease, traces the causes of illness, names the culprit, and each patient he sees is a case, to be opened and closed with diagnosis and cure. Samuel Warren's 1830s fictional series, 'Passages from the Diary of a Late Physician', published in *Blackwood's Edinburgh Magazine*, shows precisely this pattern, and indeed, one of the 'Passages', 'The Forger', is concerned with criminality as well as disease.

A closer association of a professional investigating figure, crime and the law can be seen in the slightly later (1849–52) legal narratives such as 'The Experiences of a Barrister' or 'The Confessions of an Attorney', anonymously authored pseudo-factual tales. In these, a barrister or attorney recounts cases, often criminal, many of which have some element of quasi-detection carried out by a member of the legal profession. From the 1850s to the 1880s, these proto-professional figures continue to appear, as in the physician Ezra Jennings in *The Moonstone*— where the legal figure Mr Bruff also has a small investigative role, or Mr Tulkinghorne, the lawyer, in Dickens's *Bleak House*, or Mary E. Braddon's non-practising barrister and circumstance-driven investigator Robert Audley in *Lady Audley's Secret* (1862). The secondary investigative figure in Anna Katharine Green's *The Leavenworth Case* (1878) is the young lawyer, Mr Raymond, and in the late twentieth century Linda Fairstein's serial detective figure is Alexandra Cooper, a practising attorney; Sara Paretsky's V. I. Warshawski is a lawyer-turned-private detective. But the medical strand has also remained a constant feature in crime fiction from its early days to the present.

The physician as investigator as suggested in Warren's stories returns in the quasi-Gothic tales of L. T. Meade and Clifford Halifax, which have a Dr Halifax as their protagonist. Published in the 1890s in *Strand Magazine*, these tales match the scientific and rational against the irrational and supernatural, with science triumphing every time, and frequently the motive for, or behind, the 'supernatural' event is shown to be criminal. The privileging of science responds to the post-Darwinian reliance on science to explain the world and its mysteries and to the development of scientific policing and the use of forensic science as a tool of detection. The investigative skills of the physician are, in the late twentieth and early twenty-first centuries, closely associated with crime and detection, most usually in the form of forensic pathologists such as Patricia

Cornwell's protagonist Kay Scarpetta or Kathy Reichs's forensic anthropologist heroine Temperance Brennan. And of course, Arthur Conan Doyle gives Sherlock Holmes a physician, Dr Watson, as his friend and *quondam* partner.

Doyle's debt to Poe and Gaboriau is clearly stated, positively in his autobiography, and negatively in the first Sherlock Holmes story, *A Study in Scarlet* (1887). In his autobiographical *Memories and Adventures* (1924), Doyle speaks of Poe's 'masterful detective, M. Dupin' as one of his boyhood heroes, and of his admiration for Gaboriau's plotting skills. In contrast, Sherlock Holmes in *A Study in Scarlet* (1888) dismisses Dupin as 'a very inferior fellow' and Gaboriau's detective, M. Lecoq, as 'a miserable bungler'. Doyle's knowledge of earlier periodical material concerned with crime and of the professional anecdote genre is apparent in his throwaway reference to 'Mr Sharps and Mr Ferrets', the protagonists of 'Confessions of an Attorney' and the 'The Experiences of a Barrister', legal anecdotes that appeared in *Chambers's Edinburgh Journal* between 1849 and 1852. He was probably also aware of William Russell's series, *Recollections of a Police Officer*, featuring 'Waters', the policeman of the title, which appeared in the same periodical in 1849–53.

Probably the best-known fictional detective in the world, Sherlock Holmes, is, as he himself claims in *A Study in Scarlet* (1887), in a trade of his own: 'I suppose I am the only one in the world. I'm a consulting detective.' Holmes was a new kind of detective: neither in the mould of the early 'thief taker' type of private investigator discussed earlier, nor a professional police detective; Holmes laid claim to being a professional in the science of detection in the same sense as the physician is a professional in the science of medicine. Perhaps the single most innovative aspect of Sherlock Holmes was the combination of the private detective—a figure largely absent from nineteenth-century crime fiction—with the professional. Sherlock Holmes makes his living from his detective work but in a private capacity—and privately; money or payment are not usually openly discussed. The first of the Sherlock Holmes short stories, 'A Scandal in Bohemia', is the exception to this, as Holmes, before taking on the case, asks his client, the King of Bohemia, 'Then, as to money? [...] And for present expenses?' The private detective narratives' refusal to include the commercial aspect of the profession in the early days of its emergence as a sub-genre of crime fiction blurs the boundaries between paid professional and unpaid amateur, and is perhaps related to the need to maintain the gentlemanly, middle-class aura of the detective as professional rather than as tradesman. Once the figure of the professional private detective was established, it quickly became a popular and frequently occurring feature of crime fiction, although perhaps initially more readily taken up in America.

Here, the professional private eye can be read as a progression from the frontiersmen of the Wild West, a modernisation of the Natty Bumppo figure created by James Fenimore Cooper in his Leatherstocking series, published between 1823 and 1841. The tracking and survival skills needed to survive in the wild are later transformed into the skills required to survive in the city and to track down criminals. An early American professional private detective, or 'private eye', is found in *Leaves from the Notebook of the New York Detective* (1865), 'edited' by John Williams, M.D. The text is similar in format to Russell's *Recollections of a Detective Police Officer*, but features James, or Jem, Brampton, who trains as a doctor, then works briefly as a detective police officer before finally becoming a private detective, neatly drawing together the medical, police and private detective fiction modes. The 1880s in America saw the creation of Nick Carter, who first appeared in 'The Old Detective's Pupil; or, The Mysterious Crime in Madison Square' (1886), written by John Russell Coryell (later stories were written by several different authors). Nick Carter is an amalgam of physical and intellectual strengths, using science and gadgetry in his detective work but relying also on speed and muscle power in a fashion decidedly American. This emphasis on the physical is very apparent in the 'hard-boiled' genre of detective fiction which originated in America, with Dashiell Hammett and Raymond Chandler as its best-known exponents and which clearly pits strength and intellect against corruption and crime. The term 'hard-boiled' comes from Hammett's *Red Harvest* (1929), where it is used to describe the protagonist, Continental Op.

The concept of the hard-boiled detective as the successor to the frontiersman is supported by the location of both Hammett's narratives and those of Chandler on the west coast of America, in California. This setting also allowed for the depiction of the effects of the oil boom and of Prohibition: the crime and corruption consequent on the opportunities to amass fortunes, legally and criminally, afforded by the exploitation of oil and the illegal sale of alcohol. The detective's battle is avowedly against the corruption of modern (1930s) America, usually figured as gangsters, and Hammett's detective, Continental Op, retains some of this concept of social crime. Raymond Chandler's detective, or private investigator, Philip Marlowe, has come to epitomise the hard-boiled detective with his laconic and witty speech, his readiness to resort to violence, his hard-drinking habits, his occasionally misogynistic and always chauvinistic attitude to women and his hatred of homosexuals, his knowledge of the mean streets of Los Angeles and their inhabitants and above all his strong sense of integrity and desire for justice. But while the overt threat in Marlowe's world is associated with social crime and corruption, the covert threat is nearly always from women. Marlowe is a hired man, working for money, and in this sense clearly professional, but invariably the case for which he is hired—the social crime—leads him into a second, personally motivated case involving women. This duality blurs the distinction between the paid professional detective and the unpaid investigator and can be seen in much crime fiction featuring apparently professional detectives.

The hard-boiled detective has had, necessarily, to evolve over time. Signalled perhaps by the end of Prohibition and in the aftermath of World War II, the enemies of society also change. In Mickey Spillane's novels, beginning with *I, the Jury* (1947), there is a patina of social crime, but the real enemies are those who are aberrant to a strongly masculine American way of life, particularly women. Spillane's novels later respond to the context of the Cold War by associating criminality with communism. Later still, another successor to the hard-boiled tradition, Ross Macdonald's detective protagonist, Lew Archer, finds his cases within the parameters of family, responding to the tensions between the family ideal and its lived reality and the increasing interest in the psychology of crime. The sense of social responsibility and liberalism seen in Macdonald's narratives and to some extent in those of Chandler is strongly marked in the appropriation of the hard-boiled genre by the feminist writers of the 1980s such as Sara Paretsky and Sue Grafton. Paretsky in particular uses crime fiction as a vehicle for questioning social and cultural values, especially concerning gender, race and ethnicity, and her texts return to social crime in their representation of corruption in business and government. America does not have the monopoly on the female professional private detective; in 1972 P. D. James introduced Cordelia Gray, owner of a Detective Agency, in *An Unsuitable Job for a Woman*, Liza Cody's Anna Lee, who works for Brierly Security, appeared in 1980 (*Dupe*), Sarah Dunant's Hannah Wolfe, another professional private detective, had her first outing in 1991 (*Birth Marks*). Val McDermid has Kate Brannigan, who is based in Manchester and who entered the detective world in *Deadbeat* (1992). There are, however, many more female— and often feminist—professional private detectives in America than in Britain.

Not all private detectives in American detective fiction are of the hard-boiled variety. The professional private investigator continues to appear in many forms over the twentieth and into the twenty-first century, and America seems to have made the genre very much its own. In contrast, while Britain has the archetypal private professional in Sherlock Holmes, it has produced many more fictional private detectives who fall rather into the categories of the amateur or part-time detective, that is either the individual who is drawn into investigating crime in some way, or the detective for whom detection is an important part of his or her life but who does not detect from financial motivation.

Private detectives: Amateur

The figure of the amateur detective in fiction might be said to have had its beginnings in William Godwin's *Caleb Williams* (1794), in which the protagonist, Caleb, is drawn into what retrospectively can be read as detective work by his curiosity about his master, Falkland. Caleb receives no payment or reward for his detection; proving Falkland guilty of murder results in misery for Caleb and illness and death for his master in the published ending, and madness for Caleb in the first, unpublished ending. Caleb is, then, unpaid and 'falls' into detective work as a result of circumstance or accident, and these two factors are what I am using to define the term 'amateur private detective'. Perhaps the proliferation of this figure in British crime fiction can be explained in part by the very British concept of the 'gentleman amateur', that is someone who takes his 'hobby' or sport seriously; the phrase is more usually associated with sport, where it was used to differentiate the upper/middle-class gentleman who played for personal and national pride as opposed to the lower-class professional who played for money. The amateur detective narrative also allows a space for women as active agents, particularly in nineteenth and early twentieth-century crime fiction when, in the pre-feminist era, as the title of P. D. James's novel suggests, detection was *An Unsuitable Job for a Woman* (1972).

In the nineteenth century, as early as 1856, Wilkie Collins introduced the concept of the amateur female detective in his short story 'The Diary of Anne Rodway'. Typically, Anne, an engaged girl living alone in London while her future husband earns his fortune abroad, is drawn into a detective role by the mysterious death of her friend, Mary. Anne comes close to solving the case, but final resolution is firmly back in masculine hands as her fiancé returns from America in time to see the case through to its conclusion. Collins reprised this attenuated female detective figure in *The Woman in White* (1860) with his representation of the rather masculine Marian Halcombe, whose detective activities are brought to an abrupt end by illness, ensuring that detection is again returned to the masculine domain in the hands of Walter Hartright. In 1875, Collins published *The Law and the Lady*, in which the heroine, Valeria Woodville, enters into detection in order to prove her husband innocent of the death of his first wife—and carries out the role successfully and to completion. The amateur female detective is frequently drawn into detection in order to help a friend, husband or lover either as a detecting partner or in order to save them from a wrongful accusation of crime.

Men too can be drawn into investigative action in this way. Robert Audley, in *Lady Audley's Secret* (1862), is impelled into the role of amateur detective by the disappearance of his best friend, George Talboys, but is very keen to distinguish himself from the detective police, whom he describes as 'stained with vile associations, and unfit company for honest gentlemen'. And it could be argued that Watson, whose profession is that of physician, takes on the frequently feminised role of amateur assistant detective in his relationship with the professional Holmes. However, the amateur detective figure proliferated in the 'Golden Age' of crime fiction, that is the texts produced in the years between the two World Wars, although books in the 'Golden Age' style continued to be produced after this period, and indeed, in the late twentieth and early twenty-first century a number of parodies and pastiches of the sub-genre have been published. In 'Golden Age' fiction the detective is commonly male, an amateur or later a police officer who is distinguished from his counterparts, usually by class.

Perhaps the best-known example of the amateur gentleman detective is Lord Peter Wimsey, the creation of Dorothy L. Sayers. His first appearance was in *Whose Body?* (1923), and he featured in a further 14 novels and collections of short stories. Lord Peter is a foppish, effete aristocrat, described as having a 'vaguely foolish face', but is in fact highly intelligent. He suffers shell-shock while serving in the trenches in the first World War, and is prone to nervous breakdowns; despite his effete appearance he is actually strong and athletic and attractive to women. Rather in the manner of Sherlock Holmes he detects out of interest or because he is in some way personally involved; he does not have a female assistant, at least not in the early stories, but a faithful man-servant, Bunter, who looks after him and also helps in his detective work. His fortune ensures that he can indulge himself in his detective work without requiring payment—Sayers declared that she deliberately made him wealthy as at the time of his creation she herself was struggling to make a living. In a similar mould to Wimsey is Margery Allingham's Albert Campion, first featured in *The Crime at Black Dudley* (1929), another aristocrat—there are hints that he has royal blood—superficially foolish and bespectacled, wealthy and assisted by ex-convict and now man-servant Magersfontein Lugg. Both Campion and Wimsey have close and cordial relationships with police detectives who at times assist the detectives, and this is an important aspect of both amateur and professional fictional detectives. The police contact both legitimises and enables the private detective in his or her work.

Wimsey acquires a female assistant, Harriet Vane, who is also the love interest in the Wimsey novels and whom Lord Peter eventually persuades into marriage. Campion too marries in the course of his adventures, Amanda Fitton, who also takes on the role of female assistant detective. But Golden-Age fiction also produced female detectives who worked alone. These were not the feisty feminist detectives of Grafton or Paretsky, but tended to be spinsters, often elderly, with sharp eyes, a taste for gossip, a nose for scandal and time on their hands. Agatha Christie's Miss Marple is the most famous of these figures, first appearing in a short story, 'The Tuesday Night Club' (*The Royal Magazine*, December 1927), but she has her origin in figure of Caroline Sheppard, the spinster sister of Dr Sheppard, in *The Murder of Roger Ackroyd* (1926). Caroline Shepherd plays a minor role in the narrative, assisting the central detective, M. Poirot, but her characterisation prepared the way for Miss Marple.

Jane Marple is an elderly, white-haired spinster who lives in the village of St Mary Mead, which is the location for an amazing number of murders. Miss Marple is very much the 'armchair detective', in that she is largely static, gathering information from friends, servants and tradesmen and knitting it together into a complete narrative of the crime. She is a knitter, of wool as well as narrative, and a collector of gossip whose long experience of life and of the darker aspects of peoples' characters is the foundation of her detective abilities. She travels outside St Mary Mead—to the Caribbean (*A Caribbean Mystery*, 1964), to London (*At Bertram's Hotel*, 1965) and on a coach tour around England (*Nemesis*, 1971) for example, but even in these other locations the pattern of sitting and knitting information together remains. Physically frail, nonetheless Miss Marple has a backbone of steel: she is undismayed by dead bodies and the darkest corners of the human psyche and it is perhaps this aspect of her character that can be found in later representations of the (much younger) female detective.

While Miss Marple is the best-known of the Golden-Age female detectives, she was not the first. In 1928, two years before the first Miss Marple novel appeared (*Murder at the Vicarage*, 1930), Patricia Wentworth introduced her spinster detective Miss Maud Silver in *The Grey Veil*. Miss Silver has elements in common with Miss Marple, but rather blurs the boundaries between the amateur detective and the professional: where Miss Marple 'falls' into detective work by dint of being present where crimes are committed, or is somehow drawn into the investigation of a crime, Miss Silver, a retired governess who by accident initially is involved in a series of investigations from which she profits financially, supplementing her 'meagre pension' and enabling her to acquire a pleasant and well-furnished flat and some of the luxuries of life. That she profits from her investigations, and that she sees herself as a 'private enquiry agent' locates her as a professional rather than amateur detective, but like Miss Marple she is elderly, single, knits and has a similar opinion of human nature—possibly she is a little more acerbic than her counterpart. She also has a much closer relationship with the police than does Miss Marple.

The Golden-Age female detective is an important development in detective fiction. This period saw a feminisation of what had been a very masculine genre, and the final amateur detective to whom I wish to refer is male, but hardly masculine and, similar to Miss Silver, rather blurs the boundaries between amateur and professional detective. Agatha Christie's M. Hercule Poirot, the little Belgian with his waxed moustaches, bald head and the 'little grey cells' which he uses to solve crimes, is, after Sherlock Holmes, probably the most famous detective in the world. Poirot is not superficially effete but in reality strongly masculine like Wimsey or Campion; he is actually feminised in his characterisation and in his detective methods, relying on intuition, collecting—and enjoying—gossip, and employing his extensive knowledge of domestic matters such as whether starch would be used when laundering a handkerchief (*The Murder of Roger Ackroyd*) in tracking down the criminal. There is, though, at the core of Poirot, an implacable sense of justice. As he tells Flora in *The Murder of Roger Ackroyd*, 'if I go into this, you must understand one thing clearly. *I shall go through with it to the end* [...] you may wish that, after all, you had left it to the local police' (emphasis in the text). While it is tempting to suggest that this is a masculine trait which recuperates Poirot's own masculinity, it is a trait seen also in Miss Marple, who is likened to 'Nemesis' the Roman goddess who was the spirit of divine retribution. There is still, in Christie's crime fictions, a strong, quasi-religious sense of good and evil and of divine justice, albeit channelled through human agency.

The representation of Poirot is superficially at least very different to that of Sherlock Holmes, yet there are similarities between the two. The Holmes–Watson model is reproduced in the Poirot–Hastings pairing, with Hastings performing a similar role to that of Watson (in fact Hastings appeared in only eight of the thirty-four Poirot novels), and the ineffectual but necessary police contact Inspector Japp is the literary descendant of Inspector Lestrade. As a retired Belgian policeman, it is reasonable to assume that Poirot has a pension, and monetary reward for his detective work is implied rather than explicitly discussed. As he declares, 'Money, it means much to me and always has done' (*Murder of Roger Ackroyd*), and in the well-known television series starring David Suchet as Poirot, his secretary Miss Lemon deals with all matters financial, including payment for his services. But the *milieu* in which Poirot works—property-owning professional middle class, frequently rural and always superficially respectable—and the period in which many of the books are set combine to make the mention of money distasteful. The reader is left feeling that Poirot works for the intellectual stimulation and satisfaction afforded by his detective practices rather than for financial gain.

The early part of the twentieth century saw a proliferation of variations on the detective figure epitomised by Sherlock Holmes and on his methods of detection, and this has continued up to the present day. The representation and characterisation of the detective responds to social and cultural change, as does the representation of the criminal and the type of crime. In Britain, Sherlock Holmes provided the masculine, rational certainty required in an increasingly unstable world of social, economic and cultural change; figures such as Peter Wimsey and Albert Campion reiterated and reasserted the social and moral values shaken by social revolution and world wars; Miss Marple, Miss Silver and Poirot functioned similarly but within a middle/upper-class, largely domestic frame and their role was very much to alleviate the anxieties consequent on the rapidly eroding class boundaries and the subsequent difficulties of social identification. At heart of the Christie novels is always the revelation of someone who is not what he or she seems to be, and Poirot or Miss Marple's detective work is necessary to expose the impostor and restore social stability. This function of the detective and of detective fiction, to reassure the reader not just about the threat posed by crime and the criminal but also about contemporary cultural and social anxieties, remains. Identity is still central to detective fiction, but the focus has shifted away from anxieties about social and communal identity, that is identity fixed in class, employment and location, to questions about personal and individual identity, particularly in terms of gender and of psychology.

In the United States, detective fiction in the twentieth century has taken a different path, with criminality often associated with social and political corruption; certainly from Hammett's 'Continental Op' and Sam Spade through Chandler's Philip Marlowe onwards the detective is the often alienated individual fighting against the system which generates criminality. Detection is less intellectualised than in the Golden-Age 'clue-puzzle' and more action-based with detective activity that comprises watching, following, questioning and physical violence by and against the detective. The personal and the political are inseparable in much American crime fiction, and it is often used as a vehicle to explore politics, as in Sara Paretsky's feminist V. I. Warshawski novels or BarbaraNeely's [sic] fictions featuring black amateur detective Blanche White, which combine racial and feminist themes, or Tony Hillerman's Navajo novels with Native American detectives Sergeant Joe Leaphorn and Jim Chee or Jeffrey Deaver's quadriplegic serial detective, Lincoln Rhyme. Deaver's protagonist perhaps exemplifies most clearly the need for the modern detective to have access to the techniques and technology of forensic science and medicine; confined to a wheelchair and no longer able to make forensic searches himself, Lincoln Rhyme requires an assistant to 'walk' the crime scene and recover physical evidence and then is totally reliant on technology and his own mental acuity to read and interpret that evidence. Computers and databases have now superseded Sherlock Holmes's mental 'calendar of crime' and detection is, in Deaver's novels, an intellectual, rational and scientific exercise rather than an active physical engagement with the criminal.

Clearly detection has become very much the science that Sherlock Holmes claimed it to be, and the modern detective has either to be a professional, in the police or in a connected profession such as a forensic pathologist or psychological profiler or in similar role. If working in a private or amateur capacity, the investigative figure must have or acquire contacts within and assistance from the professional world in order to realistically and effectively function as a detective. The amateur detective, who still seems very much a British figure, is seen less often than in the Golden Age, as it is increasingly difficult to make such a figure credible in the face of media-fostered public understanding of the complexities of real detection. Where there is an amateur protagonist, he or more commonly she will often work in employment which itself incorporates investigative elements, for example journalism, as with Val McDermid's Lindsay Gordon series and Denise Mina's Paddy Meehan books, or writing, as in Veronica Stallwood's Oxford-based narratives featuring novelist Kate Ivory, or academic sleuths such as Judith Cutler's Sophie Rivers, Amanda Cross's Kate Fansler and Sarah Caudwell's ungendered Oxbridge professor, Hilary Tamar. Another route to avoiding the pressures of reality in narratives with an amateur detective is to locate the fiction in the relatively recent past when such figures seemed more possible, as in Catriona MacPherson's 1920s amateur sleuth, Dandy Gilver, Gillian Linscott's turn-of-the-century suffragette Nell Bray or David Roberts's 1930s aristocratic amateur Lord Edward Corinth. A further solution is placing the narrative anachronistically in the distant past before the detective in the modern sense existed, for example in Ellis Peters's Brother Cadfael series or C. J. Sansom's Shardlake novels.

In whatever form, the detective remains central to much crime fiction. While not always as immediately recognisable or clearly defined as Sherlock Holmes, the detective function remains constant. Above all else, the fictional detective, whatever his or her guise, methods or motivation, is driven by the desire to find out, to discover, to explain and to rationalise acts and deeds which resist simple solutions. Crime in fiction is a mode of expression for contemporary social anxieties and speaks eloquently of its cultural context; the detective is the culturally constructed response to criminality and functions to reassure and restore the social status quo. In the act of detection, in revealing motives for murder and solutions to mysteries, in rationalising the irrational and in ordering the disordered, the detective is very much a creation of a modern world in which, we assume, science and human intelligence can find the answers to everything.

See also   *Contexts*: Crime and Criminality, Evidence, Gender and Sexuality, the Law, Police and Policing; *Texts*: Feminist Crime Fiction, Golden-Age Fiction, Historical Crime Fiction, Police Procedural; *Criticism*: Feminism, Cultural Materialism, Postcolonialism, Postmodernism.

Further reading

Craig, Patricia and Mary Cadogan, *The Lady Investigates: Women Detectives and Spies in Fiction* (Oxford: Oxford University Press, 1986).

Delameter, Jerome K. and Ruth Prigozy (eds), *The Theory and Practice of Classic Detective Fiction* (Westport, CO: Greenwood Press, 1997).

Emsley, Clive and Haia Shpayer-Makov (eds), *Police Detectives in History, 1750–1950* (Burlington, VT: Ashgate, 2006).

Kayman, Martin, *From Bow Street to Baker Street: Mystery, Detection and Narrative* (Basingstoke: Macmillan, 1992).

Klein, Kathleen Gregory (ed.), *Diversity and Detective Fiction* (Bowling Green, OH: Bowling Green State University Popular Press, 1999).

Knight, Stephen, *Crime Fiction 1800–2000: Death, Detection, Diversity* (Basingstoke: Palgrave Macmillan, 2010 [2004]).

Miller, D. A., *The Novel and the Police* (Berkeley: University of California Press, 1988).

Ousby, Ian, *Bloodhounds of Heaven: The Detective in English Fiction from Godwin to Doyle* (Cambridge, MA: Harvard University Press, 1976).

Rzepka, Charles, *Detective Fiction* (Cambridge: Polity Press, 2005).

Walton, Priscilla L. and Manina Jones, *Detective Agency: Women Rewriting the Hard-Boiled Tradition* (Berkeley: University of California Press, 1999).

Worthington, Heather, *The Rise of the Detective in Early Nineteenth-Century Popular Fiction* (Basingstoke: Palgrave Macmillan, 2005).

Evidence

Evidence is inextricably involved in criminal investigations real and fictional: the verbal, visual or physical proofs establish the facts of the case; evidence is essential in correctly allocating guilt. If the detective is an important and omnipresent figure in crime fiction, it is because of his/her role in seeking out evidence. In many ways the detective comes into being in reality and in fiction as the decline in religious certainty in the Western world from the eighteenth century onwards undermines and weakens the belief that God will ensure the punishment of the criminal. The detective is a product of the Age of Enlightenment, with its emphasis on reason and rationality, and the gradual ascendance of secularism over religion, an ascendance ensured by Darwin's revelation of the process of evolution in *On the Origin of the Species* (1859) and *The Descent of Man* (1871). For much of the eighteenth and nineteenth centuries, and indeed into the twentieth century and beyond, State control was not an effective substitute for religious control.

A further significant factor in the need for evidence to prove guilt and in the development of the detective is urbanisation and the concomitant loss of rural communities in which everyone was known to everyone else and aberrant behaviour was therefore very apparent. In the cities, the juxtaposition of poverty and wealth and the anonymity conferred by the large population were perceived to encourage crime and simultaneously make its prevention and detection more difficult. In these circumstances, as the old systems of visible guilt, witnesses, confession and divine justice failed to control crime and criminality, the drive to discover hard evidence that would prove guilt beyond question became more urgent.

In criminography of the eighteenth and early nineteenth century in Britain the most common ways in which a criminal was caught were, as the *Newgate Calendars* show, by being seen in the act; by behaving in a manner out of character; by fleeing the scene of the crime in a panic and implicitly admitting guilt by absence; by being overcome with guilt for the crime and confessing. This pattern is very clear in the 1697 case of Matthew Clarke, who robs and kills a former girlfriend and then flees the scene in a guilty panic; 'some men come up' as he is on the road, notice his terror and the bloodstains on his clothes and deliver him to the local justice. Clarke immediately confesses and is subsequently executed. There is no need here to seek evidence. But increasingly this system is seen to fail. Criminals conceal their guilt; there are no witnesses; there is no confession. Correct allocation of guilt begins to require other kinds of proof and this is often in the form of circumstantial evidence. If connections between the accused man or woman and the victim of crime can be made, if there is a possible motive, if the accused has no alibi for the time of the crime and if he or she has been seen acting suspiciously, all these could be woven into a narrative which seemed to prove guilt.

Sometimes this narrative would be accurate, as in the case of Joseph Richards, recorded in a broadside. In 1786, Richards was accused of murdering his ex-employer, Walter Horseman. The evidence against Richards was all circumstantial: he had been away from his lodging on the night of the murder; he had been seen to add melted lead to a stick in order to make it heavier and a similar stick had been used as the murder weapon, and he had been frequently heard threatening vengeance on his ex-master. Clearly today this would be insufficient evidence to convict, but in the eighteenth century Richards was found guilty and sentenced to death. Fortunately his subsequent confession confirmed his guilt and so the sentence was seen to be just and justified. However, as the number of crimes potentially punishable by death increased from fifty in 1688 to over 200 by 1810, public anxiety about the reliability of circumstantial evidence unsupported by confession rose—as did anxiety about capital punishment and the severity of the penal system generally, an anxiety that led men such as Sir Samuel Romilly to campaign for the reforms of the penal system that Parliament eventually undertook in the 1820s and 30s.

This anxiety was also articulated in the fiction of the period, particularly in the periodical press, as Peter Drexler has discussed in *Literatur, Recht, Kriminalität* (1991). *Blackwood's Edinburgh Magazine* published a short story by John Wilson, 'Expiation' (1830), in which a young man is convicted, solely on the grounds of circumstantial evidence, of the rape and murder of a beautiful young woman—he has no alibi for the time of the murder, he behaves strangely, he has a letter from the victim on his person and so on. He is found guilty and sentenced to hang; at the final moment his father confesses to the crime. The son had known of the father's guilt and was protecting him from the force of the law, while the father's knowledge of his son's innocence had convinced him that true justice—read God—would ensure that the son would escape conviction. A similar story appeared in the popular *Chambers's Edinburgh Journal* in 1849. In 'Circumstantial Evidence', attributed to Samuel Warren, an elderly woman dies suddenly after threatening to disinherit her nephew when he proposes to make an unsuitable marriage. The doctor called in to treat the woman suspects she has been poisoned; the grandson has had sole access to his aunt during her illness and is observed to behave strangely. The combination of motive, behaviour and the subsequent discovery of a quantity of poison in his bedroom cabinet is seen as sufficient evidence of guilt and the nephew is sent to trial and found guilty. In this story there is some minimal detective work carried out by the lawyers attending the case, and there is a last-minute reprieve when it is discovered through witness statements that actually the nephew's step-father is guilty of the offence. Both 'Expiation' and 'Circumstantial Evidence' are clearly intended to highlight the unreliability of evidence dependent on circumstance and unsupported by fact.

In the nineteenth century in Britain, the drive to acquire evidence that will definitively prove guilt—or indeed innocence—in cases of serious crime such as murder is seen to be increasingly urgent, and the detective is an active part of that process. Another important element that facilitates the search for evidence is the development of forensic medicine and science and in Britain this is relatively late. In Continental Europe the inquisitorial system of criminal justice was and is based on enquiries carried out by State-appointed investigators who directly examine evidence in order to ascertain the facts of the crime, while the jury-based adversarial English system relied, and still does to a great extent, on oath, witness statement and legal precedent. Evidence is still collected by the police and used in court, but it is filtered through the barristers acting for the prosecution and defence and is part rather than the whole of the case. The Continent, then, saw much earlier and stronger developments in forensic medicine, science and ballistics and, broadly speaking, it was not until the nineteenth century that Britain began formally to produce and record its own systems of forensic investigation. Andrew Duncan was appointed as the first Professor of Medical Jurisprudence and Police at Edinburgh University in 1807, later followed by Professor Robert Christison (1822) who was an expert in toxicology and the medical witness at many famous trials including those of the body-snatchers Burke and Hare and the alleged poisoner Madeleine Smith. In 1823, J. A. Paris and J. S. M. Fonblanque, both English despite their names, published *Medical Jurisprudence*, which was hailed as an essential guide to understanding medical evidence in trials for potential jurors, and incidentally as a sensational read for the ordinary man or woman interested in crime.

Much early forensic science was concerned with determining the cause of death rather than with the correct attribution of guilt, hence the medical aspect of the discipline. Advances in anatomy, a greater understanding of chemistry and new technology such as microscopes all contributed to the development of forensic medicine. Toxicology, or the study of the effects of chemical/poison on the living organism, was an important part of this development, with Mathieu Orfila producing his treatise *Traité des Poisons* or *Toxicologie Générale* in 1813. Before the scientific advances that made it possible to trace and identify poisons in the human body, poisoning had been a popular method of murder. The science of ballistics would make it possible to match a bullet to the weapon from which it had been discharged; matching knives to stab wounds was made possible by increasing knowledge of anatomy and the ability to look closely—microscopically—at weapon and wound; it became possible to differentiate between accidental or natural death and murder. But the focus was on the body of the victim in the search for evidence of the cause of death. What was more complex was the search for physical evidence that would link victim to perpetrator and identify the criminal.

It was not until the early twentieth century that Edmond Locard famously articulated the notion that, in every crime scene, the criminal will bring something to that scene and take something away, that there are physical traces which definitively connect criminal to crime. Initial attempts to identify criminality, if not the individual criminal in a particular case, were centred on physical characteristics. Just as there was in the nineteenth century a perception that there was a specific 'criminal class', so criminality was thought to be visible, apparent in the features of the criminal. The pseudo-sciences of phrenology and physiognomy were both briefly considered as methods of detecting criminality: phrenology claimed that the shape, the lumps and bumps that occur naturally on the human skull, corresponded to specific mental functions and modes, the skull being the housing of the brain which directed thought and behaviour. Franz Joseph Gall is considered to have proposed the theory circa 1800, and his best-known disciple is Johann Gaspar Spurzheim. Phrenology was subsequently dismissed as quackery by the scientific community, which could find no corroboration between Gall's theory and empirical examination of the brain. Physiognomy, which suggests that outer appearances, especially the face, are indicative of inner character and personality, has a longer and slightly more respectable history. This concept had been circulating in societies from the Ancient Greeks onwards, but achieved 'scientific' status in the eighteenth century, when Johann Kaspar Lavater published his essays on the subject in 1772. The idea captured the popular imagination and nineteenth-century novelists, such as Charles Dickens, Charlotte Brontë and Wilkie Collins, drew on the theory of physiognomy in their fiction.

In the second half of the nineteenth century Cesare Lombroso pursued the idea of physical markers of criminality in *L'uomo Delinquente* (1876), or *Criminal Man*, in which he proposed that individuals could be 'born criminal' in a kind of reverse evolutionary process and that such people could be identified by physical characteristics such as low, sloping foreheads, large jaws, fleshy lips, large, prominent ears and even baldness. While Lombroso's theories have been discredited, his methodological approach, involving careful measurements and consideration of sociological factors, influenced the science of anthropometry, or what became known as 'Bertillonage'. This was a system, invented by the French law enforcement officer Alphonse Bertillon, of detailed measurements of various physical characteristics of known criminals, kept in a card file—the modern equivalent would be a database. This file meant that when a crime was committed and there was a suspect it was possible to compare the measurements on file with those of the suspect and so confirm identity even if the criminal had changed his/her name or physical attributes such as hair colour. Bertillonage was widely used in France and across Europe in the period before fingerprinting came into being, but of course its drawbacks were the difficulties of achieving consistency of measurement when carried out by different officials and the limitations of having the measurements only of known criminals.

The concept of evidence of criminality being somehow physically visible on the face or body was also explored by Francis Galton who, in the late nineteenth century, devised a system of 'composite photography' in order to identify 'types' by appearance, a system that he hoped would aid medical diagnosis and potentially assist in the recognition of criminality in the individual, positing a typical 'criminal face'. He obtained these composite photographs by overlaying a series of photographic exposures of a selected group of people onto a single plate; the resulting image offered a composite of their various features in a single face, creating the 'type'. The idea clearly owed much to physiognomy, and Galton published his ideas in his 1883 text *Inquiries into Human Faculty and Its Development*. Although forced finally to admit that this system of identification did not work, Galton later devised the method of identifying fingerprints that is still in use today. He built on work by William Herschel in the 1860s and Henry Faulds in the 1880s, and his final classification system for fingerprints was influenced by the detective work of Argentine police officer Juan Vucetich. In 1900, Edward R. Henry's *The Classification and Use of Fingerprints* was instrumental in persuading a Government Committee to recommend the adoption of fingerprinting as the preferred method of identifying criminals. By the beginning of the twentieth century the body of the criminal was beginning to be perceived as equally important as the body of the victim in terms of evidence.

Combining the two narratives of evidence—of the victim and of the criminal—developed into a science over the nineteenth century and continues in the twentieth century. Advances in technology and in science have made possible the most minute examination of the scene of the crime and the body of the victim, with DNA evidence the most recent major development. Locard's theory of traces, which states that a perpetrator will inevitably bring something to a crime scene and equally will take something away from that scene, is now an accepted fact and central to any criminal investigation. But criminography shows that the seeds of the idea had been in circulation—and limited use— for a long time before the theory was articulated. In Eugène François Vidocq's *Mémoires* (1828–9) the criminal-turned-detective recounts a case in which plaster casts of a suspect's footprints are successfully matched to his shoes; Henry Goddard, in his *Memoirs of a Bow Street Runner* (written between 1875 and 1879, but not published until 1956, with an Introduction by Patrick Pringle), tells of a case where he matched bullets found at a crime scene to the mould in which they were cast, proving it to be an inside job carried out by the butler. Fiction also offered quasi-forensic examinations of the scene of the crime. Perhaps most famously, in Wilkie Collins's *The Moonstone* (1869), the crime scene is reconstructed by means of inducing an opium trance in the protagonist, Franklin Blake. In Edgar Allan Poe's 'The Murders in the Rue Morgue', the proto-detective, Dupin, visits the crime scene, works out by careful examination of the nails securing the window catch how the assailant exited the apparently locked room, considers the finger marks on the throat of one of the victims, finds a stray tuft of hair of animal origin and reaches the correct solution that the 'murderer' is an orang-utan.

French author Émile Gaboriau's *The Widow Lerouge* (in French *L'Affaire Lerouge* [1866]) featured the kind of crime scene investigation that Sherlock Holmes would later claim as his own. Gaboriau's amateur detective figure, Père Tabaret, examines muddy footprints and considers the significance of their depth, looks at and identifies cigar ash, works out the size and type of hat worn by the murderer from the marks it leaves on a dusty mantelpiece. But it is with Doyle's Sherlock Holmes stories that the scene of the crime examination and the concept of forensic investigation really catch the public imagination. Indeed, it has been suggested that the police looked to Sherlock Holmes's methods in their own detective work, but it seems more likely that Doyle was responding to the contemporary developments in forensic medicine. It is certain that he drew on his own medical knowledge and on the example of his tutor at Edinburgh University Medical School, Joseph Bell, in creating Holmes and his investigative techniques. Bell was renowned for 'detecting' the employment, personal history and likely ailment of a patient simply from his or her appearance, and in Holmes's first outing in *A Study in Scarlet* (1887) the detective similarly correctly assesses Watson's recent history: 'You have been in Afghanistan, I perceive.' In the same novel, Holmes's later examination of the murder scene in Lauriston Gardens echoes that of Gaboriau's Père Taberet, with Holmes's reading of the traces of the perpetrator and the injuries to the victim's body creating a convincing narrative based entirely on empirical and physical evidence. Later Holmes stories are littered with this kind of scientific and forensic approach to crime.

And of course Holmes is the archetypal rational, scientific detective. When he is first introduced to the reader and to Watson, Holmes is completing a successful trial of a test he has devised for proving the presence of blood in stains. He refers to 'the old guaiacum test', which was a real forensic method of identifying blood used at the time, and to 'the microscopic examination for blood corpuscles', clearly suggesting some knowledge of forensic medicine and implicitly acknowledging the necessity of this kind of concrete evidence in criminal cases. In 1901, the Fingerprint Branch of the Metropolitan Police was established; in Doyle's 'The Adventure of the Norwood Builder' (1903) a bloodstained thumbprint is used in an attempt to attribute guilt to an innocent man. While in the mid-nineteenth century the 'chain of circumstantial evidence' forged by Mary E. Braddon's fictional amateur detective Robert Audley in *Lady Audley's Secret* (1862) is sufficient to convince him of Lady Audley's guilt, by the end of the century such circumstantial evidence is clearly insufficient: forensic science has become essential to the reality of crime investigation and to its fictional representation. Even in the Golden-Age clue-puzzles of writers such as Agatha Christie or Dorothy L. Sayers, where the body of the victim is quickly removed from the scene, there is an implicit recognition of the importance of forensically verified evidence. Crime fiction is very much concerned with proving 'the facts of the case'; the collection and interpretation of evidence of all kinds and its collation into a coherent narrative is at the heart of the genre, especially in the sub-genre of detective fiction, whatever its origins or format.

As in reality the collection and interpretation of evidence became increasingly specialised, complex crime fiction rose to the challenge of incorporating this trend into its narratives in accessible form. In the USA the 1930s detective Dick Tracy, the comic-strip hero created by Chester Gould, used real and fantastical forensic science in his investigations; Erle Stanley Gardner's lawyer-detective Perry Mason, hero of over 80 novels, also utilised forensic detection in his work. The police procedurals of the 1950s and later necessarily, in the interests of authenticity, include details of forensic investigation and evidence in their stories. By the late twentieth and early twenty-first century, forensic techniques for collecting evidence have become a staple element in crime fiction and there is a positive fashion for the detective figure to be a forensic specialist in some form. This is possibly a consequence of the frequent references to forensics and the focus on the body of the victim in factual as well as fictional accounts of crime. In the fiction, perhaps the best-known forensic detectives are Patricia Cornwell's Kay Scarpetta, who is initially Chief Medical Examiner and latterly a freelance forensic specialist, and Kathy Reichs's Tempe Brennan, who is a forensic anthropologist. The popularity of the forensic investigator has resulted in numerous television series: in Britain, *Silent Witness*, featuring a team of forensic pathologists, has been running since 1996, and is credited with increasing the number of university applications to study forensic pathology; *Waking the Dead* (2000 onwards) uses forensic science to investigate old unsolved crimes; America has *CSI: Crime Scene Investigation*, which started in 2000 and is still running and in 2006, in a new twist, *Dexter*, based on the novels by Jeff Lindsay, has a protagonist who is an expert in blood-spatter analysis but also a psychopathic serial killer.

Evidence is then, a vital part of crime fiction. From the early days of the genre, when evidence was, if unreliable, simple and straightforward, relying on witnesses, aberrant behaviour, the appearance of guilt or force of circumstance, to modern crime fiction with its access to the complexities of forensic science, the drive to discover the facts of the case and correctly apportion guilt and prove innocence has in a sense structured crime narratives and the genre itself. The content of a crime fiction novel is, to a great extent, devoted to evidence and its collection and interpretation. Equally, the methods of its collection and the skills required to read evidence correctly respond to cultural change and scientific, medical and technological developments. Evidence is as much an important factor in the development of the detective in fiction as it has been in reality, and ensures that crime fiction retains its relevance and maintains its popularity.

See also *Contexts*: Detectives and Detection, the Law, Police and Policing; *Texts*: Early Criminography, Police Procedural; *Criticism*: Feminism, Cultural Materialism, Postmodernism.

Further reading

Clark, Michael and Catherine Crawford (eds), *Legal Medicine in History* (Cambridge: Cambridge University Press, 1994).

Frank, Lawrence, *Victorian Detective Fiction and the Nature of Evidence: The Scientific Investigations of Poe, Dickens and Doyle* (Basingstoke: Palgrave Macmillan, 2003).

Smyth, Frank, *Cause of Death: The Story of Forensic Science* (London: Orbis, 1980).

Thomas, Ronald, *Detective Fiction and the Rise of Forensic Science* (Cambridge: Cambridge University Press, 1999).

Gender and sexuality

Crime fiction is often considered to be a masculine and deeply conservative genre, in its subject matter and because of the formulaic nature of its narratives—at the very least there must be a crime, a perpetrator and a victim, while the narrative conventions of the form tend to insist on a movement from enigma or puzzle to solution or revelation. These fixed patterns have contributed to the perception of the genre as masculine, a perception strengthened by the underpinning of method and rationality that enable the discovery of the solution and the strong association, in the case of much crime fiction, of the detective with science and logic. This is perhaps most clearly represented in the figure of Arthur Conan Doyle's Sherlock Holmes, the self-declared 'world's first consulting detective'. The nineteenth and early twentieth-century concept of the detective as a professional and the satisfactory resolution and closure of crime narratives are also strongly gendered as masculine, and the violence inherent in crime, real and imagined, is largely considered a masculine trait. While criminals in fiction are frequently male, they tend to remain within a normative gender frame; men may behave badly, but they are deviant more usually in terms of illegality than sexuality. Certainly in nineteenth-century criminography issues surrounding gender and sexuality tend to be focused on the feminine.

Crime fiction as a genre developed mainly in white, Western, patriarchal societies in which agency was granted to men rather than women and this also has been reflected in the gendering of the genre as masculine. The apparently passive position of women in such societies results in women in crime narratives commonly being allocated the role either of the victim, the catalyst for or the cause of crime rather than its perpetrator. This idea has a long history, beginning perhaps with Eve in the Garden of Eden tempting Adam into sin—or crime—and the association of deviant femininity and crime has remained a constant feature of the genre. Inherent in this association are patriarchally fostered masculine anxieties about the feminine, particularly female agency, which is seen as a transgression of traditional gender boundaries and is often represented as criminal in early crime narratives. However, as women in reality laid claim to independence and autonomy, the gender-transgressing female figure in crime fiction maintains her association with crime but in an investigatory rather than criminal role. Women authors began to develop women detectives, appropriating the formulaic structures of the genre and making it their own. The female detective is late in developing as the masculinised genre of detective fiction is very resistant to a female protagonist and from a male perspective the female detective is seen to be equally gender-transgressing as her criminal counterpart.

As Gill Plain observes in *Twentieth-Century Crime Fiction: Gender, Sexuality and the Body* (2001), '[g]ender transgression and the disruption of "normative" sexuality have always been an integral part of crime narrative'. Plain is speaking of modern criminography, where issues of gender and sexuality have become central to the genre in terms of both criminal and detective, but, even in earlier narratives of crime, gender transgression, especially where women are concerned, is a recurring feature. Middle- and upper-class society's rigid conventions concerning gender and sexuality in the nineteenth century meant that masculine and feminine roles were clearly defined: men dominated the public and social spheres while women were firmly contained within the domestic. Men were perceived to be active, socially and sexually, women to be passive and their sexuality directed by their 'natural' desire to have children. Men were concerned with the intellectual and rational, women with the emotional and physical—although not the sexual. Clearly these roles are cultural constructs rather than realities, but the ideological constraints, particularly on women, meant that any deviance from the perceived norms of gender was condemned by society. Gender constraints on men were no less rigid in terms of their behaviour, duties and responsibilities but, while ideology advocated sexual continence for men, in reality there was an implicit acceptance that they might satisfy sexual desire outside marriage, as the number of prostitutes in the nineteenth century shows.

Criminality in men, then, was in the nineteenth and early twentieth century less commonly associated with gender or sexual deviance (with the exception of homosexuality) and more usually concerned with legal transgression—murder, theft, drunkenness, violence, fraud, embezzlement, forgery and so on—and deviation from their proper social class. But because gender roles for women and constraints on their sexual behaviour were more rigid, any transgression of these patriarchally constructed boundaries was more apparent. Women, considered to be the weaker sex, less rational and less intellectually capable than men, were therefore more likely to fall into sin and criminality and so required stricter guidance in and control over their personal lives. And, when a woman does take to crime, her criminality is accentuated; she is doubly deviant, not only acting in defiance of the (patriarchal) law but also rejecting her 'proper' feminine role. In early crime narratives the causes of female criminality are often directly linked precisely to a lack of proper masculine control and the female criminal is frequently depicted as behaving in an unfeminine fashion and of using her sexuality in the interests of crime, usually to deceive men.

This pattern can be seen in the story of Mary Young, executed for theft in 1740, which is contained in one of the *Accounts* written by the Ordinaries of Newgate Prison. Mary is an orphan, brought up by a woman; she rejects her proper role and place in society, leaving Ireland to go to London; she uses her sexual attractions to persuade her lover to pay for her journey which incidentally leads him to steal from his master. Once in London, finding no legal way of making a living, Mary is drawn into a life of crime at which she excels, eventually becoming the leader of a gang of thieves which, in a most unfeminine manner, she runs like a business. The *Account* focuses on those acts of theft in which Mary uses her femininity to trick men into parting with their money or jewels or to steal from other women, as when she fakes pregnancy with a false belly and arms which stay on view while her actual limbs are involved in picking pockets. While the *Account's* stated intention is to warn against a life of crime, its narrative is more concerned to entertain its audience with its racy representation of gender transgression and the use of sexuality in the interests of female agency. This focus on the sensational aspects of the factual female criminal's story later finds its way, in the mid-nineteenth century, into what became known as sensation fiction, a genre in which female deviation from proper gender roles and conventional sexual behaviour was central.

Perhaps the best-known example is Mary E. Braddon's *Lady Audley's Secret* (1862), in which the eponymous heroine uses her sexual allure to entice Sir Michael Audley into what for her is a bigamous marriage and then attempts to murder her first husband in order to avoid prosecution, validate her second marriage and maintain her new and elevated social status. While Lady Audley does commit criminal acts, her real 'crime' is assuming agency and controlling her own fate—and of course, using her sexuality in the process. The narrative should be seen in the context of the author's own life and of the state of the divorce laws in the period. Braddon had a long-term relationship with the editor, John Maxwell, bearing him several children, but could not marry him until his wife, who was insane and in an asylum, died, as insanity was not grounds for divorce. The 1857 Matrimonial Causes Act made it possible, for the first time, for a woman to divorce her husband, but while under the new Act the husband had only to prove his wife's adultery, the wife had to prove her husband had committed not just adultery but also either incest, bigamy, cruelty or desertion, a condition which, in combination with the fact that for many women money was also an issue, meant that divorce was still impossible. So, although in Braddon's text Lady Audley feels herself to be deserted by her first husband, she has no grounds for divorce. Significantly, *Lady Audley's Secret* cannot, finally, admit female agency and depict a female murderess, and Lady Audley's behaviour is categorised as the consequence of an inherited madness.

Contrastingly, in Arthur Conan Doyle's determinedly masculine Sherlock Holmes stories at the end of the nineteenth century, women tend to play more conventional roles and feature as victims of or catalysts for crime rather than as criminals. This is perhaps Doyle's conservative response to the rise of the 'New Woman' and the contemporary demand for female suffrage. In the first Sherlock Holmes story, *A Study in Scarlet* (1887), Lucy Ferrier is part victim of and part catalyst for the crimes committed by the male characters in the narrative; in stories such as 'The Adventure of the Copper Beeches' (1892) or 'The Adventure of the Speckled Band' (1892) women are very definitely victims—of deceit in the first instance and murder in the second—and both crimes are motivated by the desire of a male guardian to retain possession of a daughter's or ward's inherited income when it is threatened by her proposed marriage. Even in 'A Scandal in Bohemia' (1891), which features Irene Adler, who outwits Holmes and who is for him 'always the woman', Irene is less sinning than sinned against and the reader is, overall, offered a positive portrait of femininity. When women commit murder in Doyle's stories they do so under extreme provocation, usually after being badly treated by a man. In 'The Musgrave Ritual' (1893) maidservant Rachel Howells, who is 'a very good girl, but of an excitable Welsh temperament', kills the butler, Brunton, who has jilted her. However, there is a strong suggestion that Rachel, motivated by 'a smouldering fire of vengeance', is temporarily deranged. Certainly, in 'The Second Stain' (1904), Mme Henri Fournaye kills Eduardo Lucas in a jealous frenzy and then lapses into madness. These murders are then, explicable and in a way are in keeping with masculine and ideological expectations of traditional female behaviour.

In *The Hound of the Baskervilles* (1902) the representation of women is more complex. Beryl Stapleton is essentially a victim of her husband's ambition as well as of his violence; Mrs Barrymore is of the servant class and, although deceitful, is motivated by appropriate female emotions, but Laura Lyons is depicted as the improper feminine. She is separated from her husband, earns her own living by doing secretarial work and is seeking a divorce: she is clearly meant to represent masculine perceptions of the least attractive aspects of the 'New Woman'. When Watson first meets her his impression is of her beauty, but then he notices 'some coarseness of expression, some hardness [...] of eye'. Her improper femininity is evident in her appearance and her deviance is associated with crime. At the instigation of Stapleton, with whom she is in love, she writes the note that leads Sir Michael Baskerville to his death. Her motive is her illicit love for Stapleton, so she is transgressing not only gender boundaries in her independence, but also proper sexual behaviour.

The association of improper femininity and criminality is clearly present in the later, also strongly masculine, hard-boiled detective fiction, exemplified by Raymond Chandler's *The Big Sleep* (1939). While the external plots of Chandler's novels revolve around public corruption, the inner plots are concerned with private and personal corruption usually figured in the feminine. In *The Big Sleep* Carmen Sternwood appears to be the victim of blackmail, but is finally revealed to be a murderess. She has killed Rusty Regan, her sister Vivien's husband, because he has refused her sexual advances and she subsequently tries to shoot Chandler's detective figure, Philip Marlowe, for the same reason. The trend in conventional, masculine crime fiction tends to be that sexualised women who refuse to conform to their 'proper' gender role are criminalised in some way. Sometimes, as with Carmen Sternwood, they are actual criminals—although as if unable to admit that women are capable of premeditated murder the text excuses Carmen's behaviour as madness, just as Lady Audley in Braddon's text is found to be insane rather than criminal and Doyle's murderous women are thought temporarily deranged. The negative representation of the feminine acts, in hard-boiled detective narratives and other strongly masculine sub-genres of crime fiction, to valourise the male protagonist and endorse properly masculine behaviour; the invariably unpleasant fates of transgressive women function to enforce properly feminine behaviour. In Chandler's *The Big Sleep* deviant male sexuality is also negatively represented in the homosexual blackmailer and pornographer Arthur Geiger and his young male lover, Carol Lundgren, and this too serves to endorse proper masculinity.

However, in feminised crime fiction such as the Golden-Age clue-puzzles of Agatha Christie, the association of female criminality with gender transgression and deviant sexuality is less fixed and women who apparently conform to their proper gender roles are shown to be capable of committing crimes. And in Christie's texts, as the titles often advertise, the crime is invariably murder. Motives vary, but usually circulate around sex and money. In her first novel, *The Mysterious Affair at Styles* (1920), two lovers concoct a complicated plot to acquire the money they require to enjoy life together: Alfred Inglethorpe marries the elderly widow Mrs Cavendish then; with his lover, Miss Evelyn Howard, murders her in order to inherit her fortune. While superficially it seems that the man is the criminal here and Miss Howard merely his accomplice, Poirot is 'inclined to think that Miss Howard was the master mind in [the] affair'. Christie's later novels feature a variety of female criminals and motives: an older woman's overheated affection for a younger woman which leads to murder in order to prevent the object of affection from marrying (*Nemesis*, 1971); in *Sad Cypress* (1940) an apparently dedicated nurse commits murders in order to obtain an inheritance and in *The Mirror Crack'd from Side to Side* (1962) actress Marina Gregg poisons the woman who had infected her with German measles during pregnancy, causing her baby to be born mentally retarded. Christie, it seems, had a more realistic approach to the female capacity to kill.

Another Golden-Age author, Dorothy L. Sayers, creates a plot in *Gaudy Night* (1935), in which the female murderer is actually motivated by what she—and possibly much of the contemporary society—see as improper female behaviour. The killer is revealed as the widow of a male don who commits suicide after his career has been ruined by a female academic. The widow's crimes are acts of revenge against intellectual women who move away from their proper domestic feminine role, that is, who transgress the boundaries of their gender. As Sayers was herself an intellectual with an academic bent this is clearly an ironic comment on the limitations placed on women by the conventions of gender but, as with much crime fiction, the novel also articulates the contemporary cultural anxieties about gender and sexuality. Sayers's earlier *Unnatural Death* (1927) is again set within a very female domain with a female murderer seeking to ensure her inheritance. Mary Whittaker kills her elderly great-aunt, spinster Miss Agatha Dawson, a murder initially undetected because of Miss Dawson's ill health. The case is reconsidered by Sayers's detective hero, Lord Peter Wimsey. Although a spinster, Miss Dawson has had a life-long relationship—described as companionable in the text—with another single woman, while Mary Whittaker has a friend, Vera Findlater, who is clearly in love with her. Sexual deviance is suggested here in these inter-female relationships and this female world is one which the male detective finds hard to penetrate. To facilitate access, Wimsey employs another spinster, Miss Climpson, who thus has an investigative function, as does Harriet Vane in *Gaudy Night* and, in Christie's *Nemesis* and *The Mirror Crack'd from Side to Side*, Miss Jane Marple.

Women investigators are, perhaps, more effective in dealing with female criminals—although Miss Marple is equally effective when it comes to masculine criminality. While the majority of Christie's detective novels feature Hercule Poirot, a male detective, and Sayers's serial detective is Lord Peter Wimsey, both are very different from their strongly masculine predecessor, Sherlock Holmes. Poirot is a short, fussy, rather feminised figure as are his use of 'the little grey cells' and his knowledge of domestic matters in his detective work. Wimsey is represented as effete rather than feminised, but his deceptively languid manners, his hobby of collecting incunabulae, or very early printed books, his rather foolish appearance and his attacks of 'nerves' in the wake of his service in World War I conceal an athletic and essentially very masculine character. The 'feminisation' of the male detective is a strong element in Golden-Age crime fiction, seen also in Margery Allingham's amateur sleuth, Albert Campion. This is perhaps in response to the growing number of female writers and readers of crime fiction in this period, and can be related back to World War I and the hundreds of thousands of men killed in action, leaving a population in Britain in which women heavily outnumbered men.

It is in this context that the female detective begins to make her appearance. Women in this period are still associated with crime but, as women's agency increased, partly as the consequence of their undertaking men's work during the war years and with the acquisition of voting rights (for women over thirty in 1908 and all women in 1928), so women in crime fiction begin to be represented not as passive victims or innocent catalysts, nor even as perpetrators, but as active investigators. Forays into writing fictional female detectives had been made in the nineteenth century, but these imaginary and transgressive figures were few and undeveloped; in the early twentieth century, as Patricia Craig and Mary Cadogan discuss in *The Lady Investigates* (1986), more appear but often in a limited capacity or playing a secondary role to men. In the 1920s and 1930s, characters such as Christie's Miss Marple and Tuppence Beresford, Gladys Mitchell's Dame Beatrice Lestrange Bradley, Patricia Wentworth's Miss Silver and even Sayers's Harriet Vane and Miss Climpson contribute to the establishment of a discursive space for the female detective. With the exception of Harriet Vane and Tuppence Beresford, though, all these investigators are middle-aged or elderly women, widowed, divorced or spinsters and somehow asexual; Harriet and Tuppence work as helpmates to the male detective. Detection is still only a suitable job for some women, generally those apparently beyond the age of sexual desire and no longer in need of masculine protection, suggesting that the conventions of genre and gender were still strong.

As the twentieth century progressed, the active/passive masculine/feminine gender patterns of the nineteenth century begin to erode, a slow process that culminated in the feminist movement of the 1970s and 80s. Responding to reality, representations of gender in crime fiction also changed as women began to achieve some measure of equality with men. Sexual emancipation follows on from personal emancipation and, from the 1960s onwards, the sexual elements implicitly present in earlier crime fiction become more explicit, especially in terms of sexual violence, a process that continues today. And, in the wake of the feminist movement, the fully formed modern female, or even feminist, detective comes into being. This figure need not be asexual like her predecessors, but is indeed often actively sexual, and this contributes to the way in which, even while acting on the side of the law, women in crime fiction are still perceived to be deviant and transgressive creatures. While in America the female detective features in what is very much an appropriation of the masculine hard-boiled genre, seen for example in Sara Paretsky's series with the androgynously named private investigator V. I. Warshawsky and Sue Grafton's serial detective Kinsey Millhone, in Britain the title of P. D. James's 1972 novel featuring detective Cordelia Gray perhaps sums up the contemporary society's ambivalent attitude to such figures: *An Unsuitable Job for a Woman*. Sarah Caudwell's *Thus Was Adonis Murdered* (1981) avoids the problem and incidentally, perhaps, makes a feminist statement about the gendering of detective fiction with its protagonist/narrator Hilary Tamar, whose gender is never disclosed. But by 2000, the female investigator is no longer transgressing gender boundaries; women in modern crime fiction now perform all the same functions as their masculine counterparts. Female detectives, whether professional or private, amateur or police, lawyers or forensic scientists, have proliferated in the late twentieth and early twenty-first centuries and possibly now outnumber their male equivalents.

But the most significant shift has been the focus on the role of gender and sexuality in the formation of identity; the cult of personality in reality has inflected criminography and readers now demand rounded characterisation and psychological motivation in their crime fiction rather than clue-puzzle plots. The association of sexual deviance and criminality remains, but recent crime fiction has also articulated society's more liberal attitudes towards and tolerance of sexual difference. Perhaps because the genre is perceived to offer containment and conservatism, it has proved a fruitful location for the representation of non-heterosexuality in its protagonists as well as a space in which to explore, in safety, the darker side of human sexuality. Paralleling sexual diversity in reality, crime fiction has featured male and female homosexuality in a more positive light than did Chandler's Philip Marlowe novels in the 1930s and 40s. In 1970, Joseph Hansen's first Dave Brandstetter novel was published. Brandstetter is an insurance investigator and detective who is also openly gay, and the 12 novels in the series are as much concerned with his sexual orientation and his personal relationships as with the crimes with which he is involved. Hansen sets his narratives in the gay areas of California and so offers a very specific representation of homosexuality, but the text is very concerned with the politics of gender and sexuality. There had been earlier gay detectives, but Hansen's creation was the first to sell to a general audience and the novels map the history of the gay experience in America between 1970 and 1990, including the onset of AIDS and its consequences.

Crime fiction featuring gay detectives has enjoyed some success, but the gay investigator has never really had mainstream appeal, possibly because male gay ideology lends itself less well to aggressive and politicised detection than does female gay ideology. Nonetheless, Michael Nava's gay lawyer-detective Henry Rios appeared in seven books between 1986 and 2000, while Richard Stevenson's gay private investigator Donald Strachey and Josh Lanyon's amateur detective Adrien English both 'came out' in print in 1987 and 2000, respectively, and have continued to appear in novels up to the present day, suggesting a strong if minor audience for such crime fiction. By contrast, crime narratives with lesbian protagonists have achieved wider popularity. Early examples of this sub-genre were deliberately radical and transgressive, with M. F. Beal's Kat Guerrera in *Angel Dance* (1977) openly functioning to critique heterosexual, patriarchal and corrupt American society. Lesbian crime fiction is very much an American product and its political agenda was initially closely allied to that of the feminist movement, but it was not until the 1980s that the sub-genre really gathered momentum and general acceptance. Authors such as Barbara Wilson and Katherine V. Forrest incorporated the politics of gender into their crime narratives, with Wilson's first novel set in a feminist collective (*Murder in the Collective*, [1984]), while Forrest's serial detective Kate Delafield is a lesbian police officer working in the deeply masculine and heterosexual Los Angeles Police Department (first introduced in *Amateur City*, [1984]). Mary Wings' crime novels, featuring her detective protagonist Emma Victor, are less overtly political but are particularly concerned with lesbian sexuality and its modes of expression. As with the feminist detective texts, the vast majority of lesbian detective novels were and are, as Sally Munt observes in *Murder by the Book: Feminism and the Crime Novel* (1994), published in North America.

In Britain lesbian detective fiction has been brought to popular attention by Val McDermid and Stella Duffy. McDermid has openly stated that her serial amateur detective protagonist, Lindsay Gordon, was part of a wider project to introduce an openly homosexual character into mainstream fiction and so normalise gay and lesbian sexuality. Lindsay Gordon is 'a cynical socialist lesbian feminist journalist' and her lesbianism is secondary to her socialism; the novels are all concerned with aspects of contemporary British politics and society rather than the politics of gender, although they carry a feminist message. Similarly, Stella

Duffy sees crime fiction as a political forum and her private detective Saz Martin's adventures are deliberately based in present reality and respond to current social issues. Lesbian crime fiction continues to appear but, in a post-feminist world where gay sexualities have become accepted, the radical edge of the sub-genre has become blunted.

In the late twentieth and early twenty-first century the association of deviant sexuality and gender transgression with criminality continues, but the patterns have changed. When gender roles are seen, as Judith Butler's *Gender Trouble: Feminism and the Subversion of Identity* (1990) suggests, as being performative rather than biologically determined, a woman refusing her 'proper' role or a man who rejects 'proper' masculinity can no longer be seen as criminal. Equally, homosexuality is no longer considered to be a crime, or even deviant behaviour. Rather, gender and sexuality in crime fiction have become associated with extremes, usually of violence or what is still considered by society to be sexual perversion, for example paedophilia. Child abuse/abuser is the theme of crime narratives from British authors such as Ian Rankin (*Dead Souls*, 1999), Ruth Rendell (*Harm Done*, 1999), Minette Walters (*Acid Row*, 2001) and more recently Denise Mina (*Last Breath*, 2007) and Belinda Bauer (*Blacklands*, 2010). In the United States, Karin Slaughter's *Kisscut* (2003) has paedophilia at its centre, as does Australian Leah Giarratano's *Vodka Doesn't Freeze* (2007).

More common is the association of gender and sexuality with violence in various ways. Crime fiction has long been familiar with violence and it is present in nineteenth-century criminography from the *Newgate Calendar* accounts of particularly grisly rapes and murders to the harrowing story of Bill Sikes's murder of Nancy in Charles Dickens's *Oliver Twist* (1838) or the newspaper reports of the Ripper murders in Whitechapel, London (1888). Gender is significant here; women are more usually the victims than the perpetrators and sexualised violence is more sensational. In the twentieth century the Golden-Age clue-puzzle mysteries of Christie *et al.* had covert violence, both masculine and feminine, at their centre and it is overt and endemic in hard-boiled detective fiction, the crime novel, the psychothriller and the sub-genre of serial-killer fiction. Explicit violence is gendered in these sub-genres of crime fiction and is more commonly masculine, that is male perpetrators with both male and female victims. Women do kill, but are rarely depicted as violent, although Bella, the 'heroine' of Helen Zahavi's *Dirty Weekend* (1991) carries out a series of graphically described acts of extreme violence against men. The novel is a postmodern feminist revenge fantasy which reverses the more usual dominant male/subservient female relations of sexualised violence.

Male detectives use violence in the course of their work: Raymond Chandler's Philip Marlowe seems to have a positive penchant for slapping women and casually inflicts physical violence on his opponents. Detectives also suffer violence in narratives of crime and this has coded gender significance: male detectives subjected to violence never suffer penetrating wounds but often receive blows to the head that result in unconsciousness; while female victims are almost invariably penetrated in some way, the female detective will receive wounds that abrade the skin but do not necessarily pierce it. This pattern maintains the myth of unassailable masculine identity and the inviolate hero-detective and locates the female detective midway between (masculine) hero and (feminine) victim. In the late twentieth and early twenty-first century, what had been clear-cut in terms of gender in crime fiction becomes less well-defined. It is generally agreed in Western culture that men and women are equal but different and that all have the right to express and act upon their sexual preferences with the caveat that it is within legal bounds. But what exactly constitutes gender and sexuality has come into question.

This questioning of gender can be seen in Thomas Harris's *The Silence of the Lambs* (1988). Attention in the text is focused on the infamous serial killer/cannibal, Hannibal Lecter, and the junior FBI agent Clarice Starling. Lecter is strangely asexual, killing for desires that are beyond normal comprehension (Harris's *Hannibal Rising*, 2006, detracts from the mystique of his serial killer by offering rather lame psychological reasons for Lecter's habits). Starling is an interesting combination of feminism and femininity that perhaps prefigures post-feminism; determined to succeed in a masculine profession, she solves her case using her professional skills and her female empathy and intuition. But it is her quarry, serial killer Jame Gumb, or Buffalo Bill, who brings the issue of gender to centre stage. Gumb kills women in order to dress himself in their skins. He wants to be a woman and, in what accords with the concept of gender as performance and might be read as a parody of transvestism, feels he needs only their exterior in order to become female. In its detective and in its killer, *Silence of the Lambs* explores the role of gender in the construction of identity.

This is even more apparent in Val McDermid's 1995 novel, *The Mermaids Singing*. Gender and sexuality are key to the plot and to the agenda of the text and its author. Criminal profiler Tony Hill, called in to assist the police in their hunt for the 'Queer Killer' who has carried out a series of macabre murders involving sadistic torture, is described by McDermid as 'such a girl'. Hill is feminised in his use of intuition and by his sexual impotence; by contrast, police detective Carol Jordan must prove herself better than her male colleagues in her use of rationality and intelligence. But it is again in the figure of the murderer that the issues of gender and sexuality are both concentrated and confused. Postmodern anxieties about the fluidity of gender and the construction of desire combine in Angelica, the transsexual serial killer whose victims are male but whose desires seem initially to be female. The sections of the text that represent Angelica's voice are italicised, an implicit textual feminisation, there are no indicators of the speaker's gender and the discourse slips between feminine and masculine. The selection of the victims is based on a pattern of female desire, but the torture that follows what Angelica constructs as the victim's rejection of her love arouses in her/him a sexual desire that is couched in very masculine terms. Physically apparently female, but with the big feet and heavy jaw of a man, dressed in eroticised feminine apparel, but with the strength and violent tendencies of masculinity, Angelica embodies gender as a construct and questions the relationship between gender, sexuality and sexual desire.

Crime fiction offers a contained and containing world in which contemporary cultural and social anxieties can be explored. Gender and sexuality have always aroused concerns and the association of sexuality with sin ensured that, as society became secularised, sexuality was associated with criminality. Early criminography's focus on the ideological policing of deviant femininity represents masculine anxiety about feminine sexuality; the hard-boiled detective's treatment of women and of deviant male sexuality perhaps is more revealing of anxieties about masculinity itself. Feminism found in crime narratives the opportunity to appropriate a masculine discourse and used it as part of its personal and political agendas. But in recent crime fiction it is anxieties about the role of gender and sexuality in the construction of identity that are most clearly articulated. What remains constant, though, is the construction of sexual deviation and gender transgression as inherently criminal in their rejection of the ideological norms of the contemporary society.

See also   *Contexts*: Crime and Criminality, Detectives and Detection, the Law, Race and Ethnicity; *Texts*: Children's Crime Fiction, Crime Novel, Early Criminography, Feminist Crime Fiction, Hard-Boiled Detective Fiction, Golden-Age Crime Fiction; *Criticism*: Feminism, Cultural Materialism, Postmodernism.

Further reading

Craig, Patricia and Mary Cadogan, *The Lady Investigates: Women Detectives and Spies in Crime Fiction* (Oxford: Oxford University Press, 1986).

Forter, Greg, *Murdering Masculinities: Fantasies of Gender and Violence in the American Crime Novel* (New York: New York University Press, 2000).

Gunn, Drewey Wayne, *The Gay Male Sleuth in Print and Film* (Lanham, Maryland: Scarecrow Press, 2005).

Markowitz, Judith A., *The Gay Detective Novel: Lesbian and Gay Main Characters and Themes in Mystery Fiction* (Jefferson, U.S.A: MacFarland Publishing, 2004).

Munt, Sally R., *Murder by the Book: Feminism and the Crime Novel* (London: Routledge, 1994).

Plain, Gill, *Twentieth-Century Crime Fiction: Gender, Sexuality and the Body* (Edinburgh: Edinburgh University Press, 2001).

The law

The law is essential to the development of crime fiction; it is the law that constructs, or at least classifies, what is criminal. A crime is, literally, an action carried out in defiance of the law which codifies the practices and deeds that society and culture deem to be deviant from or injurious to the norm. As such, the law is ideologically inflected and culturally and nationally specific, which might be seen potentially to raise complications when discussing the role of the law in crime fiction; in the event, the law, or its letter, is curiously absent from much criminography. After all, the designation of the genre tells the reader that crime is the subject of the fiction: in modern crime fiction this crime is nearly always murder, an act that is seen as criminal across cultures although its definition— premeditated, manslaughter, justifiable homicide and so on—may differ. The law is, however, intrinsic to the genre despite its apparent invisibility; there are sub-genres of crime fiction such as the legal novel, the police procedural and the courtroom drama in which the law is overtly represented, while fictional practitioners of law often function as detectives. But it is not just at the level of plot or character that the law inhabits criminography. Crime fiction draws on the narrative structures and processes of the law in its own construction, with its drive to ascertain the facts of the case and reach a firm resolution, to create a convincing argument that reaches the right conclusion and apportions guilt correctly.

This reliance on legal discourse and structure perhaps stems from crime fiction's origins in fact. The development of crime fiction is made possible by the emergence of the novel, a form which Ian Watt and many other literary critics see as originating in the eighteenth century with the work of authors, such as Daniel Defoe and Henry Fielding, whose novels drew on reality. Defoe's *Robinson Crusoe* (1719), for example, was in part influenced by the real-life adventure of Alexander Selkirk, whose experiences as a castaway on an island in the Pacific from 1704 to 1709 had been publicised in an article in a periodical, *The Englishman*, in 1713. Writing fiction, from its origins, involved close imitation of factual narratives, and crime fiction, or the crime novel, is no exception. Early accounts of crime were factual and based on reports of trials and executions, as in many of the criminal broadsides and the *Newgate Calendar* collections. The law, then, framed and structured these narratives. The Newgate novels of the 1830s, as their name suggests, used this criminographic material as the basis for their fiction: Edward Bulwer Lytton's *Eugene Aram* (1832) was a fictionalisation of the real Aram, an eighteenth-century murderer; William Harrison Ainsworth's *Rookwood* (1834) had Dick Turpin as its 'hero' and his *Jack Sheppard* (1839) was based on the real thief of the same name who was famous for his frequent escapes from Newgate prison. These novels necessarily incorporated aspects of the law, for example the courtroom scenes in *Eugene Aram*, and represented the 'facts of the case', but did not self-consciously use the processes of the law—rather they often functioned to criticise the law as in Bulwer Lytton's *Paul Clifford* (1830).

This critical aspect of criminography is a recurring feature that will be considered later, but it is important first to look at how the novel and implicitly crime fiction draws on the law in its own narrative constructions. In *The Rise of the Novel* (1957) Ian Watt argues that:

> The novel's mode of imitating reality may [...] be summarized in terms of the procedures of [...] the jury in a court of law. Their expectations and those of the novel reader coincide [...] they both want to know "all the particulars"' of a given case [...] and they also expect the witness to tell the story "in his own words".

In the mid-nineteenth century Wilkie Collins deliberately and openly borrowed from legal discourse and courtroom procedure in *The Woman in White* (1860) and *The Moonstone* (1868) in order to locate his readers in a particular reading position. The 'Preamble' to *The Woman in White* states that 'the story here presented will be told [...] as the story of an offence against the laws is told in court by more than one witness', while the reader is very specifically placed: 'As the Judge might once have heard it, so the Reader shall hear it now.' The narrative of the text is then given as a series of first-person accounts of events from a number of characters that gradually builds, chronologically, into a complete story or case. These 'witness statements' are not confined to the main characters Walter Hartright and Marian Halcombe but include a solicitor, a criminal, a doctor and even servants—a housekeeper, a cook.

A similar idea structures *The Moonstone*, but here the 'witnesses' all tell their own version of the circumstances surrounding the same event, the theft of the diamond known as the Moonstone. As Betteredge, steward to the Verinder family and the first of Collins's multiple narrators in *The Moonstone* observes:

> In this matter of the Moonstone the plan is, not to present reports, but to produce witnesses. I picture to myself a member of the family reading these pages [...] what a compliment he will feel it, to be asked to take nothing on hearsay and to be treated in all respects like a Judge on the bench.

Collins again here openly admits his use of legalistic narrative structures. Later crime fiction tends not to draw attention to its own narrative devices, but the clue-puzzle, typified by Agatha Christie's crime novels, acts in a similar way to Collins's texts in offering to the reader all the clues and facts of the case that allow the detective to reach the right conclusion and reveal the criminal. Indeed, detective fiction generally again presents the facts of the case, if not always all the necessary clues and information that will lead to the identification of the criminal. In Arthur Conan Doyle's short crime fictions—called, using medico-legal terminology, 'cases', Sherlock Holmes's retrospective reconstruction of each case can be likened to the prosecuting lawyer's summing up of his argument.

Significantly, Sherlock Holmes's cases end at the point where the criminal has been discovered or captured, but there is no account of the subsequent trial or punishment; in some of Holmes's adventures those involved wish to avoid the attention of the law, or the 'crime' is not one that would attract a legal penalty ('A Case of Identity' (1891); 'The Adventure of the Beryl Coronet' (1892); 'The Sussex Vampire' (1924)), while in others Holmes takes it upon himself to judge and deliver sentence ('The Adventure of the Blue Carbuncle' (1891); 'The Adventure of the Abbey Grange' (1904)), or a higher authority makes the judgement, as in *A Study in Scarlet* (1887), where Jefferson Hope dies before a trial can take place, or 'The Speckled Band' (1892) where Grimesby Roylott, the murderer, is killed by the snake he has used to murder his stepdaughter. Detective fiction, as Martin Kayman has observed, prejudges cases as there can be no presumption of innocence and so the courtroom trial becomes redundant. That is not to say that the courtroom and the legal process are entirely absent. Agatha Christie's *Sad Cypress* (1940) opens with a courtroom scene; Dorothy L. Sayers's *Strong Poison* (1931) has Peter Wimsey meeting Harriet Vane as she stands trial for murder and the courtroom often functions as plot device in crime fiction. In John Mortimer's humorous crime series (1978–present) featuring London barrister Horace Rumpole, the courtroom and its practices and rituals are at the very centre of the narratives, while American lawyer-turned-writer John Grisham's novels, from *A Time to Kill* (1989) to *The Appeal* (2008), are often focused on legal matters and set in the courts.

In *The Runaway Jury* (1996) Grisham uses the courtroom and its rules in order to criticise the law and its practitioners. The plot concerns a case brought against the tobacco companies by a woman whose husband has died of lung cancer and the text is overtly focused on the debate over the liability of the companies or the individual when it comes to smoking. But the sub-text is an *exposé* of the ways in which the law can be manipulated in the interests of those involved. As the title suggests, the focus here is the jury; the narrative takes the reader through the process of jury selection in the American system, showing how the prosecution and defence teams carefully select those jurors they feel will give a favourable verdict and revealing the investigations into the private lives of individuals that this process can generate. The narrative then demonstrates how the jury, once selected, despite seclusion from the outside world, is still open to manipulation. Grisham's novel discloses how the law can be used to serve corrupt purposes. This is not a recent development; criminography, with crime at its centre and with the law always implicit in its accounts, is the ideal location for this kind of critique, as William Godwin's *Caleb Williams; or, Things As They Are* (1794), demonstrates.

Godwin's text is in part a vehicle for the writer/political philosopher's own ideas about society and social justice; Godwin's political treatise *Enquiry Concerning Political Justice* (1793) was published just twelve months before *Caleb Williams,* and the novel, despite its fictional status, incorporated many of Godwin's notions about the corruptibility of the law and its misuse by those in power. In *Caleb Williams* the aristocratic and chivalric Falkland and the socially equal but morally deficient Tyrrel are both shown to abuse their power and to manipulate the law in their own interests. Caleb Williams, the narrator protagonist, represents the ordinary man seeking to discover and reveal the truth, but his attempts are rendered ineffectual as he is made a victim of the law rather than a beneficiary. Retrospectively, *Caleb Williams* can, and is, considered to be crime fiction, although it would not have been recognised as such in its time. Nonetheless, it offered a template in which crime narrative is used as social criticism and, as seen later in Wilkie Collins's fiction, Godwin's text borrows from the narrative structures of legal discourse; Caleb's story is, essentially, a kind of witness statement in which he struggles to tell the whole truth. In the text, though, as in the law itself, truth is finally shown to be subjective rather than objective.

Employing criminography to criticise the law continues over the nineteenth and twentieth centuries; significantly it is rarely criminal law that is criticised but more usually civil law. Associated with the law, the penal system in Britain and elsewhere has frequently been the subject of criticism within crime fiction. In 1827, Henry Thomson's short story 'Le Revenant', about a young man convicted of forgery and sentenced to death by hanging—which he survives through undisclosed means—was intended as a direct attack on the death penalty for non-violent, civil crimes such as forgery. It was considered by Charles Lamb to have had more influence on the eventual abolition of capital punishment than all the work of Samuel Romilly, a well-known campaigner for the reform of criminal law and the death sentence. In the 1840s, novelists Charles Dickens and William Makepeace Thackeray published letters protesting against public executions; after 1867 executions were no longer carried out in public but privately inside prisons.

Dickens was fascinated by crime and criminals, both of which often feature in his fiction. Dickens's *Bleak House* (1853) incorporates crime but the plot is driven in part by the author's attack on the slow processes and arcane rules of the laws of Chancery. The novel was written in the context of the contemporary debates about Chancery law and may have contributed to Chancery law reform in 1870, demonstrating, as with 'Le Revenant' the way in which crime fiction not only responds to cultural and social change but may even be implicated in bringing it about. Mary E. Braddon's sensation novel featuring bigamy and attempted murder, *Lady Audley's Secret* (1862), can be read in the context of the reform of the laws concerning divorce—an Act passed in Britain in 1857 made it possible for a woman to divorce her husband, although not on equal grounds. Wilkie Collins's *No Name* (1862) is focused on the legal difficulties facing illegitimate children whose parents subsequently marry, thus effectively disinheriting their offspring; as the father of three such children it seems possible that Collins had some interest in the subject. What *Bleak House*, *No Name* and *Lady Audley's Secret* have in common, along with many other nineteenth-century novels which incorporated crime into their plots, is the presence of a legal figure. In *Bleak House* there are several legal characters of which the most important is Mr Tulkinghorn, family lawyer to the aristocratic Dedlock family, and the representation of his manipulation of the law in his own and his patron's interest has parallels with *Caleb Williams*.

No Name offers a more positive picture of the man of law with the sympathetic family solicitor Mr Pendril and *Lady Audley's Secret* has Robert Audley, who carries out a detective role within the text, but who is a qualified, if non-practising, barrister. The law in much crime fiction,

while absent in its letter, is often present in the form of its practitioners as characters in the text. This is of course reasonable—if crime is
present, a man of the law might be presumed to be of use—but the popular fictional anecdotes of professional men published between the 1830s
and 1860s may have contributed to the representation of legal men in
narratives concerned with crime. While these anecdotes featured doctors, policemen, police detectives and even eventually thieves, barristers,
attorneys and law clerks were frequent subjects, as in the anonymously
authored *Experiences of a Barrister and Confessions of an Attorney* (1859)
or William Russell's *Leaves from the Diary of a Law Clerk* (1857) or, in
America, *Pages from the Diary of a Philadelphia Lawyer* (1838). These narratives often depicted the legal figure in a quasi-investigative role and
were an important element in the development of the detective novel in
its modern form.

And it is in the lawyer, attorney or barrister that the law has its
strongest presence in crime fiction over the twentieth and into the
twenty-first century; the 'legal novel' or 'legal procedural' is a strong
sub-genre of crime fiction. The legal professional has always acted
as the point of contact between the private individual and the law,
whether in civil or criminal matters, and the lawyer, particularly those
involved with criminal cases, must in reality perform a kind of detective work as he or she constructs the case for the prosecution or
defence (at least in the adversarial systems of Britain, the United States
and other countries using common law as the basis for their legal
processes; the legal system in Europe tends to be inquisitorial and
does not therefore have the courtroom contest seen in the adversarial system). The lawyer as detective has also a credibility which is
increasingly important as the amateur detective has become, in reality,
incredible.

In the wake of Braddon's *Lady Audley's Secret*, with its barrister-
detective Robert Audley, another early first example of what will become
the 'legal novel' in crime fiction comes from America. Anna Katharine
Green's *The Leavenworth Case: A Lawyer's Story* (1872) features young
lawyer Mr Raymond, who is the narrator and who assists the detective,
Mr Gryce, in solving the murder. Green was precluded by her gender
from being a lawyer herself, but knew about the profession from her
father, who was a law practitioner. Still in America, real-life lawyer
Melville Davisson Post's fictional protagonist Randolph Mason has been
claimed as 'the first lawyer-detective' in the American literary tradition
(see Andrew F. Macdonald and Gina Macdonald, *Scott Turow: A Critical
Companion*, 2005). Post's 'shyster lawyer' first appeared in *The Strange
Schemes of Randolph Mason* (1896), a collection of stories, or cases,

where Mason spends much of his time assisting those who are actually guilty of crimes escape their just deserts.

In the early twentieth century crime writers continued to feature legal practitioners in their narratives but more often as secondary characters; there were some forays into the legal procedural form, for example G. K Chesterton, the author of the Father Brown detective stories, wrote a number of tales with retired judge Basil Grant in a detective role, and John Buchan, best known for *The Thirty-Nine Steps* (1915), who had trained as a barrister before turning to writing, produced a series of novels between 1916 and 1941 in which the protagonist also was a barrister, Edward Leithen. From 1907 to 1942, R. Austin Freeman wrote a series of over twenty novels and short stories featuring Dr Thorndyke who, like his creator, was a medical doctor and lawyer as well as a detective. Frequently authored by practising or ex-lawyers, the legal novel seems to have become part of mainstream crime fiction from the 1930s onwards; the number of law practitioners turning their hand to crime writing suggests that the narrative structures of legal discourse and the drama of the courtroom lend themselves to fiction.

The sub-genre has been, and continues to be, particularly strong in America. Perhaps the best-known and most prolific early writer of the legal procedural was Earle Stanley Gardner, another practising lawyer who turned to full-time crime writing, with his lawyer-detective protagonist, Perry Mason, appearing in eighty-two novels between 1933 and 1973. In Britain, barrister Cyril Hare wrote five novels featuring lawyer-detective Francis Pettigrew (1942–58); Henry Cecil, also a barrister, wrote 24 crime novels from 1951 to 1977, many of which, although without a serial lawyer-detective protagonist, incorporated courtroom scenes and legal issues. The legal novel seems also to have been gendered masculine in its early days; British author Lucy Beatrice Malleson's lawyer-detective Arthur G. Crook appeared in more than forty novels between 1937 and 1974, but all were written under the pseudonym Anthony Gilbert. Sara Woods, born in Britain but writing in Canada, drew on her experiences as a solicitor's clerk when writing her lawyer-detective series, with 48 books featuring lawyer-detective Anthony Maitland (1961–87); although writing under her own name, her protagonist was male.

It was not until the rise of feminism in the 1970s and 80s that more women began to produce detective novels with female protagonists working or with a background in law: Marcia Muller's investigator Sharon McCone is initially employed by a legal co-operative (1997–present); Sara Paretsky's serial detective V. I. Warshawski is a former legal aid lawyer (1982–present); Linda Fairstein, a lawyer specialising in sex crimes who is now a full-time writer, models her protagonist Assistant District Attorney Alexandra Cooper on herself (1994–present). Again, there is a strong American presence; in Britain the female investigator is more likely to be an ex-police detective than a lawyer. An exception is Natasha Cooper, whose protagonist, commercial lawyer Trish Maguire, is regularly drawn into investigative activities and so has a detective role (1998–present).

The masculine bias continues, as does the American dominance, but the serial lawyer-detective novel seems, in the late twentieth and early twenty-first century, to have been replaced by narratives that focus on the drama of the courtroom confrontation or the mechanics and machinations of the legal profession. These texts, rather in the fashion of the nineteenth-century novel, offer an exploration and often a critique of the United States justice system. Scott Turow, a practising attorney, has written eight books focused on aspects of the law in America (1987–2010); he has no serial protagonist but minor characters reappear in the novels and all are set in the imaginary mid-western Kindle County. John Grisham's numerous legal fictions (1989–present) cover ground similar to that of Turow but are perhaps less critical of and more simply interested in the workings of the law. Grisham also has a legal background, having worked as a lawyer in criminal and civil law. In America it is perhaps the dramatic possibilities of trials and courtrooms, realised in the live-time televising of important trials, which make the sub-genre of the legal novel so popular and prevalent; several of Turow and Grisham's books have been made into films and certainly Grisham's fiction often reads very much like a film script.

The law, then, is an absent presence in much crime fiction yet it underpins the genre as a whole and is intimately connected to its development. The links between law and literature have long been acknowledged; there are degree schemes in law and literature, critical texts which discuss and analyse the relationship between the two and an academic journal, *Cardozo Studies in Law and Literature*, which is devoted to the subject. Significantly, usually the literature addressed is not popular crime fiction but highbrow literary fiction and this reiterates the low status of the genre and seems a missed opportunity. Crime fiction's rapid response to cultural and social change and its sensitivity to current social issues suggest that the legal profession might find it a fruitful source of information about public perceptions of the law.

See also   *Contexts*: Detectives and Detection, Evidence, Crime and Criminality; *Texts*: American Crime Fiction, Early Criminography, Police Procedural; *Criticism*: Feminism, Cultural Materialism, Postmodernism.

Further reading

Dolin, Kieran, *Fiction and the Law: Legal Discourse in Victorian and Modernist Literature* (Cambridge: Cambridge University Press, 2009 (1998)).

Kayman, Martin, *From Bow Street to Baker Street: Mystery, Detection and Narrative* (London: Macmillan, 1992).

Leckie, Barbara, *Culture and Adultery: The Novel, the Newspaper and the Law* (Philadelphia: University of Pennsylvania Press, 1999).

Messent, Peter (ed.), *Criminal Proceedings: the Contemporary American Crime Novel* (London: Pluto Press, 1997).

Scaggs, John, *Crime Fiction* (London: Routledge, 2005).

Police and policing

As with the law, police and policing are nationally and culturally variable. The influence of the British model can be seen in those countries that were under Britain's colonial rule; the American system shares some similarities and may indeed have been in part inspired by British policing structures and methods. In Europe, police forces and policing systems vary according to the country and this is so internationally. National differences notwithstanding, the generally accepted modern understanding of the term 'police' is of a State-organised, usually civil force which is responsible for maintaining public order and enforcing the law, including preventing and detecting crime. The first use of the word 'police' in this sense is relatively recent; the *Oxford English Dictionary* has it as 1798, when it was employed to describe the privately funded body of men who patrolled the Port of London to prevent pilferage and theft and who were called the Marine Police (in 1800 this became the Thames River Police, paid by the State, and can truly lay claim to being the first English police force proper). But the concept of law enforcement is intrinsic to society and agents of enforcement in various guises and under different names have been around for as long as civilisation itself. In the context of crime fiction, the law-enforcer is a recurring, if variable, figure which consolidates and increases in importance as the genre develops.

As this textbook is concerned with Anglophone criminography, the focus here is mainly on the development and function of the police and policing in Britain and their representation in fiction. While the establishment of a State-organised police did not occur in England until 1829, with the New Metropolitan Police Force (Scotland had possibly the first, if short-lived, professional police force in Glasgow in 1778; in 1800 the Glasgow Police Act established the Glasgow Police Force), policing and agents who performed policing duties can be seen in pre-nineteenth-century crime narratives. The term 'policing' has its origins in the Greek word *politeia*, meaning all matters that affected the survival and well-being of the state, or *polis*, and this can be mapped onto society, so that policing becomes the way(s) in which society controls the individual in the interests of the wider community. In the absence of official State policing, the Church and the community-based society took on the role. The Church made rules, or laws, and the threatened punishment for breaking those laws—excommunication and eternal damnation at the extreme—served to police society. Equally, in small communities aberrant, deviant or criminal behaviour was easily discerned and quickly punished, either by the community, the law or occasionally Providence or God.

This kind of social and ideological policing is evident in the *Newgate Calendar* accounts of crime, where the criminal's actions would be witnessed by a member of his/her community, or the perpetrator of the crime would be incited by religiously induced guilt into confession or else reveal his/her culpability in unusual behaviour or even appearance. Religion is often invoked in the *Calendar* narratives, while in some of the short crime fictions in the early nineteenth-century periodicals God was shown to be on the side of the law and to ensure that the wrongdoer received appropriate punishment, usually death. Criminography itself contributed to ideological policing, with its promise of certain punishment for crime, as the execution broadsides graphically demonstrated. But the system, as the *Calendar* accounts show, was clearly not always effective and various alternatives were employed to seek out those criminals who ignored or avoided social and religious policing.

From medieval times, parishes appointed an unpaid constable, usually a man of status within his village or small town, whose duties included keeping the King's peace—a broad and inclusive remit—but more specifically, to report details of local felons and nuisances to the equivalent of the magistrates' court. The duties accompanying the post gradually increased until, as Daniel Defoe commented in 1714, 'it takes up so much of a man's time that his own affairs are frequently totally neglected, too often to his own ruin'. In towns and cities, from the seventeenth century onwards, watchmen, recruited from local householders as part of their civic duty, provided local law enforcement. Later, local taxes meant that substitutes could be paid to take on the watchmen's duties. Constables and watchmen, or 'Charlies' as they came to be known, are part of the background in criminography rather than central characters, and opinion of their effectiveness has frequently been based on their representation in literature: the comic figures of Dogberry and Verges in Shakespeare's *Much Ado About Nothing* are often given as classic examples of incompetent officers of the law; in 1751, Henry Fielding described watchmen as 'poor old decrepit people who are, from their want of bodily strength, rendered incapable of getting a livelihood by work. These men, armed only with a pole [...] are to secure the persons and households of his Majesty's subjects from the attacks of young [...] well-armed villains.' Police historians such as Clive Emsley have suggested that relying on these examples is reductive and that there were in fact probably many effective constables and watchmen.

However, increasing urbanisation and a growing population contributed to the difficulties of policing crime in society. In the late seventeenth and early eighteenth centuries the government in England introduced a system of offering rewards for the apprehension and conviction of criminals guilty of certain crimes, for example highway robbery; in the eighteenth century this system expanded as it was taken up by private individuals who offered rewards for the return of stolen property. This was not strictly policing, nor was it law enforcement, but it did lead to the creation of a semi-detective figure in the 'thief-takers' of the period. These were men who made a living from negotiating between thief and victim of theft, tracking down criminals or stolen property and claiming the rewards; the best-known is Jonathan Wild, who became known as the Thief-Taker General and whose life Daniel Defoe described in his *True and Genuine Account of the Life and Actions of the Late Jonathan Wild* (1725). Unfortunately the system was open to corruption. Thief-takers used their knowledge of the criminal underworld in negotiations to retrieve stolen property; many had criminal backgrounds; they were not averse to informing on erstwhile criminal colleagues and, in Wild's case at least, arranging the theft of goods and then profiting from the rewards for returning it, claiming protection money from career criminals in return for not handing them to the authorities and even recruiting, or grooming, children into criminality.

The character Gines in William Godwin's *Caleb Williams* (1794) is a classic fictional example of the thief-taker. Expelled from Captain Raymond's gang of robbers, Gines is described as fluctuating 'between the two professions of a violator of the laws and a retainer to their administration [...]. His initiation in the mysteries of thieving qualified him to be particularly expert in the profession of a thief taker.' In the complex plot of *Caleb Williams*, Gines is technically on the side of the law, albeit a corruption of the law by the aristocratic Falkland, who has framed Caleb, the protagonist of the novel, for a crime he has not committed. In the course of the narrative, Caleb's exploits are celebrated in a broadside detailing 'the most wonderful and surprising history, and miraculous adventures of Caleb Williams' and announcing the 'reward of one hundred guineas for apprehending him'. The criminal broadside was part of the 'hue and cry', another element in society's self-policing. Any person witnessing a crime or recognising a criminal was required to raise a 'hue and cry', that is literally cry out to attract the attention of bystanders who were then expected to assist in the apprehension of the criminal. Such broadsides described the perpetrator and his/her acts; in 1772 John Fielding (brother of and successor to the novelist Henry Fielding who had inaugurated what would become the Bow Street Runners) organised the officially sanctioned dissemination of information about criminals in this format, called *The Quarterly Pursuit of Criminals*: special editions called *The Weekly Pursuit* or, in cases of extreme urgency, *The Extraordinary Pursuit*, were intermittently published. These developed into periodicals that similarly sought the assistance of the public and which continued to appear into the twentieth century: the *Hue and Cry* until 1828—in Dickens's *Oliver Twist* (1837–9), Fagin reads a copy of *Hue and Cry*—and subsequently the *Police Gazette*.

The rapid expansion of London in the eighteenth century, from a population of around 670,000 in 1700 to 1 million, or more than one in ten Englishmen, in 1800, and the concomitant overcrowding and juxtaposition of wealth and poverty, made crime and its perceived increase a cause of real concern. In response, a small force of men dedicated to the detection of crime and the apprehension of criminals was formed in 1749 under the management of Henry Fielding, author and Bow Street Magistrate (interestingly, a Bow Street office in London is where Caleb Williams makes his deposition against Falkland in Godwin's novel). Initially in effect professional-thief takers, this force developed over the eighteenth and into the nineteenth century into the Bow Street Runners; part State-funded (after 1757) and part working for rewards, the Runners can fairly be called a prototype police force. By 1828, the Runners comprised circa 280 officers and men in various roles. While they received much attention in the press, the Runners did not feature greatly in fiction except, like the constables and watchmen, as minor, often humorous, characters such as Blathers and Duff in *Oliver Twist*. There is an anonymously authored picaresque novel, *Richmond: or, Scenes in the Life of a Bow Street Officer* (1827), but it was not popular in its time and has long been out of print. This is possibly because the low social status of the Runners and their potential—sometimes realised—for corruption, in combination with their association with criminals, made them unsuitable as literary heroes. They were, however, an effective law enforcement agency and they continued to function until they were finally disbanded in 1839 (the Runners' Horse Patrol was amalgamated with the New Metropolitan Police in 1836; in 1839 the remaining Bow Street Patrols were offered the opportunity of transferring into the new police force).

Finally, in 1829, in the face of much public resistance, Sir Robert Peel oversaw the passing of the Metropolitan Police Act. This enabled the creation of a wholly State-funded police force, located in London but with no powers over the City of London, which had its own policing methods. The New Metropolitan Police, under the command of Commissioners Richard Mayne and Charles Rowan, was established as a highly visible, highly regulated, uniformed police force, dedicated to the prevention of crime. Despite public anxieties about it being used as an extension of the armed forces and of it encroaching on civil liberties as the informer-based French police system was perceived to do, by 1851 *Punch Magazine*, which had been decidedly anti-police, declared them to be taking 'that place in the affections of the people [...] that soldiers and sailors used to occupy'. As a preventive police, the new force worked mainly through their visibility and omnipresence on the streets; Charles Dickens's *Sketches by Boz* makes frequent references to policemen as part of the London scenes the *Sketches* depict, and the newspapers featured regular Police Reports from the various London police offices in their pages. But a preventive police was not effective in investigating crimes after they had been committed, in detecting the criminal; this required a specialised body of men.

In 1842, a small plain-clothes detective department was added to the Metropolitan Police and made famous by Dickens in his 'Detective Police Anecdotes', published in 1850–3 in *Household Words*. The new department, based at Scotland Yard (actually the rear entrance to 4, Whitehall Place) comprised two inspectors and six sergeants for the whole metropolis of London. This was expanded in 1868 and subsequently reorganised in 1878 by Howard Vincent, after three of the four Chief Inspectors in the Detective Department were convicted of corruption in 1877. Vincent's restructured department had a new name: the Criminal Investigation Department, or CID, which is of course still in existence today. The corruption scandal in the detective police department and its detrimental affect on public opinion perhaps explains why Arthur Conan Doyle's detective, Sherlock Holmes, is represented as having such a negative opinion of the detective police when he first appears in print in 1887. The perceived incompetence of the police investigation into the Whitechapel Murders carried out by 'Jack the Ripper' in 1888 was equally damaging to their reputation. However, in the years between 1842 and 1868, the police detective department was seen to be efficient and capable; towns and cities outside London called on the Metropolitan detectives to assist with complicated criminal cases, as represented in Wilkie Collins's *The Moonstone* (1868), where Sergeant Cuff, who was loosely based on the real police detective Sergeant Whicher, is drafted in from London to investigate the theft of Rachel Verinder's diamond.

While police forces were set up across England and Wales from the 1830s onwards, there was no coherent approach and recruitment, numbers, structure and payment, and uniform varied from borough to borough, city to city and county to county until the 1856 County and Borough Police Act introduced some uniformity and harmonisation. Gradually this increased, although control of the police remained in the hands of local police authorities rather than central government. The 1964 Police Act defined the responsibilities and function of the Home Secretary, local police authorities and Chief Constables with regard to the police, ensured uniform service arrangements and encouraged co-operation between forces. There are now forty-three police authorities in England, Wales and Northern Ireland which are locally controlled but ultimately responsible to the Home Secretary. The other major development in the police force was the introduction of women officers.

In 1883, fifty-four years after their inauguration, the Metropolitan Police employed one woman to visit female convicts on licence; in 1889, fourteen more women were recruited as Police Matrons, whose duties included the supervision and searching of female and child offenders. The 1914–18 war saw the development of women police patrols: the Women Police Volunteers, who became the Women Police Service in 1915, and the Voluntary Women Patrols. In 1918, some of the latter were incorporated into the police forces as policewomen; it was not until 1931 that regulations defining the role of women in the police were issued, not until 1949 before women police officers were allowed to join the Police Federation and not until 1973 before they were fully integrated into the main police force. For most of the history of the police forces in England and Wales women were either absent or a barely tolerated minority and it is only in the late twentieth century that women have become an accepted and welcome part of the police. Crime fiction has responded to this; women police in criminography from the first half of the twentieth century are rare. When they do appear they play appropriately feminine, domestic and caring roles; only from the 1970s have women police *detectives* had a place in fiction.

In the nineteenth century once the police were present in fact, they began to be represented in fiction, initially more as part of the background to narratives than at the centre. But in 1849 a fictional policeman became the first 'hero' of his own narrative in William Russell's 'Recollections of a Police-Officer', a series of short stories, featuring the hero/narrator 'Waters', a gentleman-turned-policeman. 'Waters's' status as a gentleman is probably what made him acceptable to the middle-class readers of the periodical, *Chambers's Edinburgh Journal*, in which he appeared. While 'Waters' claimed to be an ordinary police officer, presenting his memoirs to the public, he worked in plain clothes and actually functioned as a detective. The 'Recollections' are set in the 1830s and so pre-date the establishment of the Detective police Department, but 'Waters' frequently, if anachronistically, refers to his fellow 'detective officers'. 'Waters's' fake 'Recollections', in combination with Dickens's 'Detective Anecdotes' and his redoubtable Inspector Bucket (based on the real Inspector Field) in *Bleak House* (1852–3), brought the policeman into fiction and opened the floodgates for the numerous fictional police 'Memoirs' and 'Casebooks' that appeared in the 1850s and 60s and beyond. But these accounts were not high literature; they appeared in periodicals aimed at the lower middle class or in the form of cheap 'yellow-back' novels, so called because of their colour and perhaps their content, which tended towards the sensational. While the police and detective police continued to appear in fiction throughout the nineteenth century, their representation remained fairly constant, becoming, perhaps in line with attitudes towards their real counterparts, more critical, at least in the case of the detective police, as the century came to its end.

Over the nineteenth century, narratives portraying the police had an ideological role, contributing to the concept of the police as an effective element in the containment of crime as well as acting to deter potential criminals with the apparent certainty of their capture should they turn to crime. But as crime fiction began to be recognised as a coherent genre, clearly apparent in Doyle's Sherlock Holmes stories, so it began to formalise its patterns, and the depiction of the police and the police detective as somewhat bumbling and ineffective that was evident in, for example Doyle's *A Study in Scarlet* (1887) continued, at least in British criminography, for some time. Many of the Golden Age crime writers continued to portray the police in this way, for example Agatha Christie with Inspectors Davis and Raglan in *The Murder of Roger Ackroyd* (1926), who can see only the most obvious solutions and who take clues at face value. Dorothy L. Sayers has a positive police detective, Inspector Charles Parker, who becomes hero-detective Lord Peter Wimsey's brother-in-law; Ngaio Marsh's hero is Detective Inspector Roderick Alleyn and Margery Allingham's Albert Campion lives in a flat which is located above a police station and works companionably with the conventional Inspector Stanislaus Oates and later with Inspector Charles Luke.

The low social status of the policeman/detective was perhaps problematic for middle-class readers seeking a point of identification with the protagonist of the narrative, something Sayers *et al.* avoided by having the police as secondary characters or, in the case of Marsh's Roderick

Alleyn, making him a gentleman as well as a police officer, rather in the pattern of 'Waters'. However, the increasing professionalisation of the police meant that by the 1920s Freeman Wills Crofts could make an ordinary police detective the protagonist of a number of novels. Inspector French first appears in *Inspector French's Greatest Case* (1925). French is a plain man who solves his cases by prosaic and practical methods; Julian Symons has the Inspector French novels as classic examples of the 'humdrum school' of crime fiction, but they suggest a growing acceptance of the police detective protagonist. In the Sherlock Holmes stories, which Doyle continued to write into the 1920s, there is also a gradual change in attitude towards the police. The early references to their incompetence end and they are recognised as useful, even if only at the level of enabling and legitimating Holmes's work and when necessary carrying out the arrest of the criminal.

Crofts's Inspector French novels can, in their focus on the practicalities of police detection, be seen as a precursor to the sub-genre of crime fiction, the police procedural, which emerged in the late 1940s and early 50s, but these narratives which had the police and their methods, as the name suggests, firmly at their centre developed first in America. However, France also had a role to play: a French police detective 'hero' had emerged in the 1820s with thief-turned-policeman Eugène François Vidocq, whose autobiographical, ghost-written *Mémoires* were published in France in 1828 and rapidly translated into English for the British and American markets. France had possessed a variety of State-funded police systems from the seventeenth century onwards and Vidocq was instrumental in setting up the *Sûreté*, the French equivalent of the CID, in 1812. While Vidocq's *Mémoires* are more interested in his criminal history than his detective methods, which are very ordinary and simplistic, the text clearly influenced Edgar Allan Poe in his proto-detective stories, 'The Murders in the Rue Morgue' (1841) and 'The Purloined Letter' (1845); the former has Poe's detective figure Dupin describing Vidocq as 'a good guesser and a persevering man' and the police as 'cunning', while in the latter Dupin observes that 'The Parisian Police are exceedingly able in their way. They are persevering, ingenious, cunning and thoroughly versed in the knowledge which their duties seem chiefly to demand.' What the Parisian Police are not capable of is incorporating imagination into their detection; their prosaic methods do not encompass crimes that lie outside the parameters of the ordinary, but it is precisely these practical police methods that will be central to the police procedural.

In post-Revolutionary France the class of the police officer seems to have been less of an issue. While much subsequent French crime fiction focused its interest on the criminal rather than the detective (Balzac's

Vautrin in Le *Père Goriot*, 1835; Eugène Sue's *Les Mystères de Paris* (1842–3) or in the late nineteenth-century Maurice Leblanc's gentleman thief Arsène Lupin), Émile Gaboriau's crime novels featuring his practical policeman M. Lecoq, *Dossier 113* (1864) and *M. Lecoq* (1868), clearly had the police detective as the hero of the narrative. Similarly, in determinedly democratic America, the police detective could play a major role without arousing any class-based antagonism: in Anna Katharine Green's *The Leavenworth Case* (1878) city detective Ebenezer Gryce is not a 'gentleman', but nonetheless he commands respect as a professional man. Gryce appeared in other detective novels by Green, suggesting he had found favour with the public. As Gryce's official designation of 'city detective' implies, while America's police system drew on the English example it developed differently, with federal, state, county and municipal, or city, police. In the early days, links between politicians and police officials meant that corruption was common, and this is apparent in the 1930s and 40s hard-boiled detective novels of Dashiell Hammett and Raymond Chandler. Later American detective fiction also features corrupt policemen, for example James Ellroy's L. A. Quartet (*The Black Dahlia*, *The Big Nowhere*, *L. A. Confidential* and *White Jazz*) and often the portrayal of the police in American crime fiction tends towards the negative, perhaps responding to reality but also to the threat to cherished American personal liberty that the police may be perceived to pose.

Nonetheless, it was in America that the police procedural first appeared. What differentiates the police procedural from narratives featuring a police detective is that, according to George N. Dove in *The Police Procedural* (1982), it is 'the only kind of detective fiction that did not originate in a purely literary tradition'; it is based on the actualities of police work carried out by ordinary men dealing with crimes that their employment *requires* them to investigate. These crimes are not solved by genius or intuition, but by practical methods and by team work, in contrast to crime fiction featuring a police detective where it is invariably the individual who finds the solution. The sub-genre is generally considered to have its first outing in Lawrence Treat's *V as in Victim* (1945), and to be most strongly realised in Ed McBain's famous 87th Precinct series which began in 1956 with *Cop Hater* and which McBain (pseudonym for Salvatore Lombino) continued to produce until 2005. The longevity of McBain's series suggests the popularity of the sub-genre; the initial positive reception accorded to the police procedural was perhaps partly a response to a post-war sense that a well-organised and disciplined body of men is the best defence against disorder; partly the immediacy with which television and radio brought the reality of crime and its detection to the public and partly the growing interest, fostered by television documentaries, in realistic narratives. The interest in realist portrayals of the police is apparent in the success of the international series *Dragnet*, which began, initially on radio, in 1949 and then transferred to television in 1952.

George N. Dove has British Maurice Procter as producing the second exemplary police procedural with *The Chief Inspector's Statement* (1951) which represented the workings of the English police: Procter was himself a police officer. Police procedural novels continued to appear throughout the 1950s and into the 1960s and beyond, but it is in televisual form that the sub-genre is perhaps most successful. The written form, having introduced the reader to the practices of the police, had difficulty in maintaining the reading public's interest; after all, the work of the police is often repetitious and boring and the tendency has been to deviate from the teamwork and method-focused police procedural to the police detective genre of crime fiction where the attention is on the individual police-detective hero rather than his—or her—team. Television afforded a more user-friendly window into the world of the police and Britain especially seems to have taken the televised police procedural to its heart, from its beginnings in *Dixon of Dock Green* (1955–76) to *Z Cars* (1962–78), *The Sweeney* (1975–78) and more recently *The Bill* (1984–). The police procedural tends to offer a positive as well as realistic picture of policing, but British series such as *Between the Lines* (1992–4) and *The Cops* (1998–2003) show the corruption and abuse that at times taint police work in the real as well as the fictional world.

The police procedural/police detective novel now spans the globe, with writers of many nationalities—French, Icelandic, Swedish, Japanese, Italian, Spanish and Australian—producing crime fiction with the police at its centre. Such texts, for example in France Georges Simenon's Maigret series (1931–72) or Fred Vargas's more recent Parisian Chief Inspector Adamsberg series, offer an insight into not only the French police system but also French culture; Michel Giuttari's Florentine Chief Inspector Michele Ferrara and Andrea Camillera's Sicilian Inspector Montalbano perform a similar function for Italy and Sicily; Arnaldur Indridason's Inspector Erlandur for Iceland; Maj Sjöwall and Per Wahlöö's Martin Beck or Henning Mankel's Inspector Kurt Wallander for Sweden; Barbara Nadel's Çetin Ikmen for Turkey; Ian Rankin's John Rebus for Scotland. The police detective in various formulations now dominates detective fiction, perhaps as a consequence of the need for reality in crime fiction.

The police and policing might also seem to be a fruitful setting for the exploration of social and cultural issues such as gender, sexuality and race. The macho and chauvinistic image of the police, consequent on its very masculine origins and its conservative conventionality, should surely make it an ideal location for showcasing feminist, gay/lesbian or racial issues and testing social and cultural conventions and boundaries. In fact this seems not to be the case. Sue Grafton's serial, female and quietly feminist protagonist Kinsey Millhone briefly refers to her past service as a police officer in *A is for Alibi* (1986) but has rejected a police career, resenting its (often masculine) constraints and preferring to work for herself as a private detective. Val McDermid's serial police detective Carol Jordan makes it clear in *The Mermaids Singing* (1995) that she has to work harder than her male colleagues to gain the respect due to her ability and rank, but this is less apparent in the later books. Feminism is inherent in narratives featuring heterosexual women police officers and is focused on their ability to function effectively in what has long been seen as a masculine profession. Non-heterosexual protagonists have a more overtly political function. Katherine V. Forrest's Los Angeles lesbian Detective Inspector Kate Delafield first appears in *Amateur City* (1984) and has since featured in a further seven novels that conform to the police procedural format; Gill Plain describes the Kate Delafield novels as 'one of crime fiction's most sustained engagements with the politics of sexuality'.

Gay police detectives are few and far between. George Batz's *A Queer Kind of Death* (1966) radically had a New York police detective, Pharoah Love, who is gay and black. Love appeared in a further four novels; more recently in Britain Reginald Hill introduced gay Detective-Sergeant Wield into his long-running Dalziell and Pascoe novels, but gay and lesbian detectives in fiction tend to be private investigators. Even in relatively recent crime fiction the gay police detective is unusual and is shown to be subject to suspicion and discrimination from fellow police officers, as demonstrated in Chris Simms's Manchester police detective novels featuring protagonist Detective Inspector Jon Spicer and his gay fellow-officer Rick Saville (2006–). Race and racial difference are integral to Chester Himes's novel sequence featuring Harlem-based black police detectives 'Grave-Digger' Jones and 'Coffin' Ed Johnson (1957–69); these are not texts that strive for racial equality but rather, pessimistically, represent the race relations and perceptions of their time. John Ball's foray into crime fiction, *In the Heat of the Night* (1965), uses black police detective Virgil Tibbs to articulate the contemporary racial tensions of the American South, responding to the civil rights movement. In Australia, Philip MacClaren's urban police procedural *Scream Black Murder* (1995) features two Aboriginal police detectives, male and female, whose backgrounds embody the darker side of the native Australian experience. But, as with gay investigators, in crime fiction the tendency is to represent black detectives—of either gender and of whatever sexuality—as working in the private sector. It seems that ultimately the conventions of and constraints on the police and their work in the real world make them less than fertile ground for fictional experimentation.

In the early twenty-first century the police are a recurring, indeed omnipresent feature in crime fiction; it would after all, lose its credibility otherwise. The amateur investigator working alone is no longer viable in an age when the police can call on cutting-edge science, information technology, surveillance systems, mass communications and where they have access to global networks of information on crime and criminality. The police in fiction function now more to add the realism required by the informed reader, and the ideological policing element of the earlier police narratives is largely absent. The actuality of surveillance in everyday life has, perhaps, rendered the imaginary version obsolete. Equally, the availability of accurate crime statistics and reports on police performance demonstrates exactly how effective—or not—the police are at containing crime. We know how the police work; the modern, often maverick fictional police detective is located somewhere between the procedural and the private detective and acts as a mediating agent between the public and the police, combining the personal and human with the bureaucracy and mechanics of the institution.

See also   *Contexts*: Detectives and Detection, Crime and Criminality, Gender and Sexuality, Race, Colour and Creed; *Texts*: Police Procedural, Golden Age Crime Fiction; *Criticism*: Cultural Materialism, Postmodernism.

Further reading

Ascoli, David, *The Queen's Peace: The Origin and Development of the Metropolitan Police 1829–1979* (London: Hamish Hamilton, 1979).

Cobley, Paul, *The American Thriller: Generic Innovation and Social Change in the 1970s* (Basingstoke: Palgrave Macmillan, 2000).

Dove, George N., *The Police Procedural* (Bowling Green, OH: Bowling Green University Popular Press, 1982).

Emsley, Clive, *The English Police: A Social and Political History* (London: Addison, Wesley Longman, 1996).

Emsley, Clive and Haia Shpayer-Makov (eds), *Police Detectives in History, 1750–1950* (Aldershot: Ashgate, 2006).

Miller, D. A., *The Novel and the Police* (Berkeley: University of California Press, 1988).

Panek, Leroy Lad, *The American Police Novel: A History* (Jefferson: McFarland, 2003).

Race, colour and creed

Criminality locates the criminal as different, Other, to the society in which he or she lives and historically this difference has been constructed as visible: crime or the signs of the guilt induced by committing crime were considered physically to mark the criminal and that inherent criminality would be apparent in his or her appearance. This concept has a long cross-cultural history and has an early literary representation in the Book of Genesis in the Christian Bible when God sets a mark on Cain after he has murdered his brother Abel, thus ensuring that Cain's guilt can be seen by all (the Muslim and Jewish faiths have similar accounts). The idea that character and personality, and hence potentially criminality, are reflected in physical appearance has a similarly long history: physiognomy, or the study of the relationship between an individual's appearance and his/her personality dates back to at least the ancient Greek and Roman civilisations and is being revisited in new forms today. Physiognomy had always had a quasi-scientific status but achieved widespread popularity in the eighteenth century when Johann Kaspar Lavatar wrote a series of essays on the subject and this continued well into the nineteenth and even early twentieth centuries. Certainly, physiognomy is a strong and recurring feature in nineteenth-century fiction as evidenced in the novels of Charles Dickens; basically, good characters tend to be attractive and physically unblemished, unpleasant or evil characters are often ugly or deformed.

Clearly this is not absolute and there are exceptions, such as Esther Summerson in *Bleak House* (1853), whose beauty is marred by small-pox in the course of the narrative but who is the heroine of the novel. In contrast, Lady Dedlock's French maid, Hortense, who proves to be a murderess, is described as 'a large-eyed brown woman with black hair; who would be handsome, but for a certain feline mouth, and general uncomfortable tightness of face, rendering the jaws too eager and the skull too prominent'. A second quasi-scientific approach to reading the physical signifiers of crime can be seen in the nineteenth-century fascination with phrenology, where the shape of the skull was held to denote particular characteristics of the individual to which it belonged, including a propensity to criminality. Phrenology was 'invented' around 1800 by Franz Joseph Gall, a physician with a particular interest in neuroanatomy, or the physical structure of the brain. Gall declared that the external shape of the skull revealed personality and the development of mental and moral faculties; he called this 'science' 'craniology', a name later altered to phrenology by his disciple, Johann Spurzheim.

Physiognomy and phrenology were influential in the development of the system of criminal anthropology championed by the Italian physician Cesare Lombroso in the late nineteenth century. Lombroso, drawing on Darwin's theory of evolution, argued that criminality was an inherited tendency that indicated a return to primal savagery in man in a form of reverse evolution. According to Lombroso's theory, it was possible to detect this criminal tendency in physical signifiers such as large jaws, low sloping foreheads, handle-shaped ears, prominent large chins, fleshy lips, long arms and insensitivity to pain among other features. Lombroso also took into account the effects of social factors as causes of criminality and this has continued to play a part in modern discussions of the subject, but his concept of inherited criminality has long been out of favour. Equally, neither phrenology nor physiognomy now have any real credibility (although facial movements and expressions are held to suggest particular psychological or emotional aspects of character), but the idea that criminality somehow physically marks or is visible in the criminal individual still occasionally occurs in twentieth and twenty-first-century crime narratives. Thomas Harris's serial killer, cannibal Hannibal Lecter, has a sixth finger on one hand and maroon eyes, for example. However, novels tend to indicate criminality through behaviour rather than appearance—the most frightening aspect of the modern serial killer is that he or she is indistinguishable from the rest of society. Visual media still rely on appearance to indicate criminality to a certain extent: the villain 'Jaws' in the James Bond film *The Spy Who Loved Me* (1977) is over seven feet tall and has metal teeth; the Joker in *Batman* (1998) and again in *The Dark Knight* (2008) is facially scarred and graphic novels, comics and cartoons use visual signifiers of criminality extensively.

Physical difference has been, then, associated with criminality for a long time, probably dating back to pre-history and inter-community hostilities: those who are from a different family or clan are automatically a threat. As civilisations developed and social groupings became wider, the threat was displaced outwards and gradually countries and nations replaced families and communities in terms of 'us' and 'them'. Issues of race and ethnicity enter the equation as there are often physical characteristics associated with a particular racial group. But within the geographical limitations of continents, differences in appearance are not always clearly visible; it is possible to distinguish between a native of China and a native of France, but less easy to tell apart a Frenchman and an Italian or a Scot and a Welshman. Skin colour and other physical signifiers of race such as eye shape and hair type/tone are clear and distinct signifiers of difference, and racial difference has frequently been part of the construction of criminality. But even within racial and ethnic groupings colouring can denote difference and potential deviance: in the West, red hair has been associated with sexual excess and fiery temper; villains are often dark haired and occasionally dark skinned; innocent women are frequently blonde. These physical signifiers are particularly apparent in nineteenth-century fiction but still carry weight today.

Thus, when in Mary E. Braddon's *Lady Audley's Secret* (1862) the protagonist's criminal acts are revealed their impact is made greater by the
fact that bigamist and attempted murderess Lady Audley is blonde and
beautiful; in Charlotte Brönte's *Jane Eyre* (1847) Mr Rochester is dark and
saturnine and 'criminalised' by his attempt to commit bigamy in marrying Jane; violent and savage Heathcliff in Emily Brönte's *Wuthering
Heights* (1847) is dark of skin and black of hair; Wilkie Collins's anti-
heroine in *Armadale* (1866), Lydia Gwilt, is beautiful, red-headed and a
forger, bigamist and husband-poisoner; famously, Fagin, one of the two
villains in Dickens's *Oliver Twist* (1839) is a red-headed Jewish fence, or
receiver of stolen goods; in Mrs Henry Wood's *East Lynne* (1860–1) dark-
haired Lady Isabel Vane is cruelly punished by disfigurement and the loss
of her husband and children for allowing herself to be seduced by the
raven-haired and criminal Captain Levinson while blonde Barbara Hare's
virtue and patience is rewarded with husband, house, children and hap-
piness. Clearly in nineteenth-century Anglophone literature darkness—or
redness—in hair or skin colour suggests deviance from the social, racial
and, in the case of red hair, religious norm and is often used to denote
criminality (red hair had long been associated with Jewish identity and
Jewishness with criminality as in Chaucer's 'The Prioress's Tale' in *The
Canterbury Tales*, circa 1385–1400, and in Dickens's later representation of Fagin, whose representation may well have been based on the
real nineteenth-century, Jewish, London money-lender and fence, Ikey
Solomon).

On a wider scale, tensions between nations influenced the literary
representation of criminality and villains in melodramas and in fiction;
for the British it was frequently the French who were characterised
as wicked, as demonstrated by Charles Dickens's choice of a French
murderess in *Bleak House* (1852–3), or his making the French Revolution the subject matter of his *A Tale of Two Cities* (1859), as did Baroness
Orczy in her Scarlet Pimpernel novels (1905–40). Within the British nation
itself the Irish were often scapegoated by the English, as were the Welsh;
'Gines', the name of the thief-turned-thief-taker in William Godwin's
Caleb Williams (1794) was originally 'Jones', a name with strong Welsh
associations, as indeed is the criminalised Caleb's surname, 'Williams'.
Equally, the Irish, Scots and Welsh, in response to English invasion,
annexation and oppression, demonised the English. In the prelude to
and during the course of World War I, as several Sherlock Holmes stories
suggest ('The Adventure of the Bruce Partington Plans' 1908; 'His Last
Bow: An Epilogue of Sherlock Holmes' 1917, among others), criminality
is associated with spying and with members of the German nation.
In fact, Doyle pits Sherlock Holmes against South African criminals in

the wake of the Boer War and against Spanish, Italian, South American and Australian criminals at various points in his career. Religious difference is also addressed with the Mormon criminals of *A Study in Scarlet* (1887).

This essentially racist association of criminality with nationality and with religion continues into the twentieth century, with writers in the Golden Age of crime fiction, such as Agatha Christie and Dorothy L. Sayers peppering their works with what seem, from a modern perspective, racial slurs. Christie's thrillers, rather than her crime fiction, are particularly prone to this, with her characters making anti-Semitic references to Hermann Isaacstein, one of the characters in *The Secret of Chimneys* (1925), as 'Fat Ikey' and 'Noseystein' and throwaway comments like 'dagos will be dagos'. But the detective novels were not without problems; in the Poirot novel *Lord Edgeware Dies* (1933) a drunken young man announces that 'I'm not a damned nigger', while in another text featuring Poirot, *Death in the Clouds* (1935), a young couple agree that they 'disliked loud voices, noisy restaurants and negroes'. Significantly, Christie avoids making the murderers in her novels Jewish or racially 'other'; to do so would have been to deviate from her pattern of the criminal being 'one of us', a member of the small white, western, middle-class social grouping that features in much of her work. While racist references such as those above have not been edited out of modern British editions of Christie's texts (some American editions have been 'tidied up'), the politically incorrect title of her 1939 novel, *Ten Little Niggers*, has been variously altered to *And Then There Were None*, after the American version, or *Ten Little Indians*, although this too is now considered unacceptable and the American title is standard.

Sayers's *Whose Body?* (1923) features several Jewish characters, including the victim, Levy, who is referred to by the highly racist and derogatory name 'Sheeny' by the medical students who dissect his body; in *Unnatural Death* (1927) a maidservant is depicted refusing to serve a person of colour and making racist remarks, even though the person in question is the Reverend Hallelujah Dawson, a man of probity and a religious minister. But Sayers and Christie also offer positive representations of and relationships with Jews and foreigners, usually articulated through the writers' investigative protagonists—indeed, Christie's best-known detective, Hercule Poirot, is a Belgian—and the seemingly racist attitudes seen in their texts must be considered in the context of the prevailing social and cultural attitudes. Anti-Semitism has had a long history in Britain and Europe; the middle-Eastern origins and appearance of the Jewish people and their different dress clearly marked them as 'other', while their religious beliefs and practices were antithetical to

Christianity as the Jews were considered to be responsible for the killing of Christ. The dislike and distrust of Jews in Europe was compounded by their long association with the trade of money-lending which historically been forbidden to Christians and anti-Semitic opinion was common and accepted in European and British society well into the early twentieth century. Both Christie and Sayers were products of the late Victorian and Edwardian periods when the British Empire still ruled much of the world; the Empire's territorial extent was greatest in the immediate wake of World War I. And it is the Empire and the merchant trade in which it had its origins, including the slave trade, which in Britain brought the nation into literal and literary contact with other peoples who were visibly different: Native Americans, Africans, Australian Aborigines, Indians, Chinese, Japanese and Asiatic.

Both the British Empire and racism flourished in the nineteenth century. Racism in this period was an odd combination of the necessary assumption of superiority over enslaved or colonised peoples, the justification, in the early part of the century, of slavery and of the act of colonisation itself, and a fear of reverse colonisation and racism was in part constructed and affirmed by the biological sciences and anthropology developed in the period, especially in the aftermath of Darwin and his theories of evolution. Slavery was abolished in the British colonies in 1833–4, but its racist discourse, which was founded in visible physical differences, lingered. Significantly, the racial 'others' who aroused such anxiety in the nation were in fact a very small section of the British population. With the discovery of the New World and the subsequent development of plantations in the Americas, which required cheap labour and consequently encouraged the entry of Europe into the already-established North African slave trade, some black Africans began to appear in England in the 1500s. But despite the first Queen Elizabeth's complaints about their numbers (in an open letter circulated in London and other cities and towns in 1596, the Queen suggested that there were too many 'blackmoores' in the country and that they should 'be transported [...] out of the realme'), the black population remained small until the abolition of slavery in 1833 and did not increase greatly until the 1940s.

Indians from the sub-continent began to appear in Britain after the establishment of trade links by the British East India Company (1757) and the later annexation of territories and imposition of British rule, effectively colonisation (1858), when India became part of the British Empire. The few Indians who came to Britain in the nineteenth century tended to be professional men, students, traders, servants or seamen and they were visitors rather than immigrants. Chinese immigration did occur, but was also limited, although the British Chinese community is the oldest in Western Europe, dating back to about 1800, and was initially focused around ports as many of the Chinese were seamen. The abolition of the slave trade meant that a new source of cheap labour had to be found, and many Chinese were recruited and travelled to Europe and to America; the 1842 treaty of Nanking opened trading routes between Britain and China and so facilitated the movement of Chinese people to Britain. Nonetheless, for Britons living outside major cities and ports, the chances of seeing a person of colour were slim. But this did not reduce or prevent racism and the fears that foreigners entering the country aroused.

The perceived threat of the oriental or African racial other was not a central feature in nineteenth-century crime fiction, but Chinese or Indian figures were sometimes used as a secondary, background element, functioning to suggest or invoke criminality, mystery, corruption, deviant sexuality, exotic drugs or simply to create atmosphere. Thomas de Quincey, whose essay 'On Murder Considered as One of the Fine Arts' (1827) can be read as an early satiric version of crime fiction, also wrote *Confessions of an English Opium-Eater* (1821), in which he recounts dreams inhabited by sometimes threatening Chinese figures located in Orientalised settings, establishing a literary link between China, opium and the criminality associated with drug-taking that would last into the twentieth century. Opium is a key element in Wilkie Collins's *The Moonstone* (1868); Chinese opium dens are a recurring feature in Dickens's unfinished crime novel, *The Mystery of Edwin Drood* (1870) and Oscar Wilde's *The Picture of Dorian Gray* (1891); Doyle's Sherlock Holmes occasionally ventures into Chinese opium dens in his search for information, as in 'The Man with the Twisted Lip' (1891). In the twentieth century Sax Rohmer's Chinese criminal mastermind, Dr Fu Manchu, epitomised what came to be seen as 'the yellow peril', that is, the perceived threat of mass Chinese immigration, particularly into America. Fu Manchu appeared in thirteen novels written by Rohmer between 1912 and 1959, and a later pastiche, written by Cay van Ash, pitted Fu Manchu against Sherlock Holmes in *Ten Years Beyond Baker Street* (1984).

Africans do not feature as criminals in nineteenth-century crime fiction, possibly because of the contemporary discourse that constructed them as simple savages and so, presumably, without the intelligence to commit crimes and perhaps also because of their scarcity, at least in Britain. The concept of the African as savage is, according to Charles Rzepka in *Detective Fiction*, evident in Edgar Allan Poe's first short story featuring his proto-detective C. Auguste Dupin. In 'The Murders in the Rue Morgue' (1841) the violent deaths of the widow Madame L'Espanaye and her daughter Camille—the former with her throat cut so deeply that on moving the body, the head falls off and the latter having been beaten, strangled and finally thrust, upside down, up a chimney—are proved to have been caused by an orang-utan. Rzepka suggests that Poe's story has been read as an expression of the fears of the slave-owning society of the Southern States of America of which Poe was a member. As Rzepka notes, 'Poe was writing in an era when analogies between Africans and apes [...] were an intrinsic part of [...] the "average racism" of the day', and the orang-utan can be seen metaphorically as an African slave attacking white women. But Rzepka goes on to read Poe's story rather more sympathetically in the context of the mid-century drive to abolish slavery in America (finally achieved after the American Civil War in 1865), suggesting that Poe uses the metaphor to show how the ape/African slave is seeking acceptance, endeavouring to become 'human', that is a member of American society, as signified by the orang-utan's attempt to shave itself in imitation of its master.

Where Africans were not a feature of crime fiction in the period, Orientals, that is Indians, Asiatics and to a lesser extent people from the Middle East, certainly were. Perhaps the best-known example is Wilkie Collins's *The Moonstone* (1868), in which a valuable yellow diamond, the moonstone of the title, is stolen from the forehead of an Indian 'Hindoo' idol by British army officer John Herncastle at the siege of Seringapatam in 1799 and brought back to England with disastrous consequences. Herncastle becomes addicted to opium and dies, leaving the diamond to his niece Rachel Verinder. The jewel subsequently disappears and suspicion immediately falls upon the trio of Indian jugglers seen in the vicinity of the Verinder house. The Indians are variously described as 'snaky', 'rogueish', 'heathenish', 'fanatically devoted' Hindus or 'lawless Mohammedan[s]', and India is represented as a place of mystery and magic, savagery and sensuousness. In this, the text can be seen to comply with the contemporary opinions and anxieties of the British with regard to India in the aftermath of the Indian Mutiny (1857). But the diamond is proved to have been stolen by a villainous white man, the aptly named Godfrey Ablewhite who, disguised as an Indian, is murdered— or executed—by the Indian jugglers, who are revealed to be high-caste Hindu Brahmin priests charged with repossessing the jewel.

Ultimately the narrative is sympathetic to the Indians, while still seeing them as radically 'other', and the text can be read as Collins's subtle critique of the Empire and its plundering of the wealth of other nations and treatment of their peoples. Collins's novel also features a man of mixed race and is suggestive of an awareness of the difficulties faced by such people and the aversion and fears of miscegenation they aroused in nineteenth-century white, Western society. Ezra Jennings is a key figure in *The Moonstone* as his quasi-detective role enables the mystery of the disappearance of the diamond to be resolved. He is not, however, a classic hero-detective in the manner of Sherlock Holmes. Jennings's mixed parentage is literally written on his body:

> [h]is complexion was of a gipsy darkness [...] his nose presented the fine shape [...] so often found among the ancient people of the East [...] thick closely-curling hair [...] over the top of his head [...] was still of the deep black which was its natural colour. Round the sides [...] it had turned completely white.

He is, as Franklin observes, 'the man with the piebald hair', the colouring metaphorically representing his mixed-race heritage. Jennings later admits that he has been born and brought up in 'one of our colonies', with an English father and a mother of unspecified race; further, he confesses to being born with a 'female constitution'. The combination of his foreign appearance, his hair and his tendency to hysterical and hence feminine emotion alienates the local rural population. Jennings is treated sympathetically in the text, but once he has performed his 'detective' work, dies before the closure of the narrative. The official detective in *The Moonstone* is the police officer, Sergeant Cuff, whose Englishness is clear in his physique and in his hobby; he is a keen gardener with a special interest in roses. In the context of the text and the time, it is hard not to read Cuff's discussion with the Verinder gardener about developing new roses using a grafting technique—which Cuff declares to be unnecessary—as a comment on the inadvisability of creating hybrids, whether floral or human.

The Moonstone is particularly redolent with racial references: Franklin Blake is represented as tainted by his foreign education and has to be educated back into full Englishness through his experiences in the narrative and his eventual marriage; there are of course the Indians; Rachel Verinder is described in frankly Eastern terms, with golden skin and dark hair; opium is a key feature in the plot; Mr Murthwaite is an expert on India and its peoples, speaking several times of their ferocity and contempt for life; even Miss Clack, the 'comic turn' of the text, makes reference to the East, declaring '[h]ow soon may our own evil passions prove to be Oriental noblemen who pounce on us unawares' in a veiled reference to her own passion for Godfrey Ablewhite. The narrative panders to as well as critiquing the contemporary construction of all those who were not strictly English, with the appropriate features, characteristics and colouring, as racially 'other', a process of racialisation that included Indians, West Indians, Africans, the Irish, the French,

Orientals, but also Jews, Catholics, Muslims, Hindus, the lower classes, women, lunatics—and criminals. But *The Moonstone* also points forwards to changes in the twentieth century in attitudes to racial difference and the relationship between race and criminality: Jennings, half black, half white, is a partial detective and an incomplete figure who cannot be fully developed in the nineteenth century, but the twentieth century sees the marginalised, racial other in crime fiction shift from a criminal role to that of the detective.

The change was gradual. The Sherlock Holmes stories at the end of the nineteenth century continue to use the East as a source of corruption and crime. Criminals in Doyle's detective fiction are not actually Oriental or Indian but have often spent time in the East and have been tainted by their exposure. Perhaps the Sherlock Holmes story that demonstrates this Eastern taint most clearly is 'The Speckled Band' (1892), in which the murderer, Dr Grimesby Roylott, has spent time in India, where he has acquired the marks of 'every evil passion' and has been yellowed by the sun. His murder weapon is 'the deadliest snake in India', a 'swamp adder', which he uses to kill his step-daughter. The second Sherlock Holmes novel, *The Sign of Four* (1890), concerns an Indian treasure—shades of *The Moonstone*—and features criminal Jonathan Small, similarly corrupted by his time in the East, and his faithful Andaman Islander servant Tonga, with his blowpipe and poisoned arrows. As discussed earlier, Doyle's villains tended, in the later 'Adventures' to be of European, South African or South American origin as the perceived threat from the East was replaced by the real threat from the South African Dutch Boers, the Austrians and Germans and the Bolsheviks in Russia.

This focus on largely European 'others' as criminal or corrupt continues throughout the first part of the twentieth century, as Christie's and Sayers's crime fiction demonstrates. A growing awareness of racism and racist ideology was fostered by the nascent multiculturalism consequent on increasing immigration, at least in Britain, in the 1950s. The majority of these immigrants were, initially, West Indians who came from the Caribbean to Britain in search of work, with the first wave arriving in 1948 on the SS Windrush, followed by others not just from the West Indies but from other countries as well which had been part of the Empire but which were now members of the Commonwealth. But the actuality of an 'other' racial presence in Britain seems not to have fulfilled nineteenth-century predictions concerning reverse colonisation, while religious tolerance followed the increasing secularisation of society from the mid-nineteenth century onwards. Certainly there were problems, but Britain generally accepted its new immigrant population and learned to live with it: the crime fiction of the 1940s, 50s, 60s and 70s shows little if any real concern with race and neither is there a proliferation of racially 'other' master criminals or murderers. In fact, there is perhaps a subtle, lingering racism in the continuing allocation of major roles in crime fiction to white, Western characters, with colour, creed and racial origin featuring only in minor players in order to accentuate criminality or suggest corruption and savagery.

But this was the British experience. In America issues of race were very different and very much focused on colour. America had been colonised in successive waves by the Spanish, the French and the British, nations whose languages and religious beliefs varied but who shared a common white, Western and European heritage. Subsequent immigration in the nineteenth and twentieth centuries was also predominantly European, often in response to natural disasters, as with the Irish Potato Famine in the 1840s, or political unrest or religious pogroms such as those against European Jews in the nineteenth and twentieth centuries. Freedom of religious belief is written into the American Constitution and consequently the religious intolerance that is exposed in, for example, the casual anti-Semitism seen in some British crime fiction is not really a factor in the American version of the genre, although links and similarities between East coast America and Britain were strong in the nineteenth and early twentieth century and both held racial and religious prejudices in common. In essence, in an already multicultural but racially similar society the most apparent signifier of difference was skin colour and the American construction of racial difference and 'otherness' was dependent on this as well as other factors such as language, a construction that began perhaps with the distinctive colouring of the Native American Indians, considered to be savages by the early colonisers, and was strengthened and compounded by the huge numbers—estimated at 11 million—of black African slaves brought, between the sixteenth and nineteenth centuries, to service the labour-intensive tobacco, cotton, sugar, coffee and other plantations in the West Indies, Brazil and the Southern states of North America.

With the abolition of slavery in 1865 the need for cheap labour was in part satisfied by workers from China and the Chinese population in the States numbered about 105,000 at the end of the nineteenth century while in the early twenty-first century they make up approximately 1.2 per cent of the population; the Chinese feature in American crime fiction largely in the same way as they do in the British version of the genre and are associated with drugs and gambling, functioning as part of the background to conventional crime fiction plots and characterisation. There is, however, an early Chinese detective; white American Earl Derr Biggers wrote six novels with police-detective protagonist Charlie Chan between 1925 and 1932. Biggers's hero proved popular and more than three dozen films were made, continuing to appear into the 1940s. But the representation of Chan has been criticised as inherently racist and a white, stereotyped version of the Chinese experience. However, the very fact that such a figure appeared at all suggests the way that in America the role of the racial 'other' developed differently, perhaps in response to the very large numbers of racially and ethnically differentiated peoples that made up American society. While the Chinese community was relatively small, in the wake of the abolition of slavery there were approximately five million free black individuals in America, or 13 per cent of the population, a percentage which has changed little over time. The process of assimilating the emancipated slaves into the general population of what had become, in the wake of the American Civil War (1861–65), the United States, was not quick or painless and racial and social segregation, official and unofficial, encouraged—forced—the new 'African Americans' to cohere into black communities and to continue the production and articulation of their own culture, which had its origins in Africa and in slavery.

African-American culture had itself assimilated much white American culture in the course of its development, including literature classical and popular, such as crime fiction. In fact, as Stephen F. Soitos suggests in *The Blues Detective: A Study of African American Detective Fiction*, the established structures and conventions of the genre, particularly the very American hard-boiled format, made it an ideal basis for creative experimentation and appropriation, as feminist writers found in the 1970s. Crime fiction set in black communities, with black detectives and black and white criminals, allowed the expression of black culture and the lived black experience but in a form recognisable and potentially more acceptable to a white as well as a black audience. And the appropriation started early in serialised form in periodicals aimed at a black readership, with Pauline Hopkins's *Hagar's Daughter* (1901–2). This is probably the earliest example of black crime fiction, written by a black (woman) author and featuring two black detectives; radically, one is also female. The sub-text of the novel is a subtle but deliberate critique of American white, racist ideology and the black female detective, housemaid Venus Johnson, succeeds where her white counterpart, federal detective Henson, fails. Venus has access to and understanding of the black community which is denied to the white, male detective and this is a trope that will recur in black crime fiction. Between 1907 and 1909, slave-born writer and historian of the African-American experience John Edward Bruce wrote and serially published *The Black Sleuth*, another crime fiction which worked as a criticism of white racist attitudes, but on a wider scale than had Hopkins, as the action takes place in America, Africa and England.

African-American crime fiction continued to appear in the first half of the twentieth century, with the early writers making possible the later introduction of an Afro-centric worldview into mainstream popular fiction: Rudolph Fisher's *The Conjure Man Dies* (1932) is a police-detective story with an all-black setting and cast and no less than four detectives. In 1957, Chester Himes published *For the Love of Imabelle*, the first of his ten-novel series featuring Harlem police detectives 'Grave-Digger Jones' and 'Coffin' Ed Johnson. The series ran until 1969, but the novels were less overtly political, representing rather the complex questions raised by portraying black police officers upholding white laws in a predominantly black community. John Ball's prize-winning novel, *In the Heat of the Night* (1965), responded to the civil rights movement in the American South with black police detective Virgil Tibbs solving a racial crime in the face of strong opposition in a racist southern town. The novel was made into a powerful film and is a major contribution to the development of politicised black crime fiction. In the 1970s, a rather less politically-aware black detective series appeared; written by Ernest Tidyman, seven novels featuring John Shaft were published between 1970 and 1975. While these were popular and well-received and quickly translated into film, Tidyman was a white writer and the depiction of Shaft lacks the African-American perspective of his predecessors. Nonetheless, Tidyman won a National Association for the Advancement of Colored People (NAACP) Image Award for his depiction of Shaft on the basis of the way his tough, smart, well-dressed private investigator more than held his own in a white world and seemed to offer a very positive image of and to black Americans.

While Shaft lacked political edge, Walter Mosley's Easy (Ezekiel) Rawlins novels in some ways chart the African-American experience from 1948 to 1967—the year of the setting for *Blonde Faith* (2007), which seems to be the final book in the series—beginning with the post-war period (*Devil in a Blue Dress*, 1990) and ending with the liberal and liberation movements of the 1960s. On the way, Mosley touches on McCarthyism in the 1950s (*A Red Death*, 1991), the apparent death of black liberal hope consequent on the assassination of Kennedy in 1963 (*A Little Yellow Dog*, 1995), the Watts Riots in 1965 (*Little Scarlet*, 2004) and the San Francisco summer of love hippy counterculture and side effects of the Vietnam War (*Blonde Faith*). Mosley's decision to appropriate and rework the hard-boiled detective novel is apparent in *Devil in a Blue Dress* which deliberately revises the opening of Raymond Chandler's *Farewell My Lovely* (1940) in which a white man enters a black bar; in Mosley's version a similar scene is set, but events and reactions are recounted from the perspective of the bar's black occupants rather than from that of the white intruder. Mosley's initially amateur detective, Easy, shares with Pauline Hopkins's Venus Johnson the access to the black community which is denied to white detectives, but Easy also has access to the white world, and his liminal positioning between black and white brings black crime writing into popular mainstream fiction; famously, Mosley is one of ex-USA President Bill Clinton's favourite authors.

In American crime fiction, race, colour and creed are still important factors, perhaps because from its relatively recent origins the United States of America has been a multicultural society in which racial, ethnic and religious differences are secondary to being American citizens. Hence, its crime fiction more fully represents its diverse population and the genre continues to be the locus in which such issues can safely be explored; American crime fiction continues to be overtly aware of the politics of race and ethnicity. Faye Kellerman, Kinky Friedman and Jerome Charyn write crime fiction featuring Jewish detectives; variously these are police detective Peter Decker (Kellerman), Kinky Friedman (Friedman) and Isaac Sidel (Charyn). All three authors weave issues concerning the dual heritage of Jewishness—as ethnicity and religion—and American-ness into their crime narratives. Native Americans are represented by Navajo tribal police detectives Joe Leaphorn and Jim Chee in Tony Hillerman's well-known and popular series of novels and in Alaskan Dana Stabenow's Kate Shugak novels; vexed issues surrounding the immigration, assimilation and ethnic/racial identity of the 'Latino' or Hispanic sector of the American population are central to Alex Abella's crime series, articulated through the Cuban-American lawyer Charlie Morrell, and Michael Nava's gay Mexican-American protagonist Henry Rios, also a lawyer-cum-detective.

In Britain questions of race and ethnicity seem to be less present in crime fiction, perhaps responding to a continuing white hegemonic ideology. Guyanan-born Mike Phillips's amateur black detective, Caribbean-born journalist Sam Dean, is more concerned with solving crimes than with black oppression, although the four novels in which Dean appears (*Blood Rights*, 1989; *The Late Candidate*, 1990; *Point of Darkness*, 1994 and *An Image to Die For*, 1995) clearly represent and explore multicultural Britain and its concomitant issues. Jamaican-born British writer Victor Headley's 'Yardie' novels (*Yardie*, 1992; *Excess*, 1993; *Yush!*, 1994 and *The Best Man*, 1999) are focused on British Caribbean crime, gangs and drugs. Well-known white crime writer Reginald Hill has a serial black detective, Joe Sixsmith (five novels), but Sixsmith, called by one reviewer 'the Miss Marple of Luton' is a comedic figure suffering from condescending

if affectionate racial stereotyping. Scots author Alexander McCall Smith's
No. 1 Ladies' Detective Agency series set in Botswana and featuring black
female detective Precious Ramotswe seems also to suffer from a certain
colonial condescension and racial stereotyping.

In South Africa where, as Geoffrey V. Davis notes, there is little, if
'any South African detective fiction', Wessel Ebersohn uses the genre to
explore issues surrounding apartheid; his detective though is not black,
but Jewish. James McClure's crime series has a white Afrikaans detective assisted by a black Bantu sergeant, a relationship that seems aptly
to sum up the issue of apartheid with which the novels are concerned.
Deon Meyer's loosely linked police detective series, originally published
in Afrikaans, is now available in translation and features both black and
white detectives in its exploration of the social, political, racial and personal tensions of being a police detective in South Africa. In Australia
a number of authors have used crime fiction to foreground the aboriginal Australian experience; the treatment has been ironic in the case of
Mudrooroo Narogin's short stories featuring Detective Inspector Watson
Holmes Jackamara but Archie Weller's more general crime stories represent a sometimes tragic aboriginal reality. Modern racial tension in
Sydney is central to Philip McLaren's *Scream Black Murder* (1995), a novel
in the police procedural style and crime fiction representing native New
Zealand seems also to represent its detectives as members of the police
rather than as private eyes. Laurie Mantell's serial Maori policeman
Steven Arrow first appears in *Murder and Chips* (1980); Maori Detective
Sergeant Rangi Roberts is the protagonist of Gaelyn Gordon's *Above Sus-
picion* (1990) and Paul Thomas's maverick Maori police detective Tito
Ihaka *Old School Tie* (1994).

In the nineteenth century 'otherness', whether facial, physical, religious, ethnic, sexual or racial, tended in crime fiction to be associated
with criminality, and criminality in turn was considered to be charac-
teristic of otherness; indeed, criminality was briefly considered to be an
inheritable trait and criminals to be not only a class but also an ethnic
or even racial group by early criminal anthropologists such as Cesare
Lombroso. But over the twentieth century this changed and increasingly the issues circulating about race, colour and creed became focused
through the figure of the detective. The established conventions and form
of the genre made it an ideal locus in which to foreground and explore
difference, and by embodying difference in the protagonist, crime fiction allows the expression of the lived experiences of others. Central
to the construction of the detective is the gaze; much is made of the
percipience of investigative figures and their ability to 'see'—clues, guilt,
motives—and the necessity for such a seeing figure, an observer, to be

located on the margins of society, to be somehow outside the society in which he or she works and so to possess an objective gaze. The 'different' detective, whether distinguished by race, creed or colour—or gender, sexuality, disability—enables and encourages the reader to see differently, while more recently the detective's often socially and racially liminal position forms a connection and makes possible communication between different social groups. Crime fiction, then, responds to and also maps changing cultural constructions of and attitudes towards issues of racial and ethnic difference: significantly, it seems that it is multicultural societies and nations that generate both the anxieties and tensions that circulate around difference and the criminography in which they are articulated.

See also *Contexts*: Detectives and Detection, Gender and Sexuality, Crime and Criminality; *Texts*: American Crime Fiction, Hard-boiled Crime Fiction, Golden-Age Crime Fiction, Police Procedural; *Criticism*: Cultural Materialism, Postcolonialism, Postmodernism.

Further reading

Arvas, Paula and Andrew Nestingen (eds), *Scandinavian Crime Fiction* (Cardiff: University of Wales Press, 2011).

Horsley, Lee, *Twentieth-Century Crime Fiction* (Oxford: Oxford University Press, 2005).

Klein, Kathleen Gregory (ed.), *Diversity and Detective Fiction* (Bowling Green, OH: Bowling Green State University Popular Press, 1999).

Krajenbrink, Marieke and Kate M. Quinn (eds), *Investigating Identities: Questions of Identity in Contemporary International Crime Fiction* (Amsterdam and New York: Rodopi, 2009).

Matzke, Christine and Susanne Mühleisen (eds), *Postcolonial Postmortems: Crime Fiction from a Transcultural Perspective* (Amsterdam and New York: Rodopi, 2006).

Reddy, Maureen T., *Traces, Codes, Clues: Reading Race in Crime Fiction* (New Brunswick: Rutgers University Press, 2003).

Soitos, Stephen S., *The Blues Detective: A Study of African American Detective Fiction* (Amherst: University of Massachusetts Press, 1996).

Turnbull, Malcolm J., *Victims or Villains: Jewish Images in Classic English Detective Fiction* (Bowling Green, Ohio: Bowling State University PMSS, 1998).

2 Texts: Themes, Issues, Concepts

Introduction

The texts that comprise crime fiction are many and varied; the genre has its origins in factual narratives that were concerned with criminals and their crime and punishment, but from the latter part of the eighteenth and into the nineteenth century the factual accounts were gradually largely superseded by fictional forms. In parallel with this change of format came a textual change as the short narratives—criminal and execution broadsides, Ordinaries' *Accounts*, entries in the *Newgate Calendars*, newspaper articles and short stories in the periodicals—were slowly joined and, in the twentieth century, overtaken by the novel. In many ways it can be argued that crime has always been implicated in the development of the novel, as seen in Defoe's *Moll Flanders* (1722), where the protagonist passes much of her life and in a considerable part of the narrative as a criminal. In *Factual Fictions: The Origins of the English Novel* (1983), Lennard Davis argues that the novel is at heart a criminal form of literature, that 'the form of the novel seems almost to demand a criminal content' and that in representing imagined events and characters as real, 'novelists become liars, perpetrators of the crime of fiction'. The criminal content of the novel is, over the nineteenth century, joined by other themes and issues and crime fiction becomes one genre among many, ameliorating the inescapable if unintended criminalisation of its writers.

Equally, as the genre evolves, the focus moves from the criminal to the detective and later from the private investigator to the police detective, as Peter Messent has described in *Criminal Proceedings* (1997). Messent is speaking of contemporary American crime fiction, but the same pattern is present elsewhere in twentieth-century crime narratives; in the interests of realism the seemingly invulnerable, indefatigable, incorruptible, independent and inevitably successful private 'I/eye' epitomised by Raymond Chandler's Philip Marlowe must disappear. The new detectives are professionals—police officers, FBI agents, psychologists, forensic scientists, pathologists—who have access to and can use the new technology and information and science and knowledge of the modern world. The evolution of crime fiction is not, though, quite as straightforward as Messent's observation seems to suggest. It is a protean genre, going through many transformations both as it begins to cohere into recognisable form in the nineteenth century and as it reconfigures itself in response to social and cultural change in the twentieth century and beyond. This has resulted in a multitude of sub-genres and (responding to technological developments in the media) other formats—film, television and computer games. Globalisation's shrinking of the world has encouraged the Diaspora of crime fiction both out of and into the Anglophone sphere as texts are translated across languages and cultures. With such wide-ranging and widespread production of crime fiction, it follows that, in the limited space afforded here, it has been necessary to be selective; the majority of the material discussed in this section will be variants of crime literature in the novel form. Equally, not every sub-genre can be discussed and I have elected to focus on those that relate to the earlier section of this volume.

The development of crime fiction as a genre also documents social, cultural and political change, as demonstrated in the **Contexts** section of this volume, while the **General Introduction** offers a general outline of the chronology of the genre and locates it in its historical context. In the following section, the broad themes, issues and concepts touched upon in the **Contexts** entries are more closely explored in the texts in which they were then and are now articulated. In some cases, the connections will be obvious—the entry on the Police Procedural clearly relates to Police and Policing; Feminist Crime Fiction has links with Gender and Sexuality. Less evident perhaps is the affinity between Detectives and Detection and Golden-Age Crime Fiction, or American Crime Fiction and Cities and Urbanisation. Nonetheless, the links are there, as the entries will show. Where the **Contexts** section takes a broad conceptual and historical approach, the **Texts'** exploration of the themes, issues and topics formulated in crime fiction is focused though genre. Some of the sub-genres discussed are practically canonical in terms of crime writing, for example Golden-Age, Hard-boiled Detective and Feminist crime fictions. Conversely, Early Criminography considers lesser-known texts, often ephemeral, that made possible the genre in its modern form and refers back to several of the Contexts entries, perhaps most closely Crime and Criminality. I have included an entry on American crime fiction because the genre's development there is similar to but different from its evolution in Britain and Europe.

There are, of course, omissions in this section; the very excess of sub-genres renders a comprehensive account impossible and is beyond the remit of this volume. But as in the previous section, each entry has a 'Further Reading' coda that will guide those readers wishing to expand their knowledge of crime fiction to other texts and where possible to critical material on, for example, Anglophone crime fiction from countries other than America and Britain, crime narratives in translation, the serial killer and forensic sub-genres. There are, however, two particular sub-genres of crime fiction that I explore which, unlike those listed above, have received little critical attention elsewhere: Children's Crime Fiction and Historical Crime Fiction. Both sub-genres are relatively recent variants that are proving hugely popular and which once again demonstrate the adaptability of the genre as well as offering new insights into the reading public and the issues and topics with which they are concerned.

American crime fiction

The development of crime fiction in America both parallels and deviates from the British pattern. The seventeenth-century English settlers brought literary culture with them, but once the new settlements were established literature became strictly delimited by religion. Despite the strongly religious foundations of the early American settlers, crimes were committed within their communities as in any other society and serious crimes such as murder attracted the death penalty; as the convicted felon waited to be hanged on the gallows, he/she and those gathered to witness the event would be subjected to what became known as an execution sermon. These early crime narratives proved popular and the first book printed in Boston reproduced the sermon given at the execution of two men who had murdered their master: *The Wicked Man's Portion; or, A Sermon* (1675), by Increase Mather. In the early eighteenth century, while America was still a colony, the influence of British criminography can be seen in the publication of ballad sheets and broadsides featuring accounts of crimes, executions and trials; 'last words' and 'dying speeches' were well-received, as were criminal autobiographies. While some of these may have been imported from Britain, the new colonies soon had their own criminals to provide the necessary material for American crime narratives.

Daniel A. Cohen suggests, however, that after the American War of Independence, or the American Revolution (1775–83), as criminography with its origins in localised crime and execution was disseminated across the vast spaces of the newly united states of America the link between social reality and crime literature was loosened and the line between fact and fiction blurred, locating crime as entertainment more rapidly and firmly than in Britain. Furthermore, the most popular crime narratives were those factual accounts dealing with alleged miscarriages of justice, perhaps representing challenges to traditional authority with its roots in a (British) colonial past. In Britain, such challenges were largely located in fiction and did not really appear until the 1830s and 40s with the Newgate novels and the short crime fiction of the periodicals. American narratives of crime such as the novels of Charles Brockden Brown, earlier than in England, paved the way for the investigative figure seeking out the facts of the case and seeking to prove innocence, and the enquiring agent quickly replaced the criminal as the centre of attention. British and European influence was not entirely lost, however; in the late eighteenth century the United States took the genre of Gothic fiction and reshaped it to fit American spaces and tastes.

This can clearly be seen in the fiction of Brockden Brown, whose seven novels were published between 1798 and 1801. Besides successfully appropriating European Gothic tropes, Brown contributed to the development of American crime fiction with his representations of investigative figures. In this he was heavily influenced by William Godwin's *Caleb Williams; or, Things as They Are* (1794), with its central theme of pursuit. Brown's *Arthur Mervyn* (1799), like Caleb in Godwin's text, discovers a secret murder and suffers persecution as he attempts to unravel the mystery; unlike Caleb, Mervyn is finally successful and is overall a more confident investigator, but the novel is more concerned with the personal development of the protagonist than with crime. In the same year, Brown published *Edgar Huntly; or, Memories of a Sleepwalker*, called by American literary historian Robert Spiller America's 'first detective novel'. Certainly the eponymous hero's pursuit of Clithero Edny, whom Huntly believes to be a murderer, involves elements of detection, but the text's interest in the Gothic themes of psychic disturbance and the seemingly supernatural predominate.

Brown's legacy to crime fiction is the strength of the American Gothic that he largely created and which recurs in later American crime writing; in terms of detective fiction a stronger claimant is James Fenimore Cooper, whose 'Leatherstocking' series (1823–41) represents the world of American pioneers in the mid-eighteenth century. Cooper's hero, Natty Bumppo, is brought up by Native Americans and acquires their skills in hunting and tracking. In *The Last of the Mohicans* (1826) he puts these skills to good use in tracing two young women kidnapped by members of the Huron tribe. In his quest, Bumppo is assisted by his Native Indian friend, Chingachgook, a pairing that prefigures the later familiar detective–assistant pattern of Poe's Dupin and his unnamed narrator-friend and of course Doyle's Holmes and Watson. Cooper's work was very influential, especially in France, where Alexandre Dumas (*père*) paid homage to Cooper's work in the title of his long crime narrative, *Les Mohicans de Paris* (1856–7). Bumppo, independent and intelligent, uses native skills to read the natural world, but this concept, relocated to the city, functions as a model for the urban detective. In America, his inheritor is Raymond Chandler's Philip Marlowe, a private investigator (private eye) who reads the unnatural world of Los Angeles.

America continued its contribution to the development of crime fiction with the work of Edgar Allan Poe. Heavily influenced by Brown's earlier Gothic fiction, much of Poe's writing is concerned with inner psychological states and quasi-supernatural events, but crime is a recurring feature in his short stories. Between 1841 and 1845, Poe wrote three tales, published first in American periodicals, which are generally considered retrospectively to articulate many of the themes and tropes of the later, established genre of detective fiction. 'The Murders in the Rue Morgue' (1841) introduced C. Auguste Dupin and his unnamed narrator-companion; brought together by a mutual love of book and learning, they live in the gloom of a decaying house in Paris and exist in a Gothic, night-time world. Dupin is not a detective, nor was this in its moment detective fiction; the story is an elucidation of a mystery and Dupin uses what he calls 'ratiocination', or a process of reasoning that combines mathematical analysis with imagination to resolve an apparently insoluble problem.

In 'The Murders in the Rue Morgue' the savage violence done to the bodies of the two female victims, the unintelligible noises heard coming from the apartment and the internally locked door and sealed window which suggest no means of escape for the perpetrator are explained by the fact that the 'murderer' is an orang-utan. 'The Mystery of Marie Rogêt' (1842–3) takes an actual and contemporary American mystery and relocates it in Paris. Mary Rogers, known as 'the beautiful cigar girl' of New York, had a history of mysterious disappearances culminating in her body being found floating in the Hudson River in 1841. Poe set out to solve the puzzle of her death using a Dupin story as his vehicle and adopting Dupinesque methods. In 'The Mystery of Marie Rogêt', Dupin relies entirely on newspaper reports and his own extensive library to discover the murderer in what is effectively the first representation of 'armchair detection'.

Dupin, and implicitly Poe, come to a rational solution to the mystery posed by Marie Rogêt, but events in America proved Poe wrong; Mary Rogers's death was shown to be the result of a botched abortion and Poe had to rewrite his ending. The final narrative featuring Dupin is considered to be the best; 'The Purloined Letter' (1845) is a purely intellectual exercise focused on discovering the whereabouts of an incriminating letter and is a reduced and refined example of Dupin's methodology. The letter, belonging to a female of clearly exalted status, is 'purloined from the royal apartments' and used by Minister D___ for political leverage. Dupin retrieves the letter from its concealment in plain view and in the process is revenged upon the Minister who at some time in the past has done Dupin 'an evil turn'. The influence and importance of Poe's Dupin stories is very clear in crime fiction later in the nineteenth century and beyond. In France, the detective novels of Émile Gaboriau, such as *L'Affaire Lerouge* (1866) or *Monsieur Lecoq* (1868), feature investigators who employ similar methods to Dupin and share some of his characteristics. Arthur Conan Doyle openly acknowledges his debt to Poe in his autobiography, *Memories and Adventures* (1924), and *A Study in Scarlet* (1887) has Sherlock Holmes dismiss Dupin as 'a very inferior fellow'. The patterns established by Poe: the Gothic atmosphere; the narrator/companion/assistant; the locked-room mystery; armchair detection; inductive (mistakenly called 'deductive') thinking; the retrospective reconstruction of the crime, all continue to shape crime fiction up to the present day.

The emphasis on and privileging of the individual in American culture perhaps explains the strong presence and valorisation of the independent investigator in American criminography from its beginnings. While in 1860s Britain there was a vogue for police-detective stories and the amateur detective existed in fiction but was not named as such, in America the private professional detective was an early innovation and a strong indicator of the direction American crime fiction would take in the future. Heavily influenced by Poe and in similar mode to the many fictional professional recollections and memoirs published in the period, *Leaves from the Note-Book of a New York Detective* (1865) asserts itself as a collection of real cases investigated by 'Jem Brampton'. Brampton has trained as a doctor, spent time as a police detective and now works as an independent agent. Prefiguring the later hard-boiled detectives, Brampton is a man of action with a strong moral sense, operating in an urban environment and choosing his own cases. In similar vein but based in fact are the eighteen detective stories, possibly ghost-written, but published from 1874 onwards under the name of Allan Pinkerton, who was the co-founder of the National Detective Agency.

Women writers in nineteenth-century America played a strong role in the development of the genre. Louisa May Alcott wrote sensation fiction anonymously or under the pseudonym A. M. Barnard, publishing stories such as 'Pauline's Passion and Punishment' (1863)', 'V. V.: or, Plots and Counterplots' (1865) and 'Behind a Mask' (1866), all of which featured crime and quasi-detective figures, in the periodicals. Harriet

Prescott Spofford's sensational stories appeared in the *Atlantic Monthly* and *Harper's Bazaar* among others from 1858 onwards. Her tales frequently incorporated crime and mystery in their melodrama, and she also created a detective, Mr Furbush, who appeared in 'Mr Furbush' (1865) and again in 'In the Maguerriwock' (1868). The detective in full-length fiction appears in 1867 with Seeley Regester's *The Dead Letter* (1866 in serial form). The gender ambiguity of the author's name conceals that the writer was a woman; Metta Victoria Fuller Victor wrote several novels but *The Dead Letter* is the only one to feature a professional detective, Mr Burton. There are Gothic elements: the action is played out against a background of nature and the land; the detective claims his investigative prowess to be the result of his quasi-mystical power to 'feel' the presence of criminality and he uses his daughter's clairvoyant skills to assist him in his work. But under this semi-supernatural guise Burton's detective skills and processes are not dissimilar to those of Dupin. Despite the gender of its author, women play a small and conventional part in *The Dead Letter*, the focus being rather on the professional detective and his amateur assistant. The detective figures are also central to Anna Katharine Green's *The Leavenworth Case* (1878), but women play much more important roles and Green is credited with having drawn together and domesticated the many and varied narrative threads of American crime fiction. Her police detective, Ebenezer Gryce, and his amateur assistant, lawyer Everett Raymond, work together largely within the domestic confines of the murdered man's house while his daughters provide both criminal and romantic interest.

Gryce appeared in later novels by Green, but she also created female detectives: at first, elderly, well-bred spinster Amelia Butterworth who works as Gryce's unofficial assistant (*That Affair Next Door*, 1897, and five other novels), and later Violet Strange, a young society woman who has a secret career as a private detective (*The Golden Slipper and Other Problems for Violet Strange*, 1915). Green's domestication of the detective novel made a major contribution to the development of the interwar 'Golden Age' of crime fiction and the female and later the feminist detective in crime fiction. Other prolific and popular women crime writers in the early part of the twentieth century were Mary Roberts Rinehart, who wrote over fifty mystery and detective novels and short stories between 1907 and her death in 1958, and Carolyn Wells, who wrote over 170 books, including at least seventy-five mystery novels. In America, women writing crime and female detectives were accepted and established earlier than in Britain, suggesting perhaps a more tolerant attitude to female independence and assertiveness. In the first half of the twentieth century, much American crime fiction was in the same mould as that in

Britain, with numerous variations on the mannered clue-puzzle mystery, or Holmesian detective fiction, with S. S. Van Dine (pseudonym of Willard Huntingdon Wright) and Ellery Queen (pseudonym of Frederic Dannay and Manfred B. Lee) perhaps the best-known and most prolific.

The other major development in American criminography was, by contrast, deeply masculine. In a return to the pioneering, macho frontiersman model of James Fenimore Cooper, Carroll John Daly created an adventurer detective, Race Williams (appeared in over fifty short stories and novels between 1923 and 1952). Daly's private eye, whose readiness to adopt violent methods located him somewhere between the police and the criminal, brought realism and violence into what had become a rather mannered genre, but his work was overtaken and overshadowed by that of Dashiell Hammett and later Raymond Chandler, who wrote what has become known as 'hard-boiled' crime fiction. Described by Larry Landrum as a 'studiously experimental' writer, Hammett used crime narratives to explore power relations in the violent, gangster-ridden world of Prohibition America in the 1920s and 30s. Chandler refined the model, focusing and articulating his sharp social critique of the 1930s and 40s Los Angeles society through his tough-guy detective hero, Philip Marlowe. Chandler stated that his intention was to reclaim crime fiction from what he called 'the cheese-cake manor' school of writing epitomised by Agatha Christie and return it to its proper place on the city streets, in a sense taking it back to its origins in the real crime seen in the criminal literature of the eighteenth and nineteenth centuries.

American crime writing was also innovative and radical in its return, from the 1930s onwards, to a focus on the criminal rather than the detective. These texts, which explore the emotions and psychology of the criminal before, during and after the crime and which have come to be known as 'crime novels' rather than crime fiction, are discussed by Tony Hilfer in *The Crime Novel: A Deviant Genre* (1990). W. R. Burnett's *Little Caesar* (1929) is an early example of the sub-genre, but a better-known author is James M. Cain, particularly his novels *The Postman Always Rings Twice* (1934) and *Double Indemnity* (1943 [1936]; as a film, 1944). Cain's protagonists fall into rather than elect to become criminal; there is a strange fatefulness about their crimes. Violent, yes, but Cain's violence is rational within its context; Jim Thompson's later crime novels, such as *Nothing More Than Murder* (1949) and *The Killer Inside Me* (1952) verge on the sadistic with their intense and repetitive scenes of brutality. The interest in the criminal continues throughout the twentieth century, modulating into the psycho-thriller. One of the earliest exponents of this sub-genre was Margaret Millar. Not strictly speaking an American as she was born in Canada, Millar wrote a variety of crime fiction in 1941–86, but in the 1940s and 50s produced several novels (*Wall of Eyes*, 1943; *The Iron Gates*, 1945; *Beast in View*, 1955; *A Stranger in My Grave*, 1960) that focused not just on the criminal's experience but also on his/her victim. These psychologically intense texts demonstrated a strong awareness of social and gender issues that prefigured the later feminist appropriation of crime fiction for political purposes.

Europe-based American author Patricia Highsmith refined and made more chilling the psycho-thriller sub-genre by making criminality and the obscenity of violence seem almost mundane. Her first novel, *Strangers on a Train* (1950), demonstrated the ease with which individuals can slip into crime and the psychological consequences of their actions, but her series of novels featuring psychopathic serial killer Tom Ripley make murder seem an everyday occurrence, justified by Ripley on grounds as flimsy as self-betterment and the protection of his deceitfully achieved and murderously protected social status (*The Talented Mr Ripley*, 1955; *Ripley Underground*, 1970; *Ripley's Game*, 1974; *The Boy Who Followed Ripley*, 1980; *Ripley Under Water*, 1991). In American crime fiction's fascination with the psyche of the killer there is a return to the early American Gothic of Brockden Brown, while the independent private detective that is another strong element in the nation's criminal literature has its origins in Fenimore Cooper's frontiersman hero and can still be found in the fiction of John D. MacDonald, Robert Crais, James Crumley and Carl Hiassen among others; Poe brings the two strands together in Dupin while women writers make an early and welcome contribution to the developing genre in the second part of the nineteenth century.

Over the twentieth and into the twenty-first centuries America continues to produce innovative and imaginative crime fiction, often grafting existing forms together into hybrids that become new sub-genres. The police procedural has its origins in America, as does the thriller of violence epitomised in Thomad Harris's Hannibal Lecter series; feminist crime fiction really takes off in the States as do the politically aware/generated crime novels focused on issues of gender, sexual orientation and race; the forensic novel, even the legal novel, find their clearest articulation in America. The proliferation of sub-genres and the huge publication figures for American crime novels demonstrate the popularity of the genre but also suggest that the tensions, social and political, consequent on the multicultural social and racial mix that is America are articulated through the medium of crime narrative.

See also *Contexts*: Cities and Urbanisation, Crime and Detection, Gender and Sexuality, Race, Colour, Creed; *Texts*: Early Criminography, Feminist Crime Fiction, Hard-Boiled Crime Fiction, Police Procedural; *Criticism*: Feminism, Postcolonialism, Postmodernism.

Further reading

Bertens, Hans, and Theo D'haen, *Contemporary American Crime Fiction* (Basingstoke: Palgrave Macmillan, 2001).

Cobley, Paul, *The American Thriller: Generic Innovation and Social Change in the 1970s* (Basingstoke: Palgrave Macmillan, 2000).

Ellis, Markman, *The History of Gothic Fiction* (Edinburgh: Edinburgh University Press, 2000).

Halttunen, Karen, *Murder Most Foul: The Killer and the American Gothic Imagination* (Harvard: Harvard University Press, 2000).

Horsley, Lee, *Twentieth-Century Crime Fiction* (Oxford: Oxford University Press, 2005).

McCann, Sean, *Gumshoe America: Hard Boiled Crime Fiction and the Rise and Fall of New Deal Liberalism* (Durham North Carolina: Duke University Press, 2001).

Messent, Peter (ed.), *Criminal Proceedings: the Contemporary American Crime Novel* (London and Chicago: Pluto Press, 1997).

Nickerson, Catherine Ross (ed.), *The Cambridge Companion to American Crime Fiction* (Cambridge: Cambridge University Press, 2010).

Pepper, Andrew, *The Contemporary American Crime Novel: Race, Ethnicity, Gender, Class* (Edinburgh: Edinburgh University Press, 2000).

Smith, Allan Lloyd, *American Gothic Fiction* (London and New York: Continuum, 2005).

Children's crime fiction

In the nineteenth century crime fiction and children's literature benefitted from the rise of the middle classes, the concomitant increase in literacy and proliferation of popular literature which fed the new reading public. Despite the apparently very different intended audiences, the two forms of literature shared a similar initial function. The early criminography from which crime fiction developed was, at least overtly, concerned with educating its readers against crime, while the origins of literature for children lie in texts intended to educate the child reader in proper behaviour. As crime fiction developed, the entertainment factor became uppermost, but the disciplinary effects were retained; the crimes committed in the course of the narrative are invariably punished. In children's literature the increasing focus on entertainment was the judicious application of the sugary stuff of pleasure to sweeten the bitter pill of learning. Juvenile fiction was and is inherently educational, teaching children not only how to read but also instructing them in how to become 'proper' adults. Yet fiction for children invariably features transgressions which form part of the educational function of the narrative.

From fairy tales to the social realism of twenty-first century writers such as Jacqueline Wilson, 'crimes' of a kind are inherent in children's fiction. In the fairy-tale world, Little Red Riding Hood disobeys her mother; Jack buys beans with his parent's money and later steals from the giant; Goldilocks breaks into the house of the three bears, robs them of their porridge and occupies their beds; the wolf murders and eats the little pigs; imaginary crime and violence are endemic in fairy tales. In Wilson's books rules are broken; secrets are kept; children behave badly to each other; children are abused by adults. In classic realist children's fiction such as Enid Blyton's *Malory Towers* school stories or Edith Nesbit's *The Railway Children* the child may misbehave or indulge in petty crimes such as 'borrowing' another child's property, but real crime and violence remain in the adult realm, although abusive adults and their effects on children are frequently the sub-text in modern juvenile fiction like that of Wilson. But minor child crimes are always rectified or justified and wicked adults are punished; sombre subjects are balanced by 'they all lived happily ever after', an ending upon which children's literature insists. Such closure mimics the plot structure of crime fiction in which the criminal is apprehended and the mystery posed by the crime is solved, restoring order to the disordered society of the text and implicitly the real world.

Away from the fantasy world of fairies, crime, in the ameliorated form of mystery, is a common feature in realist children's literature. The processes of investigating a mystery are key to the self- and world-discovery that is part of the educational function of juvenile fiction. The embargo on representing inherently criminal children in literature with child protagonists/readers has a long history: in Charles Dickens's *Oliver Twist* (1837–8), Oliver and Jack Dawkins, the artful Dodger, are clearly shown to be victims of society and their crimes to be the at the instigation of the criminal adult, Fagin. However, as the criminographic sub-genre of detective fiction evolved and gained popularity, it was possible to represent children as investigative figures; their curiosity and virtual invisibility in the contemporary adult world fitted them for this fictional role while the growing market for fiction specifically aimed at a child audience constantly demanded new material. 1866 saw the publication of the collected edition of *The Boy Detective; or, the Crimes of London. A Romance of Modern Times* (originally serialised in 71 parts, 1865–66), suggesting that child detectives were from a very early stage appearing in popular periodical fiction aimed at children.

But in mainstream crime fiction, possibly the first example is lawyer Mr Bruff's street-wise errand-boy, Gooseberry, in Wilkie Collins's *The Moonstone* (1868), whose unobtrusive presence, intelligence and sharp eyes enable him to shadow the suspected criminal. Arthur Conan Doyle enlarges on this use of London street-urchins as quasi-detectives in the Sherlock Holmes stories, where Holmes has occasional recourse to what he calls his 'Baker Street Irregulars'. This group first appears in *A Study in Scarlet* (1887) and is led by a boy called 'Wiggins'. That detective fiction and indeed the profession of detection were considered acceptable, even desirable, is evident in the fact that Doyle's contemporary and the founder of the Boy Scouts, Robert Baden-Powell, included detective skills in the Scout handbook, *Scouting for Boys* (1908). In America Samuel Clemens, better known as Mark Twain, followed up his popular *The Adventures of Tom Sawyer* (1876) with *Tom Sawyer: Detective* (1896), taking advantage of the fashion for detective fiction for children.

By the late nineteenth and early twentieth centuries, detection as a theme and detective heroes were established staple ingredients in boys' magazines and even in periodicals for girls, although here it was usually articulated as mystery-solving and set against a school background. But by the 1920s the girl detective was, like her boy counterpart, an established figure in the periodical press, epitomised in full-time sleuth Sylvia Silence, or 'the Girl Sherlock Holmes', who first appeared in the British *Schoolgirls' Weekly* in October 1922. But it was in America that the juvenile detective story in serial form firmly entered mainstream children's literature, with the Hardy Boys series for boys (1927–present), featuring teen investigators Frank and Joe, and the Nancy Drew series for girls (1929–present), with female sleuth Nancy Drew. Ostensibly written by Franklin W. Dixon and Carolyn Keene, respectively, the series were actually the product of the Stratemeyer Syndicate and were written by a number of different authors; both series continue to appear in appropriately revised formats in the twenty-first century. The Hardy Boys' and Nancy's investigations cover real crimes such as kidnapping and theft, tracing lost wills and apparently supernatural happenings, but violence is implicit and murder off limits. The narratives are intended to entertain, with an emphasis on plot, and process of investigation is central, but there are strong ideological and educational messages reinforcing as the importance of family, respect for adults, patriotism and the benefits of education. Nancy Drew can also be argued to be one of the first feminist role models, although from a post-feminist perspective she is contained within and constrained by patriarchy. Nonetheless, she demonstrates a degree of independence and freedom as well as female superiority in her triumph over frequently masculine villains.

The moral and ideological function of juvenile crime fiction is also evident in Erich Kästner's classic *Emil and the Detectives* (1929), which has Emil tracking down the adult thief who has stolen the money, entrusted to Emil by his mother, which he is taking to his grandmother in Berlin. Rather in the model of Sherlock Holmes's Baker Street Irregulars, Emil is befriended by a local boy who calls on his friends to assist Emil in his investigation, and the children successfully track down the villain, Herr Grundeis, only having recourse to adult assistance in his actual apprehension. Emil's refusal to go to the police for help in the first instance is because he feels himself to be criminal as, while drawing a moustache on a statue, he had been observed in the act of vandalism by a policeman. The text teaches the value of co-operation, persistence and honesty—Emil receives a cash award for contributing to the arrest of Herr Grundeis, who is proved to be a bank robber—and ultimately upholds adult authority and integrity; grown-up assistance in the form of the police and a bank clerk is required to restore order.

But in the twentieth century much of the literature written for children incorporated aspects of crime and detection without attracting the label of crime fiction. For example, in Arthur Ransome's juvenile fiction series, beginning with *Swallows and Amazons* (1930) the child protagonists occasionally encounter crime and criminality in the course of their adventures. But it is perhaps Enid Blyton's novels for children that most frequently exploit the narrative possibilities offered by crime. Of the twenty-one *Famous Five* adventures (1942–63), only one lacks a criminal of some kind; all the criminals are adults and in all the stories it is the children who foil the criminals and prevent the crime. The first book in the series, *Five on a Treasure Island* (1942) sets the pattern, with the children discovering a map which leads them to a secret treasure which they recover in the face of adult disbelief and opposition, finally foiling the crooks who try to make off with the gold. As in *Emil and the Detectives*, adult assistance is required in the apprehension of the thieves, but the roles of non-criminal adults in the Famous Five stories are also often questionable. Parents in particular are frequently shown to be lacking in some aspects and much of the mystery in Blyton's fiction is concerned with the children solving the puzzle of and rectifying adult behaviour. Blyton's *Secret Seven* series (1949–63) follows a similar pattern, while the Mystery Story series (1943–61) openly declares its detective function in the name given to the 'gang' of children who elucidate the mysteries the series title suggests: 'the Five Find-Outers'.

Common to all these early forays into crime/detective fiction for a juvenile market is that they were written for a pre-teenage audience; that is, they appeared in an era before the concept of teenage came into being. Thus, while they feature child detectives whose ages range up to sixteen and even eighteen in the early Hardy Boys and Nancy Drew series, their intended audience was not the modern teenager but younger children and the series underwent constant revision over the years in order to retain its audience as demographics changed. Anne, Dick, George and Julian in the Famous Five are aged between ten and twelve and attracted a similarly aged audience; the ages of the Secret Seven are never declared, but they seem to be in the same range, as are the Five Find-Outers. As teenagers became an established sector of society so writers and publishers responded; post-war social changes and the development of new media such as television and film resulted in a more-knowing and sophisticated audience.

To satisfy this new generation, more complex and darker fiction which endeavoured to represent the adolescent experience began to appear from the 1960s onwards. Such literature necessarily incorporated delinquency and violence and sometimes crime in response to the sometimes troubled realities of young adulthood, as texts such as S. E. Hinton's *The Outsiders* (1967) or Robert Cormier's *The Chocolate War* (1974) demonstrate. Juvenile detective fiction for younger readers maintained its popularity and its share of the children's literature market until the late twentieth century, but was gradually supplanted, in the 1980s and 90s, by new, hybrid forms of mystery series fiction which blended horror, science fiction and the supernatural, as in R. L. Stine's *Goosebumps* (original series 1992–7), specifically aimed at pre-teen readers, and the multi-authored *Point Horror* series (1988–present), which was marketed for an adolescent audience.

Detective fiction for children continues to appear but in new formats which often mimic those of adult crime fiction. For example, Caroline Lawrence's popular 'Roman Mysteries' series (2001–present), with girl-detective Flavia Gemina, is set in Ancient Rome, the location of the historical crime fiction of Lindsey Davis and Steven Saylor. Lawrence's stories rely on the detective fiction formula but over the series the focus has shifted from the investigation of the crime to an exploration of character. Justin Richards's 'Invisible Detective' series (2003–7) maintains the detective fiction pattern but with a time-travel twist. Increasingly, detective literature for children has become more sophisticated as the written text must compete with visual media for a share of the juvenile audience: Eoin Colfer's *Half Moon Investigations* (2006) has twelve-year-old Fletcher Moon as a detective who aspires to professionalism. Significantly, the book also introduces a child criminal, part of a delinquent family, who helps Fletcher in his investigations and in the process is recuperated back into society. It is now possible to represent the child criminal, although as in *Oliver Twist,* it is made clear that the adult world is to blame for the child's behaviour; Stephen Cole claims *Oliver Twist*'s Fagin as the inspiration for Nathaniel Coldhardt, the criminal mastermind and leader of the gang of juvenile robbers in *Thieves Like Us* (2006).

Colfer's *Artemis Fowl* series (2001–present) maintains the convention of adult blame, but the teenaged protagonist is himself a master criminal; the text avoids the difficulties associated with representing a child criminal in children's fiction by weaving fantasy and humour into the narrative and over the series Fowl seems to be reforming. More conventionally

Cornelia Funke's *The Thief Lord* (2000) features orphans in Venice sur-viving on what appear to be the fruits of crime provided by their teenage leader, the Thief Lord of the title. But he is proved to be a rich boy steal-ing from his detested wealthy father; a modern, juvenile version of Robin Hood, he steals from the rich to give to the poor. In a clever textual twist, the narrative represents the adult detective employed to seek out the orphans as childlike, while the children show decidedly adult intelligence and capability and the denouement of the plot is the literal age change, facilitated by magic, of the Thief Lord to adulthood and a detective career, while the criminal receiver of stolen goods is returned to childhood—an ending that makes an interesting comment on modern perceptions of childhood and of criminality.

Crime fiction for children, then, while not necessarily named as such, has been part of the development of the genre and of literature for chil-dren over the last two centuries. As with crime fiction written for adults, the juvenile version is quick to respond to social and cultural changes, and perhaps the modern depiction of the child criminal is a comment on the rising juvenile crime rate in reality. Young adult fiction represents crime and criminality more seriously and falls into the realm of crossover fiction, that is, fiction which is written for and attracts adults as well as adolescents. Two of the late twentieth/early twenty-first centuries' most popular dual-audience children's fiction series incorporate crime in their narratives; Philip Pullman's *His Dark Materials* sequence (1995–9) works at a more sophisticated and metaphorical level discussing issues of right and wrong, sin and crime, but J. K. Rowling's Harry Potter books (1997–2007) offer similar debates in a more accessible format. Neither series is, strictly speaking, crime fiction, but both are concerned with myster-ies and, as in Blyton's novels for children, the mysteries circulate around adult behaviour. Ultimately, it could be argued, all children's literature is about education, and that education is focused on learning how to be an adult; in juvenile detective fiction or narratives featuring crime, the child learns how to be a good adult through the example of the bad.

See also   *Contexts*: Detectives and Detection, Crime and Criminality; *Texts*: Historical Crime Fiction; *Criticism*: Feminism, Cultural Materialism.

Further reading

Craig, Patricia and Mary Cadogan, *The Lady Investigates: Women Detectives and Spies in Fiction* (Oxford: Oxford University Press, 1986).

Cornelius, Michael G. (ed.), *The Boy Detectives: Essays on the Hardy Boys and Others* (Jefferson, N. Carolina: McFarland, 2010).

Gavin, Adrienne and Christopher Routledge (eds), *Mystery in Children's Literature: from the Rational to the Supernatural* (Basingstoke: Palgrave Macmillan, 2001).

Mason, Bobbie Ann, 'Nancy Drew: The Once and Future Prom Queen' in *Feminism in Women's Detective Fiction*, ed. Glenwood Irons (Toronto: University of Toronto Press, 1995), pp. 74–93.

Nash, Ilana, 'Teenage Detectives and Teenage Delinquents' in *The Cambridge Companion to American Crime Fiction*, ed. Catherine Ross Nickerson (Cambridge: Cambridge University Press, 2010), pp. 72–85.

Routledge, Christopher, 'Crime and Detective Literature for Young Readers' in *Companion to Crime Fiction*, ed. Lee Horsley and Charles Rzepka (Oxford: Wiley-Blackwell, 2010), pp. 321–331.

Early criminography

Crime fiction's origins are closely interlinked with the development of print culture in Britain and Europe from the fifteenth century onwards. Crime is a consequence of organised society and crime narratives had of course existed and been circulated orally and in handwritten manuscript form prior to the invention of printing technology, but it is the printed accounts that offer a historical point of origin for crime fiction. Crime found its way into entertainment in dramatic productions; as sin in medieval miracle plays and as murder in many of Shakespeare's plays, but the main vehicle for crime narratives in England were the pamphlets and printed ballads which constituted a kind of early journalism. Printing technology enabled the rapid and relatively instantaneous publication of matters of public interest, and crime was certainly of interest to the public. The ballad sheets were laid out in such a way as to catch the eye and engage the reader, often with arresting headlines and a woodcut illustration, while the rhyming verses which relayed the 'news', or 'newes' (new information about very recent events), made it easier for the illiterate individual to memorise the words as they were read aloud. Accounts of crime were very popular, outselling other 'news' items; this was hardly surprising with sensational titles such as *Sundry strange and inhumaine Murthers, lately committed* (1591), which carried the woodcut illustration of a man murdering three children. Inherent in crime narrative, even in this very early format, was an element of entertainment.

The overt aim of early criminography was to warn against crime, to work as a deterrent by detailing the fate of criminals and making it seem inevitable that crime would be punished. But the motive of the writers and printers was to make a profit, and printed crime stories were also commodities; to increase sales, the accounts needed to attract readers, hence the gory illustrations and sensational titles. Murder was not the only topic; so-called 'coney-catching' pamphlets detailed how

pockets were picked, gambling games 'fixed' and described the imple-
ments used by criminals in their burglarious crimes. Another favourite
topic was the execution of criminals; while these took place in public
view in order to demonstrate the power of the State and the certainty of
punishment, not everyone could be part of the audience and a printed
version ensured wide dissemination of the event. From the fifteenth to
the eighteenth century crime narratives were randomly printed in vary-
ing formats: the most common form of publication was the broadside,
a single sheet printed on one side, made of rough paper, inexpensive to
produce and so cheap to buy. The verses or ballads that featured strongly
in the early criminography were, from the seventeenth century onwards,
largely replaced by prose and the prose broadside became the most
widely available and affordable medium for the transmission of 'news'.

Verses did not entirely disappear; writers and printers still catered
for their illiterate audience as this extract from a nineteenth-century
broadside demonstrates:

The Mother's wounds three inches deep upon her head and face,
And pools of blood as thick as mud, from all of them could trace,
None could identify the boy, his head was like a jelly;
This tragedy is worse by far than Greenacre or Kelly.

The lines are taken from a broadside account of the true case of John
Gleeson Wilson, executed in 1849 for the murder of two women and children and are cited in Charles Hindley's *Curiosities of Street Literature*, 1969
(1871). Greenacre and Kelly were two other murderers whose factual
cases were also featured in the contemporary broadsides and newspapers. Broadside accounts of crime contained none of the puzzle element
or interest in motives seen in the established genre of crime fiction; they
were simply linear narratives that offered a brief history of the criminal,
but they were also self-contained stories intended to entertain. A second
source of crime narratives, and indeed often plagiarised by the broadside
printers, were the *Accounts* of the lives, crimes and executions of the
criminals imprisoned in Newgate Gaol and published in pamphlet form
by the Ordinaries, or Chaplains, of the prison.

These *Accounts* were able to offer more detailed descriptions than
the broadsides. They purported to be the actual words of the prisoner,
but were articulated through the Chaplain who wrote the Account; as
the Chaplains were not only religious clerics but also employees of the
State and upholders of the law, the *Accounts*, unlike the broadsides, were
triply sanctioned by God, by the King or Queen in power and by the
law. A typical example is the *Account* which includes the story of Mary

Young, published under the title 'The Ordinary of Newgate, His Account of the Behaviour, Confession and Dying Words of the Malefactors, Who were Executed at Tyburn, On Wednesday the 18th of March, 1740'. Mary Young, alias Jenny Diver, is just one of the criminals whose lives and deaths are recorded in this *Account*, and her tale is not only typical in structure but also more entertaining than many of the rather prosaic criminal lives published by the Ordinaries. The narrative begins and ends in the Ordinary's voice, giving it a religious frame which recounts her early life and implicitly the causes of her criminality, and finally describes her confession and execution. The central, and longest section, is Mary's own, initially penitent, narrative. While she states that she is telling her story to warn her readers of the evils of crime and the punishment that will surely follow, the narrative quickly turns into a rattling good story that makes her life as the head of a successful criminal gang sound exciting and profitable; essentially, it reads more like fiction than fact.

Crime narratives were popular across the social spectrum. While the broadsides were aimed at a lower-class audience, Robert Altick suggests, in *Victorian Studies in Scarlet* (1972), that servants would be dispatched to buy broadsides for the covert entertainment of the master of the house and his family. The *Accounts* were more expensive, at six old pence, than the broadsides (a half-penny or so), more respectable and less sensational, and required a higher level of literacy from the reader and so were popular with the wealthier classes. In the eighteenth century another format of criminal reading specifically aimed at this propertied audience came into being with collected criminal lives published as anthologies, in book form. These collected editions became known as the *Newgate Calendars*, although one 1779 edition bore the grand title of *The Malefactors' Register or the Newgate and Tyburn Calendar*. As the readers of the expensive *Newgate* anthologies (they often comprised five or six volumes) were more likely to be victim than the perpetrator of crime, the function of the narratives was to suggest the containment of crime; these were, after all, the stories of convicted criminals. But there was still an element of sensationalism and entertainment. Not only that, but also with the repetition and rewriting of long-past accounts, the 'facts of the case' became dubious, locating the narratives more as fiction than fact and emphasising their amusement value. Furthermore, in the later editions of the *Calendars*, especially into the nineteenth century, the criminals did not always confess to the crimes of which they were accused before they were executed, bringing the validity of the guilty verdict, the sentence and implicitly the legal system into question.

Increasing uncertainty about the safety of criminal convictions was one of the factors that contributed to the development of investigative figures—detectives—and of forensic science in the nineteenth century. Certainly, in some of the accounts from *The New Newgate Calendar* (1826), revised and edited by lawyers Andrew Knapp and William Baldwin, individuals in some way connected to the crime committed or the accused undertook active investigations that helped to prove guilt or innocence. Anxiety about criminal convictions, especially where capital punishment was involved, was discussed in newspapers and periodicals but is particularly evident in fiction concerned with crime in the nineteenth century. Here, the emphasis tends to be on proving the wrongly accused to be innocent, although the courts in reality were required to assume innocence and to prove guilt. However, what the broadsides, the Ordinaries' *Accounts* and the *Newgate Calendars* had in common was their focus on the criminal and this is also true of what might reasonably be called the first 'crime novels', or, as they became known as in their own time, Newgate novels.

In some ways these were rather like lengthy versions of the Ordinaries' *Accounts*, blending fact and fiction together; some of the writers of the Newgate novels based their protagonists or other characters on real-life criminals. These exclusively male-authored crime narratives enjoyed a relatively brief period of popularity in the 1830s and 1840s; texts with criminal or criminalised protagonists had previously been published in the eighteenth century, for example Henry Fielding's satirical novel *The Life of Jonathan Wild the Great* (1754 [1743]) which was based on the real Jonathan Wild, Thief-Taker General. Daniel Defoe also wrote on Wild, although his *True and Genuine Account of the Life and Actions of the Late Jonathan Wild* (1725) was largely factual; Defoe drew on his knowledge of London's criminal fraternity in *Moll Flanders* (1722) with its female quasi-criminal heroine. William Godwin's *Caleb Williams; or, Things as They Are* (1794) has a criminalised hero in Caleb Williams, but Caleb is purely fictional; Godwin did, however, read up on criminal lives from the *Newgate Calendars* and other sources for his novel.

The nineteenth-century Newgate novels took their name and sometimes their protagonists and plots, from the *Newgate Calendars*, but presented their criminal heroes sympathetically as victims of society or circumstance, or as glamorous adventurers in the Robin Hood mode. The novels were perceived to make a life of crime seem attractive and exciting to the reader; although there were relatively few of these texts published, their authors were well-known, and their works attracted a large audience. Edward Bulwer Lytton began the trend with *Paul Clifford* (1830) and consolidated his reputation as a Newgate novelist with *Eugene Aram* (1832); where Paul Clifford was a fictional hero, Aram was based on a real eighteenth-century murderer. Bulwer's 1828 novel,

Pelham, introduced many of the tropes[1] of Newgate fiction, but its eponymous protagonist was not himself a criminal. Other writers whose books
attracted the label or who deliberately chose to write in this genre were
Charles Dickens (*Oliver Twist*, 1837–9) and William Harrison Ainsworth
(*Rookwood*, 1834, featuring the notorious highwayman Dick Turpin, and
Jack Sheppard, 1839–40, whose hero is based on the real Sheppard,
convicted thief, repeated prison-escapee and victim of Jonathan Wild).

The Newgate novels were considered very controversial in their heroisation of and sympathy for the criminal, their depiction of the criminal
underworld and mingling of lower- and upper-class characters. William
Makepeace Thackeray was one of the most vocal critics of the genre. Best
known for *Vanity Fair* (1847–8), Thackeray wrote an anti-Newgate novel,
Catherine: A Story (1839–40). He modelled his protagonist on Catherine
Hayes, executed by being burnt at the stake in 1726 for murdering
her husband, in the hope that such an unsympathetic character would
expose the problems of the Newgate novels. However, *Catherine* actually reads more as a Newgate fiction than a critique of the form and the
reader is engaged rather than repelled by its heroine.

While the broadsides and *Newgate Calendars* continued to appear well
into the nineteenth century and to maintain their focus on the criminal, in novels and short fiction in the periodicals from the late 1830s
onwards interest shifted to the process of investigation and exculpa-
tion of the wrongly accused. The investigative figure—not immediately
the detective—became the hero, exemplified in American Edgar Allan
Poe's short stories, set in Paris, featuring C. Auguste Dupin. In 'The Murders in the Rue Morgue' (1841), 'The Mystery of Marie Rogêt' (1842–3)
and 'The Purloined Letter' (1845), Dupin undertakes investigations into
murder and blackmail, providing solutions to mysteries that the police
cannot solve and, in the case of 'Murders in the Rue Morgue', ensuring
the release of a wrongly accused man when the 'murderer' is revealed to
be an orang-utan.

In England, short fiction featuring investigations into crime appeared
in the periodicals; anonymously authored but frequently attributed to
Samuel Warren, 'Experiences of a Barrister' (*Chambers's Edinburgh Journal*, 1849–50) was a series of 'cases' in which the barrister, or his
assistant, the aptly named Mr Ferret, undertake the task of proving
the innocence of their clients. Narratives such as these paved the way
for the detective proper, as did the officers of the Metropolitan Police
Detective Department, inaugurated in 1842, and their representation in
Charles Dickens's factual 'Detective Police Anecdotes' (*Household Words*,
1850–53) and William Russell's fictional 'Recollections of a Police-Officer'
(*Chambers's Edinburgh Journal*, 1849–53; later reissued in a collected

edition as *Recollections of a Detective Police-Officer*, 1856). By the mid-nineteenth century, the criminal is no longer the hero but instead the foil for what will become the brilliance of the detective in Arthur Conan Doyle's Sherlock Holmes stories.

See also   *Contexts*: Cities and Urbanisation, Crime and Criminality, Detectives and Detection, Police and Policing; *Texts*: American Crime Fiction, Police Procedural; *Criticism*: Cultural Materialism, Postmodernism.

Further reading

Ascari, Maurizio, *A Counter-History of Crime Fiction: Supernatural, Gothic, Sensational* (Basingstoke: Palgrave Macmillan, 2007).

Bell, Ian A., *Literature and Crime in Augustan England* (London: Routledge, 1991).

Kayman, Martin, *From Bow Street to Baker Street: Mystery, Detection and Narrative* (Basingstoke: Macmillan, 1992).

Knight, Stephen, *Form and Ideology in Crime Fiction* (Bloomington: Indiana University Press, 1980).

Mandel, Ernest, *Delightful Murder: A Social History of the Crime Story* (London: Pluto Press, 1984).

Rzepka, Charles, *Detective Fiction* (Cambridge: Polity, 2005).

Worthington, Heather, *The Rise of the Detective in Early Nineteenth-Century Popular Fiction* (Basingstoke: Palgrave, 2005).

Feminist crime fiction

The appropriation of crime fiction for openly declared, politicised, feminist purposes occurs relatively late in the history of the genre, coinciding with, or following on the heels of, the feminist movement of the 1960s and 70s. The canonical account of the development of crime fiction and especially detective fiction was—and still is, for some critics—strongly masculine, following a fairly direct path from Godwin to Poe to Doyle and on to Chandler. Even with the arrival of the women writers of the Golden Age of crime fiction, Agatha Christie, Dorothy L. Sayers, Margery Allingham *et al.*, the masculine gendering of the genre seems to linger on in the male detective and his individualism, the conservative, conventional plot structure, the emphasis on logic and rationality. While Christie's Poirot relies on gossip and domestic detail in his detection, he also uses his 'little grey cells' and his retrospective reconstruction of the case is faultlessly logical and founded in fact. Sayers's Lord Peter Wimsey's feminine tendency to hysteria is balanced by the fact that it is the consequence of shell-shock subsequent on his experiences in the Great War and by his deceptive masculine strength; Allingham's Albert

Campion has a foolish appearance and foppish manners but they conceal an analytical mind and physical power. So strongly gendered is the genre that the fictional feminist private detectives of the 1970s and 80s, such as Sara Paretsky's independent, assertive V. I. Warshawski, were described by Susan Geeson as 'Philip Marlowe in drag'.

Yet crime fiction's marginalised literary status, which locates it as 'other' to canonical literature, and its subject matter—criminals and criminality—which are 'other' to normal society, in some ways align it with the feminine. Women too have long been marginalised and considered to be 'other' in patriarchal society in reality and in literature, whether as female authors or in their written representations. But while women may be marginal in crime fiction, they are nonetheless essential: there are some limited early attempts at depicting female investigators, but women in criminography prior to the twentieth century appear in the roles of victim, criminal or catalyst for the crime. In each of these roles—and indeed as investigators—they are shown to be deviant from social expectations and norms. Even as victims, it seems that often their own behaviour contributes in some way to their downfall and the real crime of the women in the genre is frequently that they refuse to conform to and comply with masculine notions of proper femininity: narratives of crime all too clearly demonstrate the place of women in patriarchy. Written into the representation of women in crime fiction there is a narrative of the female struggle for autonomy, for recognition of equality as well as acknowledgement of difference, and in the late nineteenth and early twentieth centuries women writers began openly to foreground this narrative. However, it was not until the 1970s and 80s that female authors finally and fully appropriated the hyper-masculine private-eye form in a demonstration of feminist politics in fiction.

There is, then, a counter-history of crime fiction, a female narrative that interrogates and subverts masculine dominance over and the masculinity of the genre and which culminates in the late twentieth century in the refutation of the title of P. D. James's 1972 foray into the depiction of a female detective: *An Unsuitable Job for a Woman*. By 1995, Val McDermid, crime writer and feminist, can claim that, as her book on real women private investigators shows, detection is *A Suitable Job for a Woman*. But the acquisition of detective agency and implicitly equality in crime fiction as in reality was the result of a long process; early criminography lacks investigatory figures of either gender and it is only in the nineteenth century that the male investigator appears and that some tentative steps towards a female detective are made. But women, crime and literature seem inseparable from an early stage; crime narratives from the sixteenth century onwards sold better when they featured femininity in some form. For example, in the broadside *Horrid Murder, Committed by a Young Man on a Young Woman* the narrative implies that the female victim, Fanny Price, deserved her fate. Price had sought to raise her social status by marrying into a higher class. Unfortunately, in pursuit of this goal, she becomes pregnant and her lover, George Caddell, not only declines to make an honest woman of her but also murders her so that he can marry the pure, unsullied and socially superior Miss Dean. Price's modest social aspirations and her decision to use the only bargaining chip she possessed, her chastity, are punished by death.

Based on a real murder and first appearing in an early *Newgate Calendar*, the Caddell case is significant because it reappears in several versions and sympathy shifts from the murderer in the first accounts to the victim in the later, suggesting that Fanny Price is seduced rather than seducer and implying a shift in attitudes towards women. But in relocating Price as victim she is firmly brought back into the masculine control from which the earlier version represented her trying to escape by taking control of her own future. Cadell's story also features woman as catalyst for crime in the form of Miss Dean, the unwitting cause of Caddell's act of violence to Price, and the catalyst role recurs in fiction as women are frequently represented as the (usually innocent) causes of crime. In Henry Thomson's 'Le Revenant' (1827), the anonymous protagonist's forgery is consequent on his need for the money that will enable him to marry; indirectly the object of his affections is the cause of his crime.

Masculine anxiety about the perceived threat of deviant femininity is evident in the eighteenth-century punishment meted out to women in England who, for whatever reason, murdered their husbands: they were not hanged, but burned at the stake. Women such as Phoebe Harris, who was convicted of 'coining' (forging coins/defacing coins to alter their value) in 1786, suffered the same fate as their crime was considered to be an attack on the King, that is, an act of treason: husband murder was equated with treason. But the eighteenth-century criminal underworld afforded women opportunities for independence denied to most of their honest sisters. Mary Young, hanged for theft in 1740, was the leader of a very successful gang of thieves which she ran as a business, controlling not only her own life but also that of the men in the gang. However, in the Ordinary's *Account* in which her story appears, the frame narrative spoken by the male Ordinary (prison Chaplain) condemns her for unwomanly behaviour as much as for her crimes. Daniel Defoe's *Moll Flanders* (1722) offers a fictional version of female criminality as the narrative's deviant heroine resorts to crime in order to survive and prosper in a man's world.

In the nineteenth century social constraints on women increased in parallel with the rise of the middle classes and in fiction women continued to be punished for any deviation from the passive, obedient, feminine norm. Yet that very passivity and compliance can result in crime. In an anonymously authored short story, 'Pages from the Diary of a Philadelphia Lawyer: The Murderess' in *Burton's Gentleman's Magazine* (1838), the murderess is persuaded into a life of crime by her husband; despite the lawyer-narrator's attempts to depict her as doubly deviant—she kills her husband and her child—an alternative reading, from a modern, feminist perspective, locates her as the victim of patriarchal society. Women continued to appear as victims, criminals and catalysts throughout the nineteenth century, but a new, if limited, development was the prototype female investigator. Lower-class women were less constrained by conventions and had greater freedom of movement than the middle classes, and perhaps the first fictional female proto-detective is a servant. Catherine Crowe's *The Adventures of Susan Hopley, or, Circumstantial Evidence* (1841) has maidservant Susan Hopley as its key investigative figure, a conscious move by Crowe, who frequently gave her fictional female characters the agency women lacked in reality.

Susan Hopley is an early feminine-authored foray into the depiction of a female investigator, a textual territory initially more usually owned by men. In 1856, Wilkie Collins's 'The Diary of Anne Rodway' offered what would become a familiar trope in crime fiction: the attenuated female investigator. Anne Rodway is poised between lower and middle class; educated, she has been forced by circumstances to sew for a living while her *fiancé*, Robert, seeks his fortune abroad. When her friend Mary is murdered and the police refuse to investigate on the grounds of lack of evidence, Anne accrues sufficient information to lead to the killer. But her detective work is curtailed when her *fiancé* returns from America and takes the case out of her hands. Nonetheless, Anne is, briefly, an independent and effective investigative agent. Collins recycled the attenuated female investigating figure in *The Woman in White* (1859–60 (1860)) with Marian Halcombe. This time clearly a member of the upper-middle class, Marian's investigative abilities are in part explained or excused by her appearance: '[T]he lady's complexion was almost swarthy, and the dark down on her upper lip was almost a moustache. She had a large, firm masculine mouth and jaw [...] altogether wanting in those feminine attractions of gentleness and pliability.' Marian proves herself an able investigator until the rainstorm which interrupts her eavesdropping activities soaks her to the skin, resulting in an illness which quickly renders her properly pliable with appropriate feminine weakness. Collins would continue to feature attenuated women investigators in his fiction with Magdalen Vanstone in *No Name* (1862–3) and the rather more fully realised Valeria Woodville in *The Law and the Lady* (1875).

Collins's narratives fell into the category of sensation fiction, a genre originating in the 1860s in which crimes, especially murder and bigamy, were essential. In Mary E. Braddon's *Lady Audley's Secret* (1862), the eponymous heroine manages both, committing bigamy and attempting murder. Braddon's text is a sharp critique of the contemporary constraints on women and Lady Audley is ultimately a sympathetic figure, driven to her crimes by society; the narrative can be read as an early, proto-feminist crime novel. But while the representation of women as criminals or victims affords a social commentary on the position of women, it is in the figure of the detective that the struggle for female agency is most clearly articulated. Such figures are few and far between; pseudonymous Andrew Forrester's Mrs G—, in *The Female Detective* (1864), is a middle-aged woman whose gender allows her access to the domestic sphere, but while she possesses agency it is within masculine bounds. In William S. Hayward's *Revelations of a Lady Detective* (1864) the heroine, Mrs Paschal, is cast in a similar mould but is strikingly less feminine in her actions and attitudes. These male-authored texts insert a conventional, implicitly sexually unthreatening female figure into an essentially masculine narrative decorated with domestic discourse.

By the end of the nineteenth and into the early twentieth century there is a proliferation of female detectives, particularly in the (marginal) short fiction of the periodicals, perhaps influenced by the fame and popularity of the Sherlock Holmes stories and in response to the phenomenon of the 'New Woman' and the drive for suffrage. But despite their numbers, these female investigators, whether written by men or women, almost invariably retain an amateur status and remain within the generic and cultural bounds of masculinity and, unless middle-aged/ageing spinsters like Anna Katharine Green's Miss Amelia Butterworth or Mary Roberts Rinehart's Letitia Carberry, have their detecting adventures and then return to proper femininity in marriage. The Golden-Age writers essayed female detectives but again were constrained by the masculine conventions of the genre and the contemporary society. Christie's Miss Marple is an elderly spinster, as is Patricia Wentworth's Miss Silver; Sayers's Harriet Vane contributes to Peter Wimsey's detective work but when in *Gaudy Night* (1935) she undertakes her own investigation its final solution is reached only with Wimsey's help. Gladys Mitchell's psychoanalyst-sleuth, Mrs Beatrice Lestrange Bradley (*Speedy Death*, 1929), seems to break the mould, being ruthless, reptilian and as likely to commit murder as solve one, but is equally constrained within a masculine order, despite her eccentricity and independence. Rather like her male-authored pre-decessors, Mrs G— and Mrs Paschal, Mrs Bradley seems at times more masculine than feminine in her habits.

The 1940s and 50s saw the development of the determinedly mas-culine hard-boiled detective genre and the equally masculine police procedural, and the female detective rather disappeared from view. How-ever, in 1972 P. D. James deserted her male protagonist, police detective Adam Dalgleish and, in *An Unsuitable Job for a Woman*, replaced him with Cordelia Gray, a professional private detective. But despite the backdrop of second-wave feminism in the 1970s, while Cordelia succeeds in her detective work and the novel articulates female communality, the nar-rative is framed and contained by the masculine. Cordelia inherits her detective business from her male ex-police mentor, Bernie Pryde, and the closure of both case and text sees the return of Dalgleish. Ultimately, it seems, detection is still a problematic vocation for a woman. Cordelia Gray returns in *The Skull Beneath the Skin* (1982), but her Detective Agency is reduced to dealing with lost pets and Cordelia's own detect-ing agency is shown to be curtailed as she finally requires masculine aid not to solve the case but simply to survive.

It is in America, where the feminist movement was more active and more vocal, that the fully formed female detective with real agency first appears. While Sara Paretsky is perhaps the best-known writer of fem-inist crime fiction, it was actually Marcia Muller who, with her serial professional investigator Sharon McCone, set in place the format for the female private eye. In her first outing, *Edwin of the Iron Shoes* (1977), Muller's protagonist is not stridently feminist, but the text transposes the reality of the 1970s professional working woman into the world of crime fiction. By contrast to the hard-boiled male private detective, the female investigator is a more fully-fashioned figure, with family and friends; a sexual identity which is expressed and explored; the ability to empathise with the victims of crime; realistic physical vulnerability to violence. The crimes the female detective will investigate are based, as in the hard-boiled genre, in urban corruption but there is personal betrayal woven into the feminist version. Feminist crime fiction impor-tantly locates the job of the detective simply as one of the previously male-dominated professions such as the law, the police, medicine, pol-itics and business, to which women were claiming equal access and in which they could demonstrate equal efficiency and achieve equal success.

Muller's detective articulated the softer side of liberal feminism in 1970s America; Sara Paretsky's serial female private investigator, V. I. Warshawski (first appeared in *Indemnity Only*, 1982), took a harder and more abrasive feminist stance, openly and directly contesting masculine dominance and patriarchal social structures. Yet, while appropriating the hard-boiled detective format, far from being a 'Philip Marlowe in drag', Paretsky represents Warshawski as determinedly feminine when not working and her cases often focus on the contemporary sexual and racial issues. In successfully combining the personal with the political, Paretsky's detective novels offer a fictional representation of a central tenet of second-wave feminism. By the end of the twentieth century women in crime fiction have achieved detective and self-agency; their successful representation as private investigators and their fictional example of lived feminist politics opened the way for other marginalised groups such as gay, lesbian, ethnic and racial minorities similarly to use detective fiction as a vehicle for articulating their difference and asserting their right to equality.

Women writers and female detectives perhaps now dominate the market for crime fiction. But there is a potential downside to sexual and gender equality: now the fictional female detective is an established and establishment figure, will the female criminal demand equality with her male counterpart, particularly the popular and recurring figure of the serial sexual killer? Val McDermid's *The Mermaids Singing* (1995) gestures towards this with its male-to-female transsexual murderer, but at the time of writing a sexually motivated female killer still seems to be beyond literary imagination.

See also *Contexts*: Detectives and Detection, Gender and Sexuality; *Texts*: Golden-Age Crime Fiction, Hard-boiled Crime Fiction; *Criticism*: Feminism, Postmodernism.

Further reading

Irons, Glenwood (ed.), *Feminism in Women's Detective Fiction* (Toronto: University of Toronto Press, 1995).

Johnsen, Rosemary Erickson, *Contemporary Feminist Historical Crime Fiction* (Basingstoke: Palgrave Macmillan, 2006).

Makinen, Merja, *Agatha Christie: Investigating Femininity* (Basingstoke: Palgrave Macmillan, 2006).

Munt, Sally R., *Murder by the Book? Feminism and the Crime Novel* (London: Routledge, 1994).

Plain, Gill, *Twentieth-Century Crime Fiction: Gender, Sexuality and the Body* (Edinburgh: Edinburgh University Press, 2001).

Reddy, Maureen T., *Sisters in Crime: Feminism and the Crime Novel* (New York: Continuum, 1988).

Walton, Priscilla L. and Manina Jones, *Detective Agency: Women Rewriting the Hard-Boiled Tradition* (Berkeley: University of California Press, 1999).

Golden-Age crime fiction

The so-called 'Golden Age' of crime fiction can justifiably be said to have been made possible by Arthur Conan Doyle's Sherlock Holmes and his adventures in detection. Doyle's creation, perhaps more than any other previous foray into crime fiction, consolidated the public's liking for, expectations of and familiarity with the genre. Doyle's stories also firmly established narrative patterns and plot conventions that would, at least initially, be staples of Golden-Age crime fiction: the detective's assistant, the focus on the detective process, the early occurrence of the crime and the retrospective reconstruction. Golden-Age fiction built on these basics and added new elements, but the Holmes stories arguably fostered the enormous and inventive outpouring of crime fiction, particularly the stylised 'clue-puzzle' narratives, produced in Britain and America between the two world wars (1918–39). And of course, Sherlock Holmes continued to appear until 1927, seven years after the first Agatha Christie novel, *The Mysterious Affair at Styles* (1920), was published.

The dates of the Golden Age are contested; Golden-Age-style fiction continued to be produced after 1940 by established and new writers. Indeed, in the twenty-first century authors such as Catriona McPherson and David Roberts continue to play with the form. In terms of origin, crime fiction critic Leroy L. Panek proposes E. C. Bentley's *Trent's Last Case* (1913) as a starting point. Bentley's text subverted the Holmesian myth of the super-detective by having its own detective come to the wrong conclusion based on apparently sound evidence and rational thought. This foregrounding of the importance of correctly reading clues prefigures the later clue-puzzle narratives, in England most famously exemplified in the novels of Agatha Christie and in America by S. S. Van Dine (pseudonym of Willard Huntington Wright). This form, where the reader is given access to all the same clues and information as the detective, unlike in the Sherlock Holmes stories where Holmes frequently withholds information or metaphorically obscures his thought processes with blue clouds of tobacco smoke, was not the only sub-genre that appeared in this fertile period of crime writing, but it came to dominate the crime fiction market and had a strong influence on later criminography. Julian Symons (*Bloody Murder*, 1985) divides the Golden Age into two decades; the 1920s when the form becomes established, and the 1930s when writers begin to elaborate on and deviate from the original. Howard Haycraft, credited with coining the phrase 'Golden Age', makes a similar division, with the Golden Age covering the years 1918–30 and the 1930s as 'The Moderns'. Haycraft also separates the American version from the British; while the American contribution to the form was significant, it was later in beginning and seems to have ended earlier, perhaps because of the rise of the hard-boiled detective novel in the 1930s and 40s.

The development of Golden-Age crime fiction and particularly the clue-puzzle was concomitant with the gradual demise of the short story which had been the nineteenth-century norm for detective fiction and the preferred form for many writers in the genre, for example, Doyle and his Sherlock Holmes; G. K. Chesterton's Father Brown; Jacques Futrelle's Professor S. F. X. Van Dusen; R. Austin Freeman's Dr Thorndyke. In the wake of the Great War, the previously largely masculine audience for crime fiction had been drastically reduced and the predominantly female post-war readership required a different kind of fiction; not short stories in the periodicals purchased on the way to work but longer fiction, in Britain often borrowed from one of the increasing number of public lending libraries. Short stories continued to appear and many of the Golden-Age authors wrote both short and long fiction, but the longer format allowed space for more complex puzzles, greater—if still limited—characterisation, multiple suspects and more detailed detection/examination of evidence. Perhaps above all, the clue-puzzle form, with its rigid structures, carefully defined rules, satisfying closure, frequently serial detective and its representation of a static society that contrasted sharply to the rapidly changing reality of the interwar years offered a sense of security to its readers.

As the genre developed it became formulaic, to the point where 'S. S. Van Dine' could produce an article, 'Twenty Rules for Writing Detective Fiction' (1928) in America and Ronald Knox, a British crime fiction writer, publish his 'Decalogue', or 'Ten Commandments' of detective fiction in 1929. But before these 'rules' were established, writers of detective fiction took their inspiration from existing crime narratives. Christie was a self-confessed reader of crime fiction, mentioning in her autobiography Anna Katharine Green's *The Leavenworth Case* (1878), Doyle's Sherlock Holmes stories, Arthur Morrison's *Martin Hewitt, Investigator* (1894), the first 'ordinary' contemporary detective-alternative to Holmes, and Gaston Le Roux's *The Mystery of the Yellow Room* (1907) as contributing to her decision to write detective fiction. She acknowledged that she felt unable to emulate Doyle's Sherlock Holmes, and indeed, her detective hero was to be the antithesis of Holmes the hero detective. But she followed the Holmesian pattern nonetheless, with the detective, his narrator/friend and the ineffectual policeman: where Doyle had Holmes, Watson and (usually) Lestrade; Christie had, at least initially, Hercule Poirot, Captain Hastings and Inspector Japp.

Christie gathered together the various detective narrative threads of earlier crime, detective and mystery stories and wove them, in her first novel, into the distinctive clue-puzzle features that are standard in Golden-Age crime fiction. Perhaps most significant was the crime; in much late nineteenth-century criminography, typified by the Sherlock Holmes stories, the crimes usually circulated around money and property and murder was the exception rather than the rule. In Golden-Age fiction, possibly in part responding to and influenced by the early twentieth-century American mystery novels by authors such as Carolyn Wells, this changed and murder became the rule: money, property and their owner-ship continued to provide motive, along with sexual jealousy, revenge and the concealment of past misdeeds and crimes. Furthermore, the book titles began to declare their subject; many of Christie's titles con-tained the words 'death', 'murder', 'evil' or 'body'. Despite this, the violence implicit in such titles is, in the narratives, very limited and the murdered body is briefly described and quickly removed from the scene. Its function is purely to initiate the subsequent action. A further signifi-cant change, and one that is strongly associated with the English rather than the American clue-puzzle, is the location of the crime in a rural rather than an urban environment: Sherlock Holmes's cases can take him into the suburbs and the country, but he is essentially an urbanite, while in 1902 G. K. Chesterton declared the detective story to be the romance of the modern city. However, contrary to popular belief not all Golden-Age fiction is set in country houses, but it is located in small or enclosed com-munities: little villages or suburban streets, islands, hotels. The country house is a recurring feature, but it is often necessarily connected to the local community.

While isolating the characters from the community is a common trope in Golden-Age fiction—Christie's *And Then There Were None* (1939, orig-inally *Ten Little Niggers*) takes place on a private island; in *The Sittaford Mystery* (1931) the country house where the action takes place is isolated by snow—the multiple suspects which are another feature of the clue-puzzle novel require that the author provides more characters than are perhaps believable in a very enclosed setting. The clue-puzzle insists that suspicion must plausibly fall on practically all those close to or involved with the victim, with only the detective and his/her assistant clearly innocent. In order to ensure plausibility, the potentially guilty charac-ters must be concealing something from the detective; there are multiple personal motives and any amount of alibis. This, in combination with the need to ensure that the reader has access to all the same information and clues as the detective, means that 'red herrings' abound in the clue-puzzle. The conventions also require that the characters share a similar social background to the reader, usually middle or upper middle class; it went against the conventions of the genre to have a member of the lower classes as the guilty party, although sometimes, as in *The Murder of Roger Ackroyd* (1926), a character may masquerade as a servant. In Christie's novels the danger and threat are shown to come from within, rather than from some 'other' part of society, hence vicars and their wives, retired army officers, doctors, lawyers, an occasional film star, businessmen, poor relatives and wealthy widows function as murderers and victims. The serving class is represented; indeed their omnipresence offers a rich source of information for the detective figure.

Detection is rational, based on often circumstantial evidence and on careful consideration of motive. Exact details of times and places are integral to the plot, hence the frequent representation of sketches of rooms or plans of houses and references to railway timetables in the earlier examples of the genre. In Christie's work domestic detail is also significant; servants' routines, mealtimes and postal deliveries, all contribute to providing detective and reader with the clues that will lead to the killer. As again demonstrated in Christie's novels, the tendency in the early texts is to have a male private detective—Hercule Poirot for Christie—and a police presence which adds realism and provides otherwise inaccessible information to the detective, but which also functions to showcase the clear intellectual superiority of the private investigator. Christie's amateur spinster-detective, Miss Jane Marple (first appears in a series of short stories, 'The Tuesday Night Club' in 1928 then in *The Murder at the Vicarage*, 1930) develops a working relationship with the police, while in Patricia Wentworth's novels another spinster sleuth, Miss Maud Silver (cameo role in *The Grey Mask*, 1928; central character in *The Case is Closed*, 1937 and continued to appear until 1961), seems to act in a consultative role to the police. Dorothy L. Sayers's detective Peter Wimsey has a sister who marries Chief Inspector Charles Parker, bringing the police into the family.

Marriage in Golden-Age crime fiction is more likely to be a source of crime than of domestic bliss and romance is either a red herring or a motive for murder. Above all, the detective must remain detached, again in the Sherlock Holmes pattern, rejecting emotional entanglements. This aspect of the clue-puzzle in combination with the focus on the plot has led to criticism that the characters tend to be rather flat and two-dimensional, mere literary tools and, with perhaps the exception of the detectives in Christie's novels, this is generally a fair comment. Later Golden-Age writers fleshed out their characters rather more, but with a resultant loss of focus. For example, Sayers, who openly declared that romance had no place in the detective novel, famously has her detective, Peter Wimsey, fall in love with Harriet Vane, whose case he undertakes in his sixth outing, *Strong Poison* (1930), and who finally accepts his proposal of marriage in *Gaudy Night* (1936). In the course of charting the love affair between the two, Sayers's texts at times struggle to balance the romantic with the detective elements and the strong clue-puzzle structure is weakened. Sayers also departs from the convention that the clue-puzzle novel usually ends merely with the discovery/revelation/confession of the guilty party; in some of his cases, trial and conviction follow the capture of the murderer and Wimsey is shown to be suffering a *crise de nerfs* caused by his awareness of the fate (execution by hanging) that awaits the convicted perpetrator.

Christie and Sayers are perhaps the best-known of the British Golden-Age writers, but there were many others: Margery Allingham, Anthony Berkeley Cox (his novels were a satirical take on the genre and he also wrote what are more strictly speaking crime novels under the pseudonym Francis Iles), Freeman Wills Crofts, Nicholas Blake (pen-name of Cecil Day Lewis), Gladys Mitchell and Georgette Heyer are some of the authors whose work remains in circulation. As the genre evolved in the 1930s and 40s, variations on the basic patterns emerged; Anthony Berkeley Cox and Sayers both suggested that the story of the detective and detection was gradually developing into a narrative concerned with murder and, rebelling against the 'rules', later Golden-Age fiction is more concerned with some psychological depth. There is less interest in detection than in the motivation of the criminal and the effects of the crime. America too had its Golden Age of crime fiction, with a similar emphasis on the clue puzzle and the art of detection. By contrast to the British version, American detective fiction of the 1920s and 30s tended to be located in the city, specifically on the East Coast; the West Coast would be the setting for the later hard-boiled detective fiction of Hammett and Chandler. Willard Huntington Wright, writing under the pseudonym S. S. Van Dine, adopted the clue-puzzle form and produced a series of novels featuring his Europhile intellectual detective Philo Vance (first appeared in *The Benson Murder Case*, 1926). Set in New York, the densely plotted texts can at times feel like an extreme version of the English clue-puzzle form, to the point almost of parody, but they were phenomenally popular in their time.

Van Dine was followed by Ellery Queen, actually a writing team of two cousins, Frederic Dannay and Manfred B. Lee; their detective was also called Ellery Queen and his first outing was in *The Roman Hat Mystery* (1929). Dannay and Lee continued to produce Ellery Queen stories until 1971 and were, like Van Dine, crime fiction critics. Their adherence to the clue-puzzle form extended to a formal 'Challenge to the Reader' once all the clues had been given in the narrative. Rex Stout, with his deskbound, orchid-loving detective Nero Wolfe (*Fer de Lance*, 1934, was the first in a long series), offered a less formulaic clue-puzzle structure but maintained the New York setting. American-born John Dickson Carr took the polished US clue puzzle back to England, where he lived for many years, creating another sedentary, fat detective, Gideon Fell, who was clearly modelled on G. K. Chesterton. Carr's Gideon Fell texts have an English setting, as have those he wrote under the pseudonym Carter Dickson, but they differ from Christie's classic model in their predilection for sometimes gory and grotesque violence. The clue-puzzle form, in both its English and American incarnations, suggests that danger comes from within the society and class in which the narratives are set and the American version strongly intimates the potential for violence within the cityscape of New York.

The usually muted violence implicit in the plot-driving murders of the classic clue puzzle becomes a key element in the psycho-thriller which developed in the same period; Anthony Berkeley Cox, writing as Francis Iles, focused on the murderer and on his victim in two novels, *Malice Aforethought* (1931) and *Before the Fact* (1932). The same crime is at the centre of both texts, but the former is seen from the perspective of the killer and the latter from that of the victim. Another strong feature in the evolving clue-puzzle form was the focus on the police detective which would feed into the police procedural, which had its origins in the 1940s and 50s. Freeman Wills Crofts's Inspector French novels, beginning with *Inspector French's Greatest Case* (1925) take detection back into the public domain and out of the hands of the private investigator. Ngaio Marsh also made a police detective, the aristocratic Inspector Roderick Alleyn, the hero of her crime novels, as did Michael Innes (pseudonym of J. I. M. Stewart), with Inspector John Appleby (another aristocrat, later Sir John). The Golden Age was, then, not simply a period when crime writing proliferated; it was a key period in the history of the genre in which new forms were developed.

It was also a period in which criminography reached new heights of popularity, and the reasons for this have been long debated. Suggestions include the attraction of the clue-puzzle form at a time when intellectual games were coming into being—the crossword puzzle, for example—and the simple satisfaction that results from solving a puzzle. This can be mapped onto wider society; by capturing the amoral and abnormal member of society, the detective restores the proper order of things. The texts also represent, respond to and offer a comforting illusion of the containment of contemporary social anxieties. Geraldine Pederson-Krag and Charles Rycroft have offered Freudian readings of crime fiction which associate it with the sexual dynamics of the family; Tzvetan Todorov focuses on the structural significance of crime narratives; W. H. Auden saw Golden-Age crime fiction as representing the religious conflict between guilt and innocence; Stephen Knight reads the form in terms of the contemporary ideology. All these readings are valid and all demonstrate the importance and influence of the fiction produced in this Golden Age. But perhaps the most important element is that the pleasure and consolation afforded by the comforting closure of the classic clue-puzzle narrative, combined with its frequently serial detective, incited the reader to return again and again in order to satisfy his or her addiction to crime fiction.

See also   *Contexts*: Detectives and Detection, Gender and Sexuality; *Texts*: American Crime Fiction, Historical Crime Fiction; *Criticism*: Feminism, Cultural Materialism, Postmodernism.

Further reading

Horsley, Lee, *Twentieth-Century Crime Fiction* (Oxford: Oxford University Press, 2005).

Knight, Stephen, *Form and Ideology in Crime Fiction* (Bloomington: Indiana University Press, 1980).

Makinen, Merja, *Agatha Christie: Investigating Femininity* (Basingstoke: Palgrave Macmillan, 2006).

Panek, Leroy L., *Watteau's Shepherds: The Detective Novel in Britain 1914–40* (Bowling Green, OH: Bowling Green University Popular Press, 1979).

Rowland, Susan, *From Agatha Christie to Ruth Rendell* (Basingstoke: Palgrave Macmillan, 2001).

Rzepka, Carles J., *Detective Fiction* (Cambridge: Polity, 2005).

Symons, Julian, *Bloody Murder: From the Detective Story to the Crime Novel* (London: Viking, 1985).

Hard-boiled detective fiction

The term 'hard-boiled' is, when not applied to eggs, peculiarly American, denoting toughness and durability. Mark Twain used the descriptor when speaking of grammar in 1886 while in 1919 American Edward Bullard invented the 'hard-boiled hat', which was safety headgear made from steamed canvas intended to protect workers in industry and on construction sites. Specifically American definitions are, when related to business, 'hardened, callous, hard-headed, shrewd' or, when speaking of clothing, 'stiff and hard'. All these terms and definitions seem appropriate when applied to the detective figure that is generally at the centre of the hard-boiled sub-genre of crime fiction. The private investigator protagonist of the form is professional; tough; shrewd; at times callous and hard; durable, surviving assault and injury; is often bound by a rigid, if very individual, moral code, and works in a protective capacity. It is a very American form; Julian Symons suggests that it was the first genuinely non-derivative crime fiction in the United States, implying that prior to its development the Americans had largely imitated or appropriated British patterns of crime writing.

Hard-boiled detective fiction is generally considered to come into existence in America during the 1920s and 30s, initially in the pulp magazines of the period, so-called because the cheap, rough paper on which they were printed was made from wood-pulp. These magazines, of which the best-known was *Black Mask*, were aimed at a blue-collar, or working-class, male audience, and so contained material written in a discourse that represented and responded to the world in which such an audience existed. In contrast to the mannered, middle-class bourgeois material of Golden-Age crime fiction, which offered comforting resolution and in which even the violence inherent in the act of murder was muted and discreet, the pulp magazine stories delivered hard-hitting, often graphic and frequently sadomasochistic and misogynistic representations of crime and its omnipresence in society which more closely resembled reality. In the face of such realism, the rarefied intelligence of a Sherlock Holmes or the little grey cells of a Poirot were clearly going to be ineffectual, inappropriate and incredible. The man—and it was always a man—who investigated the crime and corruption on the city streets of America during the 1920s and 30s, the time of Prohibition (1920–33) and the Great Depression (1929–39), facing gangsters and corrupt police and government officials, needed to be tough and to understand the streets; to speak the right language and possess the right skills for the job.

The best-known pulp magazine *Black Mask* initially offered adventure stories and Westerns as well as detective fiction; it was only after Joseph Shaw became the editor that the magazine was devoted mainly to detective fiction. Shaw considered that realistic crime fiction could promote the ideal of justice to its readers and so possibly even contribute to the control of criminality. The original juxtaposition of cowboy stories and detective narratives foregrounds the literary and historical links between the two figures; as George Grella has argued, the private detective came to epitomise the traditional American hero previously represented by the frontiersman/cowboy. The hard-boiled detective shared with antecedents such as James Fenimore Cooper's Natty Bumppo in the early nineteenth-century Leatherstocking series a strong sense of justice and morality combined with individuality and physical and mental toughness; he was a 'real' man in a very masculine world. The violence and dangers of the Wild West and its corrupt frontier towns were, in the twentieth century, transposed onto the mean city streets of interwar America. The nineteenth-century detectives—the fictional Jem Brampton and Nick Carter, or the real-life investigator Allan Pinkerton, for example—also contributed to the development of the hard-boiled detective. But where Brampton, Carter and Pinkerton were implicitly agents of the law-abiding community, protecting it against threats to the social order, the hard-boiled detective, while paid for his investigations, is alienated from the community and essentially works to satisfy himself and his personal sense of justice. Although overtly depicted as cleansing the city of gangsters and corruption, a common theme in hard-boiled fiction is the detective's personal quest, which may be initiated by the criminal case he has been hired to investigate but which finally subsumes it.

The urban setting of the city is central to the hard-boiled crime narrative as it had been to the nineteenth-century detectives in Britain and America, if for different reasons. For the earlier detectives the city brought wealth and poverty into close proximity and so encouraged crime; it provided the anonymity which enabled the criminal to avoid capture by the police, so creating work for the private investigator. For the later hard-boiled detective, the city retained these functions, but was also a breeding ground for corruption in the forces of law as well as criminals, the ideal location for gangsters to carry out their business, and an environment that fostered alienation and placed the detective as the outsider and observer, the 'eye' as well of the 'I' of the narrative. The nineteenth-century investigators were located mainly in the Eastern states of America. Pinkerton was based in Chicago, Brampton was the 'New York Detective', serial sleuth Nick Carter initially investigates his cases in the same city and the short story which has been claimed to be the prototype for the hard-boiled genre is also set in East Coast New York. Carroll John Daly's 'Three Gun Terry', featuring private investigator Terry Mack, appeared in *Black Mask* in May 1923. He was quickly replaced, in June 1923, by Daly's longer-lived and better-known protagonist, Race Williams, who continued his investigations, still in New York, until 1952. However, Race is perhaps closer to the gangster than to the lawman, less the classic hard-boiled detective than simply an adventurer prone to excesses of violence and lacking the moral sense/code of honour of the later, fully developed investigative figure represented by Raymond Chandler's protagonist, Philip Marlowe. But Chandler's creation was preceded and indeed made possible by the crime fiction of Dashiell Hammett, whose numerous short stories and five novels were published between 1922 and 1934.

Hammett took the crude material found in the pulp magazines and refined it without losing its immediacy and realism, producing hard-boiled narratives that were considered by their readers to represent honestly and accurately the social disorder, criminality, violence and tensions of the time. Hammett had personal experience of investigative work, having himself been an agent for the Pinkerton Detective Agency. Politically aware and with left-wing sympathies, Hammett resigned from the Agency when it became involved in union strike-breaking. Originally from Maryland and raised in Philadelphia, he later moved to San Francisco and it was here that he began writing detective fiction, much of which he set in West Coast America, a location which is still strongly associated with the hard-boiled crime fiction genre. Hammett's two best-known detectives are the 'Continental Op' and Sam Spade. The Continental Op, so named because he is an operative for the Continental Detective Agency, may be a short fat man but he is tough and capable. Unemotional, his moral code is shaped by his profession; he is dedicated to his job and it is this that renders him immune to bribery and corruption. The Op appeared in a number of short stories, but his (and Hammett's) fame was established in Hammett's first novel, *Red Harvest* (1929, first serialised in *Black Mask*), in which the Op almost single-handedly brings the law to the lawless imaginary city of Personville (called and pronounced 'Poisonville' by the characters in the novel, suggesting its corruption and evil). The Op also appeared in Hammett's second novel, *The Dain Curse* (1929, also first serialised in *Black Mask*), set in San Francisco.

Where the plot of *Red Harvest* is relatively straightforward and features graphic violence, *The Dain Curse* retains the violence but is more complex and sensational. The Op is employed to solve a diamond heist, but in the process uncovers a strange religious cult, a family curse, psychosis and drug addiction. This pattern, of the detective's employment on a criminal case leading to his involvement with personal, often family problems, will become a strong theme in the established hard-boiled detective novel. Hammett's second influential investigator was Sam Spade, a younger, more attractive character than the Op; Spade is a man who survives in a world of random violence and corruption by following a self-imposed code of honour, in contrast to the Op whose moral code is shaped by his profession. Spade appeared in only one full-length novel, *The Maltese Falcon* (1930, first serialised in *Black Mask*), and his longevity is perhaps due to the cinema rather than the book, particularly the 1941 film version with Humphrey Bogart in the lead role (the first version, released in 1931, starred Ricardo Cortez). Capitalising on the success of the novel, Hammett later wrote three short stories with

Spade as the protagonist, 'A Man Called Spade' (*American Magazine*, July 1932); 'Too Many Have Lived' (*American Magazine*, October 1932) and 'They Can Only Hang You Once' (*Collier's Weekly*, November 1932). In his biography of Hammett, *Shadow Man* (1981), Richard Layman describes these stories as 'lazy, inadequately developed pieces'.

The Maltese Falcon builds on and develops the patterns introduced in the Continental Op stories and Sam Spade is the archetype for the hard-boiled detectives who will follow him. The lead female character, Brigid O'Shaughnessy, is the model for the *femme fatale* essential to the hard-boiled detective novel, providing an erotic element and contributing to the personal and emotional involvement of the detective that is part of the genre. In what will become another familiar trope, the wicked woman is punished and the detective remains free and single; Spade falls in love with Brigid, but she is a murderess and a criminal, and he cannot, finally, compromise his personal code of values, and hands her over to the police in the knowledge that she may potentially face execution. Unlike the Continental Op novels, *The Maltese Falcon* is less concerned with depicting violence than with revealing its effects: the violence implicit in the dialogue intensifies the suspense of the narrative.

Hammett, then, sets in place a number of the conventions of the hard-boiled detective novel: the lone, incorruptible agent with a highly individual code of honour; the personal investigation within the external crime; the dangerous woman; the gangsters and the corrupt police. He also takes the genre to the West Coast of America, the furthest frontier, confirming the historical and literary relationship between the detective and the traditional American hero represented in the early nineteenth century by the frontiersman. Hammett's writing style was a clear influence on the genre; inspired by Ernest Hemingway's terse prose, in the interests of realism Hammett used dialogue rather than description and made every word count. The violence in his texts was not gratuitous but intended to represent the lived reality of the city and its criminals; his gangsters are not evil geniuses but corrupt or criminal businessmen and the desire for money is shown to be the root of all evil.

Hammett wrote two further novels which have been called 'hard-boiled', but *The Glass Key* (1931) does not have a professional detective as its protagonist, although it deals with crime, and *The Thin Man* (1934) features an ex-detective, Nick Charles, unwillingly drawn into a criminal investigation with his wife, Nora, while both narratives are set on the East coast rather than on the West. Hammett had set the precedent, but it is perhaps his successor, Raymond Chandler, whose crime narratives have come to epitomise the classic hard-boiled detective genre. Chandler was born in America but educated and briefly worked in Britain. He returned to the States in 1912 and from 1919 he worked in the oil business until his drinking and womanising led to his dismissal in 1932 and he turned to writing for a living. He cited Hammett as the main influence on his own work, stating that Hammett 'took murder out of the Venetian vase and dropped it in the alley [...] gave it back to the people who commit it for reasons, not just to provide a corpse'. Chandler followed Hammett in his choice of a venue for his foray into detective fiction, with his first story, 'Blackmailers Don't Shoot' (1933), published in *Black Mask*.

Chandler went on to write more than twenty short stories centred on crime and detection, mostly published in *Black Mask* and later the *Dime Detective Magazine*, between 1933 and 1959. He experimented with several detective protagonists before settling on 'Philip Marlowe', the eventual hero of his novels. While there are clear similarities to Hammett's Sam Spade, Marlowe is a more rounded, sophisticated, wittier and sympathetic character. There are other differences: Chandler's narratives are set in Los Angeles, home of Hollywood, and while representing a very real cityscape are much concerned with revealing the illusion, artifice and façades of both city and inhabitants. Perhaps the most significant difference is the use of the first-person narrative; in contrast to Hammett's third-person omniscient narrator, Marlowe speaks directly to the reader and he/she sees characters and events through his eyes—the private I/eye. The detective is a private man and the reader is given little direct information about him, having to rely instead on the clues offered by the dialogue, which is witty, stylish and enormously evocative of place and people. Chandler conjures a scene and sets a mood seemingly effortlessly in a few words, revealing aspects of Marlowe's character in his interactions with others in the narrative. Chandler was also a self-consciously stylised and stylish writer and his novels introduced the hard-boiled genre to a new, more literary audience. As with Hammett's fiction, Chandler's work was popularised in cinematic form; all his novels have been filmed, including *Poodle Springs* (1989) but strangely excluding *Playback* (1958), despite the fact that this began life as a screenplay and was only produced as a book when it became clear that the film was never going to be made.

The basic structure and themes of Chandler's hard-boiled fiction are established in his first novel, *The Big Sleep* (1939). Here, the overt case is when Marlowe is hired by oil baron General Sternwood to investigate the blackmail of his daughter, Carmen. In the process, Marlowe is drawn into a personal quest to solve the mystery of the disappearance of Rusty Regan, the husband of Carmen's elder sister, Vivian. Crime and corruption are represented by the homosexual pornographer and blackmailer, Arthur Geiger, and his lover, handsome murderer Carol Lundgren, and by the racketeer Eddie Mars. The police are not actually corrupt, but are not far from it, turning a blind eye to Geiger's pornography business. There is a good (unavailable) woman, Mona Mars, who with Vivian Regan provides a suggestion of a love interest, and a wicked woman, Carmen, who is revealed as (literally) the *femme fatale*. The real criminal or source of criminality is always a woman in Chandler's texts, responding to contemporary masculine anxieties about female—and male—sexuality. The missing Rusty Regan, whom Carmen has murdered, is the prototype for a recurring male character in Chandler's novels, a man who initially appears to fulfil Marlowe's ideal of masculinity but who proves flawed in some way and who perhaps represents a repressed homoerotic desire in the misogynistic Marlowe; a later example is Moose Malloy, who appears in *Farewell My Lovely* (1940). In *The Big Sleep* Marlowe finds solutions to both the blackmail case and the personal quest, inflicting and suffering physical violence in the process; in a further recurrent theme, he undergoes a period of unconsciousness which seems to assist him in solving the mystery.

A further strong and recurring trope is that of the quest and the knightly figure who undertakes it. The association is made clear in the opening of *The Big Sleep*, where a stained glass window in Sternwood's house shows a knight attempting to rescue a maiden in distress; there is a further reference to the knight in a game of chess. The name 'Vivian' resonates with the Vivien, or Nimue, of Arthurian myth who brings about Merlin's downfall; Chandler's first choice of a name for his detective was 'Mallory', a reference to the Malory who wrote *Le Morte Darthur*, while the surname Marlowe brings to mind Christopher Marlowe, the Renaissance poet and playwright; the title of Chandler's fourth Marlowe novel, *The Lady in the Lake* (1943) is a further Arthurian reference, as is the name of the female lead, Helen Grayle, in *Farewell My Lovely*. The surname of Orfamay Quest, the false maiden of *The Little Sister* (1949) foregrounds the concept of the quest while her first name is reminiscent of Morgan Le Fay. Chandler's construction of his detective as a knightly figure has been commented on by literary critics Stephen Knight and Charles Rzepka among others, and is tacitly acknowledged in Chandler's own critical essay on detective fiction, 'The Simple Art of Murder' (1944):

> But down these mean streets a man must go who is not himself mean, who is neither tarnished nor afraid. The detective […] is the hero, he is everything. He must be a complete man and a common man and yet an unusual man. He must be […] a man of honor […]. He must be the best man in his world and a good enough man for any world.

In all, Chandler wrote seven novels featuring Philip Marlowe; an eighth text, *Poodle Springs*, was begun by Chandler in 1958 but was unfinished at the time of his death in 1959. It was later completed by Robert B. Parker, himself a writer of detective fiction in the hard-boiled tradition, in 1989. Parker seems a reasonable choice; his own detective is called Spenser in homage to another Renaissance poet and so by inference to Chandler's Marlowe.

Poodle Springs sees Marlowe married in direct contradiction of Chandler's diktat that the detective must remain emotionally and sexually unattached and so perhaps was intended to signify Marlowe's demise. But the hard-boiled tradition continued; the political edge of the left-wing Hammett's texts modulates through the semi-liberal attitudes seen in Chandler's narratives into a fully-fledged liberalism in John, later Ross, Macdonald's (real name Kenneth Millar) eighteen crime novels, written between 1949 and 1976. The serial detective here is the divorced Lew Archer, whose name is a direct reference back to Sam Spade's partner, Miles Archer. While the texts adhere to the hard-boiled formula and the setting is still the West Coast, the detective moderates, responding to a changing social climate and, in the wake of Chandler's literary elevation of the genre, a more cultured and higher-class audience than that of the pulp magazines. Archer is a gentler, less physical man, more interested in the mind and motives of the criminal, and is perhaps the last detective in the Californian private-eye tradition. The last one firmly to adhere to the original format of the genre, possibly the strong narrative and plot conventions of hard-boiled detective fiction and the social commentary and politics inherent in its immediacy and realism—in the early novels the exposure of the corrupting effects of wealth and the consequent implicit critique of social inequality—have resulted in the form being appropriated and reworked by later writers with different agendas.

The political possibilities of the form were explored by feminist writers, who took the deeply masculine hard-boiled detective format and used it in part to demonstrate that women too could succeed in this strongly male-gendered literary domain, whether in the form of the woman writer or the fictional female private eye. Perhaps the best-known and earliest feminist writer consciously to rework the form was, in the early 1980s, Sara Paretsky. She states that she initially attempted simply to reproduce the hard-boiled genre, replacing the male detective with a woman, but quickly realised that this would not work. Nonetheless, her serial private eye, androgynous V. I. Warshawski, functions very much in the hard-boiled mode; the major difference lies in the emotional attachments and family history that are part of the female detective's persona and a closer interweaving of the public and private in the cases which she undertakes. Feminist and liberal politics are also more overtly present, with a strong focus on the poor, the underprivileged and ethnic minorities as well as women. Paretsky acknowledges her debt to the hard-boiled tradition; in *Burn Marks* (1990), Warshawski comments that 'being a private investigator is not the romance of the loner knight that Marlowe and Spenser like to pretend'.

Writers concerned with racial as well as gender politics have appropriated the form; Walter Mosley's detective series featuring black, initially amateur investigator 'Easy' Ezekiel Rawlins reverses the hard-boiled tradition. Mosley sets his narrative in black rather than white Los Angeles and in the first of the series, *Devil in a Blue Dress* (1990), reprises the opening of Chandler's *Farewell My Lovely* where a white man enters a black bar; in Mosley's version the scene is seen from the perspective of the black occupants of the bar rather than that of the white intruder. This 'seeing otherwise' shapes all the Easy Rawlins books; significantly, by contrast to the emotionally detached detectives of Hammett and Chandler but in keeping with the feminist rewritings of the genre, Mosley's investigator has family responsibilities, emotional and sexual relationships with women and fraternal attachments to men. The Easy Rawlins novels offer a 'history from underneath' in their representation of the African-American experience of Los Angeles life from post-World War II (*Devil in a Blue Dress*) to the 1960s and the aftermath of the Watts Riots (*Little Scarlet*, 2004) or the 'summer of love' (*Blonde Faith*, 2007). As Mosley and Paretsky's serial detectives suggest, the influence of the hard-boiled detective genre can still be seen in modern crime fiction, particularly in the privileging of the private investigator and as a vehicle for the exploration of personal as well as social politics.

See also *Contexts*: Cities and Urbanisation, Detectives and Detection, Race, Colour, Creed; *Texts*: American Crime Fiction; *Criticism*: Cultural Materialism.

Further reading

Cassuto, Leonard, *Hard-Boiled Sentimentality: The Secret History of American Crime Stories* (New York: Columbia University Press, 2008).

Horsley, Lee, *Twentieth-Century Crime Fiction* (Oxford: Oxford University Press, 2005).

Knight, Stephen, *Form and Ideology in Crime Fiction* (Bloomington: Indiana University Press, 1980).

Lehman, David, *The Perfect Murder: A Study in Detection* (Ann Arbor: University of Michegan Press, 2003 (1989)).

Messent, Peter (ed.), *Criminal Proceedings: The Contemporary American Crime Novel* (London: Pluto Press, 1997).

Walton, Priscilla L. and Manina Jones, *Detective Agency: Women Rewriting the Hard-Boiled Tradition* (Berkeley: University of California Press, 1999).

Historical crime fiction

Over time, crime fiction itself becomes historical; that is, part of literary history. Crime fiction written and set in the nineteenth century speaks of and for its historical moment, as does Golden-Age fiction, the hard-boiled detective fiction of the 1930s and 40s or even, more recently, the early feminist detective fiction of Sara Paretsky, and in that sense is historical. Criminography has, though, often used past crimes or located crime in the past, from the *Newgate Calendars* to the Newgate novels and from sensation fiction to the Sherlock Holmes stories which, represented as Casebooks and Memoirs and retrospectively reported by Dr Watson, are visits to a recent and familiar past. The genre is based on the investigation of past events; the crime in crime fiction necessarily takes place before the investigation and the detective has often been likened to the historian in their common endeavour to construct a coherent narrative from the relics (evidence) of a previous time. Much crime fiction may be considered to write the recent history of the present, but it is only in the later twentieth century that the increasing and deliberate use of the often distant past as the setting for crime narratives has led to the acknowledgement of 'historical crime fiction' as a recognised sub-genre.

It is, perhaps, the desire to find new ways of writing crime, the need to maintain the readers' interest in and the popularity of the genre which in recent times has led writers into locating their narratives in an earlier historical period. Placing their criminal narratives with their equally criminal protagonists in the past had been, for writers such as William Godwin (*Caleb Williams*, 1794), Edward Bulwer Lytton (*Paul Clifford*, 1830; *Eugene Aram*, 1832) or William Harrison Ainsworth (*Jack Sheppard*, 1839), a way to distance their narratives from the present of their publication in order to make them more acceptable to a public critical of the criminal content of the texts. With the advent and eventual dominance of the detective as hero rather than the criminal, this became an unnecessary ploy, and the use of historical settings was replaced by a more recent and recognisable past whose proximity to the present increased the sensational effect of the crime narrative. In the twentieth century, however, writers have once more turned to the historical past, placing their detectives rather than their criminals in previous eras ranging across the ancient worlds of Rome, Greece and Egypt, the medieval and Renaissance periods and the Victorian and Edwardian years of the nineteenth and early twentieth centuries.

Within the sub-genre there are variations; crime fiction that writes the recent history of the present is in a sense 'historical', but more generally the term is ascribed to narratives that are set in a distant past. Walter Mosley's early Easy Rawlins novels conform to the recent history pattern: *Devil in a Blue Dress* was published in 1990 but set in the Los Angeles of 1948; the distant past is the location of Lindsey Davis's Falco novels, which are set in Ancient Rome and its Empire in the reign of Vespasian (69–79AD); Ellis Peters's Brother Cadfael series is set in medieval twelfth-century Shrewsbury and Anne Perry has created two Victorian detective series, featuring police Inspector Thomas Pitt and police detective-turned-private investigator William Monk, respectively. Equally, writers can appropriate an actual crime from the past and revisit it in its moment, as in Bulwer Lytton's *Eugene Aram* or in the twentieth century James Ellroy's *The Black Dahlia* (1987), where the real murder of a young woman known by that name is woven into a fiction that also offers a historical snapshot of 1940s Los Angeles. Another way is to investigate a past crime from the present, a ploy perhaps most famously used by Josephine Tey in *The Daughter of Time* (1951), where her serial detective, Alan Grant, confined to a hospital bed, 'investigates' the role of Richard III in the deaths of the Princes in the Tower. More recently, Tey and her text have themselves been appropriated and written into historical crime fiction in Nicola Upson's *An Expert in Murder* (2008). Upson has Tey in a quasi-investigative role when a series of murders occur, all of which seem to be connected to the fictional Tey's play about Richard III and the murdered princes.

Using real figures from the past has long been the practice of authors seeking to create a sense of period and add authenticity to their historical fiction and crime fiction is no exception. Representing famous people, especially royalty, who are widely recognised by the reading public, fixes narratives in specific time frames and raises certain expectations in the reader. Tey references Richard III; Patricia Finney's spy fiction and her historical detective fiction (written under the pseudonym P. F. Chisholm) use Elizabeth I as a referent and weave real people such as Shakespeare into their plots; the hunchbacked lawyer protagonist of C. J. Sansom's Shardlake novels (2003–present) works variously for Thomas Cromwell and Archbishop Cranmer in the reign of Henry VIII. Peter Lovesey, who had already written a crime series with Victorian police detective Sergeant Cribb (eight novels, 1970–8), perhaps with tongue-in-cheek goes further and has the then future King Edward VII as his detective. In his 'Bertie' series, the prince, Albert Edward, carries out investigations himself (three novels, 1987–93). Lovesey also uses real-life Mack Sennett, the 'King of Comedy' film director, in his 1983 novel, *Keystone*, set in the movie world of the early 1900s and based *The False Inspector Dew* (1982) on the famous case of British murderer Dr Crippen.

Sigmund Freud, whose theory of psychoanalysis has been compared to the process of detection, has also appeared in historical crime fiction. Jed Rubenfeld's *The Interpretation of Murder* (2006) is based loosely around Freud's one and only visit to America in 1909, surmising that during the course of his visit he is drawn into events surrounding a series of horrific murders which led him, after his return to Vienna, to refer to Americans as savages. In similar vein, Frank Tallis's detective series is set in the early 1900s Vienna and features the young psychoanalyst, Dr Max Liebermann, a disciple of Freud, whose Wednesday night meetings he attends in *Mortal Mischief* (2003). Freud plays a part in the Sherlock Holmes myth in Nicholas Meyer's *The Seven-Per-Cent Solution* (1974), in which Dr Watson tricks Holmes into visiting the psychoanalyst in search of a cure for his cocaine addiction. Modern pastiches of Holmes stories are very common (see Peter Ridgway Watt and Joseph Green, *The Alternative Sherlock Holmes: Pastiches, Parodies and Copies*, 2003) and cannot really claim to be historical crime fiction, but their writers use the techniques of the sub-genre. Their narratives are clearly set in the past, and are authenticated by references to actual people, places and events. Nicholas Meyer returns to Holmes in *The West End Horror* (1976), pitting him against Jack the Ripper in the wake of the Ripper murders of 1888–9, as does Michael Dibdin in *The Last Sherlock Holmes Story* (1978).

A further variation is the use of real nineteenth-century authors as investigators, as in Dan Simmons's *Drood* (2009), where Wilkie Collins and Charles Dickens, both known for incorporating crime into their fiction, become part of a fiction of crime. Simmons's title is, of course, a reference to Dickens's unfinished detective novel, *The Mystery of Edwin Drood* (1870), while John Dickson Carr had already used Wilkie Collins as a detective in *The Hungry Goblin* (1972). Stephanie Barron has author Jane Austen investigating crime in a series of novels (1996–present) set in a period of Austen's life about which little is known (1800–4), a clear case, as John Scaggs notes, of utilising the reality of the author's life to give verisimilitude to the fiction. As well as using actual historical persons and ensuring authentic period details such as clothing, food, transport, housing, technology and so on, some crime fiction set in the past is authenticated by being introduced as the published version of actual historical accounts of events acquired by the 'editor' (the author), and/or supported as 'factual' by the use of footnotes. Many historical crime fiction writers use epigraphs and/or footnotes or offer forewords, afterwords, glossaries and appendices which enhance, explain or simply demonstrate the historical accuracy of the backgrounds they have selected for their narratives.

Laurie R. King's Mary Russell series (eleven novels, 1994–forthcoming), in which the heroine meets the retired Sherlock Holmes, becomes his detective partner and later marries him, claims to be the published version of Russell's own manuscript memoirs which have been sent to a writer of mystery novels. In a doubly fictive frame, the writer embarks on a quest to discover the identity of the mysterious sender of the manuscripts. Stephanie Barron's Jane Austen stories are alleged to have been original manuscripts by Austen found in a trunk and transcribed by a fictional editor. Perhaps the best-known text that follows this frame pattern is Umberto Eco's *The Name of the Rose* (1980). Here, the fourteenth-century original account of events in 1327, transcribed by the young apprentice monk Adso of Melk, is contained within the frame narrative of an eighteenth-century translation discovered by an unnamed historian. Hans Bertens and Theo D'haen suggest Eco's medieval 'whodunnit', *The Name of the Rose* (English edition 1983), established historical crime fiction as a recognised sub-genre although, as they admit, forays into history had been made prior to this.

But while the fame of Eco's text and his literary reputation can be considered to have brought historical crime fiction to international and critical attention, Britain in particular already had an established tradition of using historical settings for crime fiction, with a very early twentieth-century example from Agatha Christie in *Death Comes as the End* (1945). Inspired by her interest in archaeology and encouraged by Egyptology specialist Professor Stephen Glanville, who gave her the necessary information on the period, Christie chose ancient Egypt circa 2000 BC as the backdrop for her crime narrative. In *Death Comes as the End* an apparently amicable extended family is revealed to be rotten at the core when the patriarch, Imhotep, returns from a trip away with a new, beautiful and youthful wife, Nofret. She deliberately turns the father against his sons, and he disinherits them. In desperation, and goaded by his wife, one of them turns to murder. One killing leads to another as he seeks to cover his tracks until Hori, described as the patriarch's 'man of business', investigates the crimes and discovers the culprit. The narrative is focalised through the young and beautiful daughter of the house, Renisenb, who, newly widowed, has returned to her father's house. Renisenb also provides the romantic sub-text of the novel. Described by Robert Barnard as '*Hercule Poirot's Christmas* transported to Egypt', *Death Comes as the End* is in essence a Golden-Age clue-puzzle fiction weakened by the incongruity of relocating the stock characters, crimes and motives of Christie's contemporary clue-puzzle plots in a distant and foreign past. The historical details are accurate, but the use of Egyptian names and the stilted dialogue consequent on trying to invoke a sense of cultural and temporal difference through language results not in narrative credibility but simply alienation from text and characters.

The difficulties of conveying a strong and recognisable sense of period and place while portraying characters that are credible and acceptable to contemporary readers have generally been overcome by the later exponents. With an established, multi-format yet clearly identifiable crime fiction corpus on which to draw, and with greater and easier access to facts about the past, authors such as Ellis Peters, Lindsey Davis and Anne Perry have in effect inserted modern fictional investigative figures into their historical narratives. The past is invoked by the use of accurate period detail, often based on actual historical documents, events, places and people as fact is woven into the fiction. Ellis Peters (pen-name of Edith Pargeter) is considered by Rosemary Erickson Johnsen to be the originator of the contemporary market in the sub-genre and more specifically, to have inspired other writers to turn to the medieval period as the setting for crime fiction. Peters, who had already written many straight historical novels under her real name, began her long-running medieval crime series, featuring Benedictine monk and herbalist Brother Cadfael, with *A Morbid Taste for Bones* (1977). The twentieth and final novel was *Brother Cadfael's Penance* (1994), but it was Peters's death, not her protagonist's, that ended the series. In the fiction, Peters drew on her knowledge of Shrewsbury and its Abbey's long history; the first Cadfael story was loosely based around the actual twelfth-century removal of St Winifred's remains from Gwytherin Abbey, where she had been the Abbess, to Shrewsbury, as described in Owen and Blakeway's *A History of Shrewsbury* (1825).

While Peters's Cadfael narratives demonstrate meticulous research into the period and show clear knowledge of the Benedictine Order and its rules, the history is secondary to the characters and to the mystery, which is usually but not always criminal, at the centre of the text. Each novel is set against the backdrop of actual historical events in the years or even months portrayed; the stories are chronologically ordered from 1137–45 and offer continuity as Cadfael ages, old monks die and new ones arrive, the seasons change, Cadfael's investigative partner, Deputy Sheriff Hugh Beringar (introduced in *One Corpse too Many*, 1997) marries and has children and is promoted to Sheriff. By contrast to Christie's foray into the sub-genre, Peters tried, and succeeded, in making her medieval characters seem real and accessible, sharing the needs and motives of their twentieth-century readers and speaking what Peters called 'a kind of universal speech which could be understood in any time'. What Peters's medieval series does have in common with Christie's non-historical crime fiction is its representation of strong female characters. Peters did not consider herself to be a feminist, but women in the Cadfael novels are not stereotypical medieval damsels in distress. Rather, they are rounded, capable and often self-willed figures. Peters makes no claim to be representing the actuality of the female experience in the medieval world, but later writers of historical crime fiction have used the form deliberately to suggest precisely that these women had more independence and autonomy in some parts of their circumscribed lives than is popularly imagined. Rosemary E. Johnsen argues that the historical crime fiction of Sharan Newman, for example, 'combines credible historical information, a strong mystery, and a feminist imperative'.

Newman's twelfth-century serial heroine, Frenchwoman Catherine LeVendeur, has a detective role and she investigates crimes herself; more commonly women in medieval crime fiction assist active male investigators as in Candace Robb's Owen Archer series, where Archer's wife Lucie Wilton has the supporting role. Robb's Margaret Kerr series, as the name suggests, has a female detective protagonist, as does the Dame /Sister Frevisse series (1992–present) of Margaret Frazer (initially the joint pen-name of Gail Frazer and Mary Monica Pulver Kuhfeld; latterly just Gail Frazer). Frazer inserts her narratives into the medieval tradition in part through the use of book titles that resonate with Chaucer's *Canterbury Tales*: *The Novice's Tale* (1992), *The Squire's Tale* (2000) and even *The Prioress's Tale* (1997). Significantly, Newman, Frazer and Robb are all American authors; as with the US-driven feminist appropriation of the hard-boiled crime fiction genre of the 1980s, it seems that historical crime fiction also lends itself to the expression of gender politics. In Britain, the feminist possibilities of the sub-genre are openly demonstrated in Gillian Linscott's Nell Bray series (1991–2003). Nell is a suffragette in the first decades of the twentieth century, and the first novel in the series, *Sister Beneath the Sheet*, opens with her leaving Holloway Gaol after being imprisoned for throwing stones at the Prime Minister's residence. While the texts are concerned with crime and Nell is an amateur detective, her suffragette status is central to her characterisation.

Linscott's Nell Bray and Laurie R. King's Mary Russell are both Oxford-educated, intelligent and independent women whose representation is clearly intended to convey a feminist message which seems appropriate in the context of the issues of female emancipation circulating in the early twentieth century. Anne Perry's Victorian detective fiction is equally in accord with the gender politics of its historical setting, with her strongly masculine serial protagonists, amnesiac police detective-turned-private investigator William Monk (1990–present) and police Inspector Thomas Pitt (1979–present). Women have a role to play in both series, as Pitt is helped in his investigations by his wife, Charlotte, while Monk has ex-Crimean nurse Hester Latterly (later his wife) as his assistant. The women's secondary role accords with Victorian ideas of proper feminine behaviour; they have some agency but always within the constraints of a patriarchal society. Perry's texts offer a credible and familiar representation of Victorian London with its juxtaposition of wealth and poverty; as with the Cadfael novels of Ellis Peters, the historical detail is accurate and Perry references actual persons and events and follows a chronological structure in the series. Perhaps the most interesting aspect of her historical crime fiction is the creation of an amnesiac detective. In the first Monk narrative, *The Face of a Stranger* (1990), William Monk regains consciousness after a carriage accident and discovers that he has no memory of who he is or what he has done. A police officer, he conceals his amnesia and is subsequently assigned to investigate the murder of a Crimean War hero. His detective work leads him to suspect that he himself may have committed the crime; he is eventually proved innocent and the real perpetrator is apprehended. Monk's investigation into his own past continues into the series and John Scaggs has suggested that this process mimics the research of the historian/writer of historical crime fiction.

The narratives in the Monk series often circulate around issues of class and the detective is frequently shown to be critical of the upper classes and their abuse of privilege. It is perhaps because of this that Perry quickly has him dismissed from the police; an actual police detective in the 1850s would have concerned himself with the crimes of the lower classes and had little contact with his social superiors. As a private agent, Monk can plausibly become socially mobile and so gain historical credibility. Perry's Inspector Thomas Pitt is less credible in that, although lower class with a gamekeeper father who is wrongly accused of poaching game and transported to Australia, he marries into the upper classes. This gives him the social mobility that the fictional crime plots require, as does the education he gains when as a child he is given the opportunity to share lessons with the son of his father's gentleman employer. Perry's detectives are only superficially Victorian, bearing little resemblance to the actual police officers of the time. But if the detectives are lacking in historical credibility, this is more than compensated for by a historical background which is at times so detailed that it overwhelms the narrative and blinds the reader to the somewhat repetitive plots. Perry is a prolific author, with, by 2011, twenty-seven Thomas Pitt novels, seventeen in the William Monk series, five books in her more recent crime series set in World War I and nine Victorian Christmas crime novellas. She has also written a number of stand-alone historical novels, but her focus in her crime narratives is very much the period from 1850–1920.

The Victorian and Edwardian periods are a popular choice for the writer of historical crime fiction, perhaps because it has been made so familiar to the public with television and film adaptations of nineteenth-century and early twentieth-century novels and because of its relative temporal closeness. The early nineteenth and eighteenth century are less popular, although Richard Falkirk (pseudonym of Derek Lambert) wrote a series of crime novels set in London in the early 1800s, featuring Bow Street Runner Edmund Blackstone (six novels, 1972–77). Alexander Bruce (pen-name of Bruce Cook) selected real-life Sir John Fielding, who with Henry Fielding, his elder brother and predecessor at Bow Street Magistrates' Court, created the Bow Street Runners in the 1750s and 60s, as his detective protagonist in the eleven books published between 1997 and 2005. More recently, Andrew Pepper has Pyke, an ex-Bow Street Runner/ex-crook as the protagonist in his crime series (five by 2011), set in the period following the inauguration of the Metropolitan Police Force in 1829.

But, broadly speaking, the majority of historical crime fiction is set after 1800, or in the medieval and Renaissance period, or in ancient times. Elizabeth Peters (pen-name of Barbara Mertz) manages to combine the nineteenth century with Ancient Egypt in her Amelia Peabody series (nineteen novels, 1975–present), in which the Victorian proto-feminist protagonist undertakes a number of investigations set in Egypt in the company of archaeologist/Egyptologist Radcliffe Emerson. Ancient Egypt, indeed the ancient world, has been successfully if anachronistically used as a setting for crime fiction by numerous authors: Paul Doherty writes under several different names and has many historical crime fiction series, some set in the medieval/Renaissance periods, but also in the time of Alexander the Great, Egypt circa 1479BC, Imperial Rome and in the reign of Tutankhamen; Margaret Doody sets her novels in the Ancient Greece of Aristotle; Anton Gill, Lauren Haney and Lynda S. Robinson all use Ancient Egypt; in the 1960s Robert van Gulik located his Judge Dee series in China, circa 600AD; Rosemary Rowe chooses Roman Britain.

Rome provides the backdrop to two of perhaps the best-known ancient history crime fiction series. Lindsey Davis has been writing her Falco novels since 1989 and the twentieth in the series was published in 2010. Marcus Didius Falco, to give him his full name, is an ex-legionnaire of the plebeian rank, working initially as an informer and later as the Roman equivalent of a private detective. The novels are set in Rome and its Empire, with the first, *The Silver Pigs* (1989) moving from Rome to Britain and back in AD 70. The subsequent texts follow chronologically, with the action sometimes located in Rome and sometimes in other parts of Vespasian's Empire. The historical background is meticulously researched and made vivid and credible and the focus on the ordinary, plebeian citizens of Rome and their daily routines gives the narratives a strong sense of reality. Davis interweaves the lives of actual people into the fiction, not merely to give colour but at a deeper level. As Ellen O'Gorman observes, in *The Silver Pigs* the murder of the beautiful young Sosia Camillina which, in the style of Chandler's hard-boiled narratives, is the private case set within the broader case which the detective is hired to solve, draws on fact. Sosia Camillina is stabbed by an inky pen and the murderer proves to be Domitian, Vespasian's son. History, in the form of the writings of Seutonius, recounts that Domitian was in the habit of stabbing flies with his pen.

The Falco novels are replete with descriptions of Roman food, clothing, culture and architecture. The city itself is carefully mapped as is the Roman Empire. Social structures are carefully observed and equally carefully explained; Falco's plebeian status is an obstacle which prevents his marriage to Helena Justina as she is the daughter of a Senator and Falco must attain equestrian rank in order to legalise their relationship. Despite the volume of factual and historical information the reader is given, it is subtly conveyed; the interest is always on Falco and his relationships with those around him. The narratives are often comic and imbued with irony, while Falco's personal life gives depth to the characters. His extended and humorously dysfunctional family play an increasingly important role as the series progresses and the characters and their lives are, finally, of more interest than the crimes which, as in Golden-Age fiction, are there to make possible the rest of the narrative. The Falco series is, finally, skilfully using history, but as a setting for a very modern investigator: Falco is a variation of the hard-boiled detective with the misogyny removed and the cynicism moderated. As in the Los Angeles of Chandler's Philip Marlowe, corruption in Falco's world is ubiquitous and omnipresent, especially in the higher ranks of citizens, and social and political issues are touched upon. But their articulation is muted, often voiced by Falco himself and evident in the crimes with which he deals. Ultimately it is the protagonist and his life that holds the attention of the reader rather than the setting and the series makes no attempt to use the past to comment upon the present.

By contrast, American writer Steven Saylor's Roma Sub Rosa books (beginning with *Roman Blood*, 1990, with a further eleven novels in the series to date) implicitly draw political parallels between the ancient Roman world and modern America. The series is set in the first century BC, the Rome of the late and decaying Republic before Julius Caesar comes to power. The 'detective' is Gordianus the Finder. Saylor's academic background in history and his fascination with Roman history in particular is evident in the meticulous period detail of the books, which are peopled with actual Roman citizens of the time such as Cicero, Pompey, Mark Anthony and even Julius Caesar, all of whom are mediated to the reader through their involvement in Gordianus's investigations. Indeed, many of the cases on which the fictional Gordianus is employed have their origins in actual, or plausible, activities of real historical figures. As the series title suggests, the novels purport to offer a secret history of Rome, that is, a criminal history which reveals the corruption at the heart of the crumbling Republic. Each text in the series takes its inspiration from Cicero's published works or accounts of his oratory and Saylor freely references other contemporaneous literary figures, for example Plutarch and Sallust.

Clearly Saylor fictionalises both people and place, but the evocation of Rome is colourful and powerfully convincing, working with and extending the reading public's preconceptions and knowledge of the period in its skilful use of social, cultural and political history: as a review in *Archaeology Magazine* states, 'The detail is meticulous'. Each of the texts in the series deals with a different 'case' for Gordianus, but the series offers continuity in its adherence to historical chronology and, at a human level, with its development of the character of Gordianus. This is represented in his gradual acquisition of personal responsibilities; property, a wife, a cat, a child, other young people rescued and 'adopted' in the course of Gordianus's investigations, servants, slaves and so on. Gordianus is openly political in his support for the Republic and for democracy; his Alexandrian wife is an ex-slave and his antagonism towards the rule by dictatorship that the concept of an Emperor represents is clearly articulated. He is a pacifist and much angered by the often violent side-effects that the political machinations of the powerful have on the ordinary citizen. The crimes in the narratives invoke political and social topics such as citizenship and rights, immigration, slavery and incest. While firmly set in the past, Saylor's historical crime fiction is very much a commentary on a modern America that faces many of the same issues.

Historical crime fiction is in many ways anachronistic, with its insertion of often very modern investigating figures into settings from the past and, as Christie's *Death Comes as the End* demonstrates, can be unpersuasive and lack credibility. But this kind of time-travel tourism in crime fiction can also be informative, educational as well as entertaining in its exploration of personal and political history and even use crime in the past to comment on crime and other issues in the present. It is perhaps this last aspect that has led to and maintained its current popularity: crime, its perpetrators and its motives, history and historical crime fiction seem to suggest, have not really changed over millennia, a suggestion that affords a comforting sense of human continuity.

See also *Contexts*: Crime and Criminality, Detectives and Detection, Gender and Sexuality; *Texts*: Children's Crime Fiction, Feminist Crime Fiction; *Criticism*: Feminism, Cultural Materialism.

Further reading

Bertens, Hans and Theo D'haen, *Contemporary American Crime Fiction* (Basingstoke: Palgrave Macmillan, 2001).

Browne, Ray B. and Lawrence A. Kreiser Jr., *The Detective as Historian: History and Art in Historical Crime Fiction* (Bowling Green, OH: Bowling Green State University Popular Press, 2000).

Christian, Ed and Blake Lindsay, 'Detecting Brother Cadfael: An Interview with Ellis Peters, 17th August 1991', *Clues: A Journal of Detection*, 14:2 (Fall/Winter 1993), pp. 1–30.

Erickson Johnsen, Rosemary, *Contemporary Feminist Historical Crime Fiction* (Basingstoke: Palgrave Macmillan, 2006). Should be Johnsen, Rosemary Erickson here and elsewhere and so later in alphabetical order.

Geherin, David, *Scene of the Crime: The Importance of Place in Crime and Mystery Fiction* (Jefferson, N. Carolina: MacFarland and Co., 2008).

Knight, Stephen, *Crime Fiction 1800–2000: Detection, Death, Diversity* (Basingstoke: Palgrave Macmillan, 2004).

O'Gorman, Ellen, 'Detective Fiction and Historical Narrative', *Greece and Rome*, Second Series, 46:1 (April 1999), pp. 19–26.

Scaggs, John, *Crime Fiction* (London: Routledge, 2005).

The police procedural

In G. K. Chesterton's 'A Defence of Detective Stories'(1901), the author, himself the creator of the fictional detective Father Brown, speaks of 'the romance of police activities'. Chesterton's paper draws a parallel between detective fiction and the heroic quest narratives, with the detective equating to the knightly figure of romance. In the course of his 'Defence', Chesterton firmly locates the police detective in the same narrative sphere. In actuality, the work of the police is far from romantic. Rather, it is frequently repetitive and boring, occasionally dangerous, often frustrating, highly regulated, hierarchical and subject to all the personnel and management problems associated with large organisations.

Yet it is precisely the actualities of policing that distinguish the sub-genre of the police procedural from crime fiction that simply features the police. In the police procedural, as the name implies, the police and the procedures they follow in their pursuit of criminals are absolutely central; the police detectives, working as a team, are substituted for the traditional individual hero-detective typified by Sherlock Holmes. But despite the existence of the police in reality and the very real role they play in the detection of crime and the apprehension of the criminal, it was not until the 1940s that texts appeared which were entirely focused on the police and the procedures which enable, guide and control their detective work.

In Britain, the police have played a role in crime narratives almost from the inauguration of the New Metropolitan Police in London in 1829; prior to that date, different bodies undertook what might loosely be termed the policing of crime, for example the Bow Street Runners, parish constables, nightwatchmen and thief takers, and these too had their place in the contemporary criminography. Many early accounts of crime were factual, or at least based in fact, and the 'police' agents played a relatively minor role in narratives that tended to be focused on the criminal rather than those who apprehended him or her. In fact and fiction, policing figures tended to be marginal to the plot. There were exceptions to this: in Britain the anonymously authored *Richmond: Scenes in the Life of a Bow Street Runner, Drawn Up from His Private Memoranda* (1827) offered a fictional account of the delinquent youth and subsequent employment as a Runner of its hero. In his guise as a Runner, Richmond offers details of the Runners' methods of detection, which often verged on the criminal. The book had very poor sales, suggesting that the public considered it unacceptable to have a Runner of dubious social status and with criminal associations as the hero of a novel. By contrast, a factual account of a French policeman's activities achieved widespread popularity. The (probably ghost-written) *Mémoires* of François Eugène Vidocq, the Chief of the *Sûreté* in Paris, were published in France in 1827 and in translation in Britain in 1829.

While much of Vidocq's *Mémoires* was, like its fictional counterpart *Richmond,* concerned with the protagonist's early life as a criminal and his recruitment into the French police as an informer, the text contains accounts of Vidocq's 'cases' which can be read as early examples of police procedures and so might be considered to be a forerunner of the very much later police procedural. France, specifically Paris, is also the setting for American author Edgar Allan Poe's three short stories featuring his proto-detective C. Auguste Dupin. In 'The Murders in the Rue Morgue' (1841), 'The Mystery of Marie Rogêt' (1842) and most clearly in 'The Purloined Letter' (1845) with its detailed account of police search procedures, the police are shown to be perfectly competent in finding the solutions to ordinary crimes with ordinary criminals, but to require the assistance of the cerebral and analytic Dupin when the crimes are out of the ordinary. This model of limited competence would continue to appear over the nineteenth century; in the Dupin stories, set in post-Revolutionary, socially egalitarian France, the limitations are associated with intellectual ability and imagination rather than, as in the British model, class.

Vidocq's status as a police chief, the distancing of the criminal narrative to France and the pleasure of having British suspicions about the spying activities of the French police justified all contributed to making Vidocq's *Mémoires* popular in Britain, but most important was its adaptation for theatre, with its socially broad and so larger audience. While police began to feature in British criminography after 1829, their lower-class origins, social position as public servants and necessary association with criminality seem to have limited the potential for them to be literary heroes. Charles Dickens's fascination with the police and its articulation in his series of articles about the Metropolitan Police Detectives and their work, published in *Household Words* (1850–53), helped popularise the police; the anecdotes gave details of police detective methods and focused strongly on teamwork. A fictional counterpart was William Russell's 'Recollections of a Police Officer' (1849–52), a series of stories in *Chambers's Edinburgh Magazine* which featured the pseudonymous police officer 'Waters'. This policeman, by contrast to actual police officers of the time, was socially mobile; he is a gentleman fallen on hard times who joins the police as a last resort. 'Waters's' social status made him acceptable to his middle-class audience and both his narratives and those of Dickens familiarised the public with the activities of police detectives. However, even in these positive accounts, there is an element of condescension towards the police consequent on their role as public servants and their (generally) lower-class status.

Significantly, in the fictional 'Waters' stories and in the many pseudo-autobiographical police-detective diaries and casebooks that appeared in the 1860s, the focus is less on teamwork than on the activities of the individual and the police detective is differentiated from the later private detective only by his official standing. This privileging of the individual police officer prefigures what George N. Dove, in his analysis of the police procedural form, will refer to as 'the Great Policeman', that is, a police detective who effectively functions in the same way as the Sherlockian hero detective and solves the case essentially by himself. Early prototypes are Dickens's Inspector Bucket in *Bleak House* (1852–3) and more obviously Sergeant Cuff, the police detective in *The Moonstone*

(1868). But while both these detectives eventually solve their cases, their treatment in the novels illustrates the condescension with which the nineteenth-century middle and upper classes regarded the police and emphasises their lower-class status, especially in the representation of Cuff. His investigations in the upper-class Verinder household not only result in his incorrect identification of the culprit but also contribute to the disruption of the domestic social structure. It is made clear that Cuff cannot understand the upper class individual, nor is his knowledge of criminality relevant in elevated social circles. Cuff later correctly identifies the real criminal, but only after his retirement from the police, while the guilty Godfrey Ablewhite is revealed to have lower-class and so potentially criminal origins; his father is not of the gentry but a self-made man.

Practically contemporaneously with Collins's *The Moonstone*, again it is in France that the police detective is, if only briefly, more fully heroised. Émile Gaboriau's Monsieur Lecoq—a name reminiscent of his predecessor, Vidocq, and, like Russell's 'Waters', a man of good birth fallen on hard times—is the police-detective hero of three novels: *Le Crime d'Orcival* (1867), *Le Dossier no. 113* (1867) and most significantly the two-volume *Monsieur Lecoq* (1868), in which the young and energetic detective carries out quasi-forensic investigations in the first volume, capturing what the evidence suggests is the criminal, who subsequently escapes without accounting for his suspicious actions. The second volume is largely devoted to the history behind the crime and the supposed criminal, who is revealed to be innocent; Lecoq only returns towards the end of the novel in time to identify the real culprit. The figure of Lecoq brings together the practical and imaginative elements of detection, as will the later 'Great Policemen'; while using information/evidence garnered by his fellow police officers, the 'Great Policeman'—or here Lecoq—resolves the case independently. A later example of this figure in French crime fiction is the Belgian writer George Simenon's Inspector Maigret, who appeared in seventy-five novels and twenty-eight short stories between 1931 and 1972.

Increasingly, as the genre of crime fiction becomes more formalised and the police a part of society, they become a necessary presence in the narratives but are usually in secondary or supporting roles. The advent of Sherlock Holmes sets in place a format that will continue into the Golden Age of crime fiction. In the early Holmes stories the police function to accentuate the brilliance of the hero-detective, to allow him access to information and indeed crimes and often to provide a legal framework for his actions as in *The Hound of the Baskervilles* (1901). Here the police, in the form of Inspector Lestrade, are called down from London to Dartmoor in order to provide an arrest warrant for the capture of the criminal. But, while the police incompetence apparent in Holmes's first adventure in *A Study in Scarlet* (1887), it is not overtly apparent in *Hound*, where Lestrade is described as 'the best of the professionals', the condescending attitude towards the police seen in earlier texts is covertly expressed. When the hound of the title comes bounding out of the mist towards Holmes, Watson and Lestrade at the climax of the narrative, Lestrade yells in terror and throws himself 'face downwards upon the ground' while the socially superior Holmes and Watson quickly recover from a moment of fear-induced paralysis and shoot the beast.

In the wake of Sherlock Holmes, the private, professional or amateur hero-detective dominates crime fiction. However, while continuing, by their limited intelligence, inability to see beyond the obvious and their occasional incompetence, to show the brilliant detective to advantage, the police become increasingly necessary in order to add a level of verisimilitude to crime narratives. The Golden-Age fiction of Agatha Christie retains the mythology of the private/amateur detective's superiority in the Poirot and, to a lesser extent, Miss Marple stories, but the police are called in to investigate the crimes, do provide information that would otherwise be inaccessible to the detective and can, according to the demands of the plot, arrest the criminal. Dorothy L. Sayers accords a more positive role to the police, making police Inspector Charles Parker (first appears in *Whose Body?*, 1923) not only an effective investigator but also a part of Lord Peter Wimsey's family when Parker marries Wimsey's sister, Lady Mary (Parker finally proposes to Mary in *Strong Poison*, 1930). While Parker's role is still very much as a supporter for the central figure of Wimsey, he is credited with intelligence and ability and works with the aristocratic detective on most of his cases.

Another Golden-Age writer, Margery Allingham, follows and develops Sayers's pattern. Her detective, Albert Campion, is assisted in his early cases by police detective Stanislaus Oates who, while portrayed as competent, is very much the facilitator and assistant figure. But in Allingham's later Campion novels, she introduces Detective Inspector Charlie Luke and allows him to take a leading role in two stories, *The Tiger in the Smoke* (1952), which features a savage serial killer, and *Hide My Eyes* (1958). In both these novels the focus is on Luke; Campion makes crucial contributions but the police detective does the work and Luke may be considered a prototype 'Great Policeman'. The criminal in these texts is represented differently to those more usually found in Golden-Age plots, where the motive for murder is comprehensible and if more than one murder is committed the later deaths are to conceal the identity of the killer. There is, in these later Allingham narratives, the recognition that sometimes the police are better equipped to deal with certain kinds of criminal such as the psychologically motivated serial killer. By the 1950s, radio, film and television had made visible the actualities of violent crime and the police work it generates, and crime fiction had to respond accordingly.

While the police are an important element in some Golden-Age fiction, the actualities and procedures of police work are implied rather than articulated. Even in Ngaio Marsh's crime fiction, with her serial police-detective hero Roderick Alleyn (32 novels between 1934 and 1982), the prosaic details of police procedure are glossed over: Alleyn is perhaps an exemplary 'Great Policeman'. He can be the hero of the novels because he is a gentleman, educated at Eton College and Oxford University; he is the character with whom the reader engages and he brings intelligence and imagination to his investigations while his subordinate, the lower-class Sergeant Fox, carries out the necessary legwork. In British crime fiction in the first part of the twentieth century, class, it seems, still plays a part in keeping the police in a supporting rather than central role.

It is in America where the police procedural first comes into being. As with the British tradition, the police had been part of the crime genre as it developed in the United States in the nineteenth century; John B. Williams's investigator Jem Brampton is an ex-police detective and Seely Regester's (pen-name of Metta Fuller Victor) Mr Burton, in *The Dead Letter* (1867), is a man of private means who works with/for the police on occasion but is careful to declare himself a member of the business class. In 1878, Anna Katharine Green's *The Leavenworth Case* has Mr Gryce, a New York metropolitan police detective, in a major role. The potential problems of class and audience are solved by having a young lawyer, Mr Everett Raymond, as the narrator, providing the necessary social mobility and acting as a point of identification for the middle-class reader. Raymond assists Gryce in his detective work, as does 'Q', or Morris, an investigative operative employed by the police officer. The model is similar to its British counterparts, and the manipulative Mr Gryce functions more as a 'Great Detective' than as part of the team central to the police procedural.

It is perhaps the development of the hard-boiled detective novel in America in the 1930s and 40s that made possible the police procedural. The sub-genre brought an element of reality to crime fiction that was absent from the Golden-Age narratives with their focus on plot, and it is this reality that is so important to the procedural. In the wake of the war and as a consequence of the crime generated by the Depression, there was perhaps a perception that an organised, disciplined and well-equipped body of men might provide the best defence against the disorder of crime. Television and radio brought the unpalatable reality of urban crime generated by city living directly into the domestic space, making the amateur or private detective of fiction less credible. But the media also made the public more aware of the police forces which defended them against crime and criminality. In 1945, an experienced crime writer, Lawrence Treat, created what has come to be considered the first police procedural in *V as in Victim*. Treat not only read extensively on criminal investigation and forensics, but also spent time with the San Diego homicide police and in the New York Police Department forensics laboratory, familiarising himself with not only police procedures but also the realities of life in the police.

According to George N. Dove in *The Police Procedural* (1982), while *V as in Victim* followed the conventional crime fiction structure of problem, complication, solution and explanation, it introduced the elements that would come to define the police procedural: the police were shown to follow routines and procedures such as questioning witnesses/suspects, completing paperwork, organising and carrying out surveillances and so on. The characterisation of the police officers and the descriptions of inter-police relationships and their personal lives gave the reader an insight not only into police routine but also into the mindset of the men who did the job. And, even in this very early example, there is an emphasis on the role of forensic science, although in *V as in Victim* the police detective, Mitch Taylor, is clearly resistant to this, preferring traditional methods of detection in contrast to those of police scientist Jub Freeman. Significantly, in the context of the realism of the police procedural, while Treat went on to write a further eight novels with Taylor and Freeman, forensically minded Freeman quickly replaced Taylor as the protagonist. Another early police procedural and one that even more closely than Treat's texts focused on the minutiae of police investigation and teamwork was Hillary Waugh's *Last Seen Wearing . . .* (1952). Waugh's procedurally detailed account represented the police detectives working their way to a successful conclusion in the case of the rape and murder of a young college girl in small town America.

The British version of the police procedural appeared in the 1950s with the publication of ex-police detective Maurice Procter's *The Chief Inspector's Statement* (1951). The text purports to be the first-person account of Scotland Yard Chief Inspector Philip Hunter, focused on his investigation of crimes in a Yorkshire village. The police procedures and forensics are there, as are the teamwork and police relationships and aspects of Hunter's personal life. Procter went on to write a series of novels set in a fictional Yorkshire city in which Detective Inspector Harry Martineau works with his fellow officers, using police methods familiar to the modern eye. Better-known and longer-lived is John Creasey's George Gideon. The series was written under the pseudonym 'J. J. Marric', and Gideon is a Commander of police at Scotland Yard; it is interesting that the British police protagonists all hold higher ranks in the force. Gideon is to some extent in the 'Great Policeman' mode, but Marric's use of multiple cases in each novel not only responds to the reality of police work where an officer may be dealing with several cases at any one time, but also suggests the importance of organisation and procedure in successful police investigations. The popularity of the Gideon books led Creasey to reformulate his earlier series, featuring Inspector Roger West, who had first appeared in *Inspector West Takes Charge* (1942), from what was essentially a private detective in the guise of a police officer into the team player of the police procedural.

Creasey/Marric continued to produce his police procedurals until the 1970s and the sub-genre continued to attract an audience. But in Britain the 'Great Policeman' model and its variations dominates, at least in literature. The model has developed and the police detective protagonist is now marked as idiosyncratic in some way; the individuality of the detective is paramount and the police are merely a frame for his or her activities. P. D. James's Adam Dalgleish is marked as different by his creative talents—he writes poetry; Colin Dexter's Inspector Morse drinks whiskey, does crosswords and listens to Wagner; John Harvey's Charlie Resnick is a jazz fan and creative sandwich maker. Ruth Rendell's Inspector Wexford is more conventional but marked by his uxorious domesticity while Ian Rankin's John Rebus is a maverick with contempt for authority and a tendency to work on the margins of the law. These detective stories are set against the background of the police but are not police procedurals. It was, once again, in America where the sub-genre was brought into the mainstream of crime fiction with Ed McBain's 87th Precinct series.

Ed McBain (born Salvatore Lombino, he also wrote mainstream fiction as Evan Hunter) was a prolific writer and had already published a number of mystery novels and short stories, including police stories which he confessed to be heavily influenced by the radio, later television and police procedural series *Dragnet* (radio 1949–57; television 1951–9 and 1967–70). McBain was invited by Herbert Alexander, the editor-in-chief of Pocket Books, to produce a mystery series with an original and fresh lead character. McBain felt that a police detective would make a good series hero; as he wryly observed, 'any other character dealing with murder was unconvincing. If you came home late at night and found your wife murdered [. . .], you didn't call a private eye and you didn't call a little old lady with knitting needles'. The author understood the necessity for realism, and considered that a single 'cop hero' would lack credibility; real police work was carried out by a team. So he decided upon 'a squadroom full of cops, each with different traits, who—when put together—would form a conglomerate hero.' Each text in the series could then foreground a different cop, but retain the sense of a team. He also decided on a city setting, initially New York, but quickly changed this to the imagined city of Isola in order to allow himself more freedom; Stephen Knight suggests that Isola is the map of New York turned ninety degrees clockwise, while the name suggests the isolation and alienation of city living.

McBain carried out extensive research, spending time with the men of the New York City Police Department, including laboratory technicians and forensics specialists as well as police officers. By the time he came to write the first novel in the series, *Cop Hater* (1956), which introduced the cops of the 87th Precinct of Isola, McBain felt that he 'knew what being a cop was all about'. *Cop Hater* not only introduces the reader to the men of the 87th Precinct, their characters and relationships, their personal lives and opinions and their methods and procedures, but also locates them as 'other' to the rest of the city's population and even the cops from other Precincts in the city by making the victims of the murders at the centre of the text the detectives' fellow officers. This has the effect of bonding together the members of the 87th Precinct as they hunt down the cop-killer and ensures that they obey what Dove later designates as 'The Tight Enclave', that is, the police bound together against, in *Cop Hater*, the criminal world, but also as the series progresses and the police procedural develops, against a sometimes hostile public and the Police Establishment. *Cop Hater* opens with a domestic scene as a police detective on night duty leaves his sleeping wife and children; two pages later he is dead, shot through the head at close range. The novel closes with a wedding which promises domesticity for Officer Steve Carella as he marries his deaf and dumb girlfriend, Teddy, but between these two scenes the narrative is strongly focused on the work of the detectives as they seek the killer of Mike Reardon.

Two more cops are murdered in the course of the narrative, both of whom have been made familiar to the reader, rendering their deaths more shocking but, simultaneously, more real. The aftermath of violent death is described; the effects of losing a friend as well as a co-officer on the men of the Precinct are made clear. But what dominate the narrative are the procedures the police follow in their investigation: interviewing possible suspects; establishing alibis; examination of the crime scenes; checking police files for potential matches to the killer's methods; interviewing the victims' families for possible motives; working with police informants; using forensic science to match bullets and preserve footprints. The text itself is interspersed with what purport to be police documents such as forensic reports, suspect details or gun licence applications, precisely the kind of paperwork that takes up police time. The evidence gradually accrues, but as in many police procedurals it is one of what Dove calls 'The Fickle Breaks' that results in the capture of the criminal. Carella is the intended victim; the killer forces his way into Teddy's apartment and waits for Carella to arrive for a lovers' tryst, meaning to shoot him, but Teddy, despite her handicaps, manages to warn Carella in time.

Cop Hater feels somewhat dated to the modern reader, especially in its representation of women, who are often represented as the sexualised objects of the masculine gaze—Reardon contemplates his sleeping wife's semi-naked body; Bush is forced to watch his wife as she slips the clothes from her body but refuses to let him touch her; Teddy is described in very physical terms, while her name and the silence imposed on her by her deafness and inability to speak reduce her to the status of a sex toy. But *Cop Hater* introduces what will become the criteria for the police procedural: its officers are ordinary men who work for a living and are not heroes; their job is seen by the public and by the cops themselves at times as unrewarding and unpleasant; the officers are closely bonded together by their role and profession; there is a reliance on coincidence/accident/luck to break cases and the police must race against time to capture the criminal before he/she strikes again. The procedures of police work are balanced by insights into the personalities and the personal lives of the detectives, and perhaps most importantly, while one or another detective may take a leading role, the men of the 87th Precinct work as a team. McBain made his police representative of the diversity of America's citizens, with black and white detectives of, amongst others, Italian, Irish and Jewish origin. In all, there are fifty-five 87th Precinct novels, with the last, *Fiddlers*, published in 2005, the year of McBain's death and, while the characters, especially Steve Carella, are constants, the crimes and the police methods respond to changes in society and the novels have retained their popularity.

The police procedural was not confined to Britain and America. In Sweden, Maj Sjöwall and Per Wahlöö wrote ten novels featuring police detective Martin Beck (1965–75), which were translated into English for the Anglophone crime market. The Swedish writers used the series as political commentary, with a Marxist stance; in South Africa James McClure used the police procedural to explore the ramifications of apartheid in his series with Afrikaans police detective Kramer and his Bantu assistant Sergeant Zondi in seven novels published between 1971 and 1991 while more recently Deon Meyer's crime novels have been translated from Afrikaans into English and several other languages (1999–present); Tony Hillerman's series with Navajo tribal police detectives Joe Leaphorn and Jim Chee implicitly considers the place of and problems facing Native Americans and their culture in the modern United States; Barbara Nadel is English but her police detective Çetin Ikmen is Turkish; British writer Michael Dibdin's Aurelio Zen series, set in Italy, has elements of the procedural and offers a subtle critique of Italian politics and society (eleven novels, 1988–2007), as does Sicilian Andrea Camilleri's Inspector Montalbano series (2002–present, twelve novels in translation) and American Donna Leon's Commissario Brunetti series, set in Venice (1992–present).

The procedural in some ways lends itself to social and political criticism as the police, in whatever country, deal with the crime that often arises from social problems and yet are part of the Establishment; exposing the internal workings of the police can also expose political and even police corruption. Increasingly, however, the police and their procedures provide a frame within which individual police detective protagonists function. The 'Great Policeman' has to some extent been subsumed in this way. Reginald Hill's long-running series featuring Yorkshire detectives Dalziel and Pascoe (1970–present) is procedural in form and at times demonstrates political awareness in content, but the focus is firmly on the working and personal relationships between the two detectives; Dalziel's detective work in particular relies on intelligent speculation, analytical flair and an understanding of human nature as much as it does on proper police procedures.

The police procedural in its original written form has to a great extent vanished; the format is now almost entirely confined to television, where it thrives on both sides of the Atlantic and indeed across the globe. The accuracy of procedural and forensic detail in series such as the American *Crime Scene Investigation* (2000–present) has led to claims that criminals use it as a guide on how to avoid leaving evidence at the scenes of their crimes. However, even in the televisual renderings of the police procedural, it is the individual characters rather than their procedures which maintain the public interest. The police detective is now an established, respected and important figure in crime fiction, still functioning to give the genre credibility in a modern, scientifically and technologically advanced world and to provide a realistic framework to books about crime. Elements of the procedural remain, but the emphasis is on the individual police detective rather than on the team.

There are, in the early twenty-first century, many variations in the representation of the police in fiction, but perhaps the most significant is the prevalence of police across all criminography, Anglophone, non-Anglophone, in translation and in crime fiction written in English but set in countries other than Britain. Just as all societies designate certain practices as crimes and so categorise those who carry out those practices as criminals, so it seems that the police in some form are common to a diversity of cultures. In the crime fiction of the modern world it is perhaps the presence of the police, not the criminal or the crime, that forms the connective tissue between cultures and perhaps because we feel we know what the police do, there is no longer any need to describe their procedures. But no matter in which country the police operate, their presence in fiction not only offers comfort in the suggestion that crime can and will be contained and the public will be protected. There is also an ideological narrative function: the omnipresence of the fictional police covertly disciplines the reader through the illusion that the police will, in the end, always get their man—or woman.

See also   *Contexts*: Detectives and Detection, Police and Policing; *Texts*: American Crime Fiction, Hard-Boiled Crime Fiction; *Criticism*: Cultural Materialism, Postmodernism.

Further reading

Dove, George N., *The Police Procedural* (Bowling Green, OH: Bowling Green State University Popular Press, 1982).

Klein, Kathleen Gregory (ed.), *Diversity and Detective Fiction* (Bowling Green, OH: Bowling Green State University Popular Press, 1999).

Knight, Stephen, *Crime Fiction since 1800: Detection, Death, Diversity* (Basingstoke: Palgrave Macmillan, 2010).

Nickerson, Catherine Ross (ed.), *Cambridge Companion to American Crime Fiction* (Cambridge: Cambridge University Press, 2010).

Panek, Leroy Lad, *An Introduction to the Detective Story* (Bowling Green, OH: Bowling Green State University Popular Press, 1987).

Panek, Leroy Lad, 'Post-war American Police Fiction' in *The Cambridge Companion to Crime Fiction*, ed. Martin Priestman (Cambridge: Cambridge University Press, 2003), pp. 155–171.

Worthington, Heather, *The Rise of the Detective in Early Nineteenth-Century Popular Fiction* (Basingstoke: Palgrave Macmillan, 2005).

3 Criticism: Approaches, Theory, Practice

Introduction

This introduction is intended to give a broad survey of literary criticism and its relationship to crime fiction generally. Covering briefly the main critical approaches and offering succinct explanations of the theories, it will give the reader a sense of the breadth and complexity of the topic, as well as demonstrate the interrelationships between different schools of literary criticism as it has developed over the twentieth century. The Introduction will also point readers towards other sources of information about the various theoretical perspectives. I have limited the entries on particular approaches to criticism to those that are particularly appropriate in the context of crime fiction and which are deliberately fitted to the Texts and Contexts discussed in the previous sections. Cultural materialism, feminism, postcolonialism and postmodernism are all products of, influenced by or incorporate aspects of the theoretical positions outlined below. Limiting the number of theoretical approaches in this way allows for a more detailed account of theory in practice which will, I hope, prove more useful to the reader than a longer series of necessarily attenuated accounts.

Literary criticism of crime fiction in the early days of the genre was, as with much nineteenth-century criticism, focused mainly on artistic merit measured by adherence to reality, uplifting moral message and educational impact. Consequently, crime fiction was generally roundly condemned for its subject matter, its potentially pernicious effect upon its readers, especially the lower social classes, younger generation and women, and as with sensation fiction for its privileging of plot over character and hence distance from reality. Literary luminaries such as Edward Bulwer Lytton defended the representation of crime in fiction, arguing that it permitted the exploration of the deepest modes of emotion and suffering in humanity; Charles Dickens was fascinated by crime and accounted for his frequent recourse to the subject by reasoning that crime was often evidence for or the consequence of social deprivation, while the motives that drive individuals to crime are part of the human condition.

It is not until the Golden Age of detective fiction, from the 1920s onwards, that there was a reconsideration of the literary status of the genre and consequently a recognition of the critical potential of crime fiction, although that recognition was often tinged with defensiveness and guilt at admitting one's addiction to detection. In 1901, G. K. Chesterton argued that detective fiction 'expressed some of the poetry of modern life' in his short article, 'In Defence of Detective Stories'. Dorothy L. Sayers's lengthy Introduction to the criminally inflected tales she selected for her *Great Stories of Detection, Mystery and Horror* (1928) offers a history of the genre but also implicitly makes the case for its literary significance. As she notes, 'it is remarkable how strong is the fascination of the higher type of detective story for the intellectually minded, among writers as well as readers'. T. S. Eliot acknowledged his interest in the genre with his comment, in the *Times Literary Supplement* of 1927, that Wilkie Collins's *The Moonstone* (1869) was 'the first and greatest of English detective novels'; W. H. Auden's interest resulted in 'The Guilty Vicarage' (1948), which drew parallels between crime fiction and the drama of Christian guilt; Sigmund Freud made comparisons between the work of the psychoanalyst and of the detective.

But it was to be those elements that had initially elicited the strongest opprobrium that finally made crime fiction a suitable literary case for treatment by critical theory. The very conventions, the strict structural patterns, the lack of emphasis on character, the revelations about society inherent in this popular and immediate genre brought it to the attention of academics and literary critics as the twentieth century progressed. Nonetheless, crime fiction was not part of the literary canon that, for many years, was the focus of academic literary criticism. The Victorian concentration on the worthiness of a text, often based on its closeness to 'real life' and its moral messages as well as its artistic merits, developed in the 1940s into what has become known as the 'Leavisite School' of criticism. A Cambridge academic, F. R. Leavis and his influential *The Great Tradition* (1948) were instrumental in forming the canon of English literature—a canon that certainly did not include crime fiction. Leavisite criticism valorised 'Englishness', realism and temporally transcendental humanistic enquiry, epitomised in fiction by Eliot, Austen, Conrad and James; Dickens was initially disregarded as populist (and occasionally criminal) writer but later admitted to the canon because of the moral qualities of his fiction. While Leavisite literary criticism has fallen into disuse—and in some critical circles disgrace—because of its liberal humanistic aspects, it is precisely the reading techniques employed in liberal humanism criticism that made possible later modes of literary theory.

Liberal humanism is, very loosely, a school of thought that evaluates literature's ability to represent timeless and universal truths about an essentially unchanging 'human nature'. While later criticism is more concerned with the ways that literature is implicated in the very formation and promulgation of the ideologies of humanism and realism and with the cultural politics of literature's social context, liberal humanist Leavisite criticism's insistence on close readings of (carefully selected) texts was instrumental in the development of textual reading and analysis that is central to many of the modern critical 'isms': Marxism; Cultural Realism; Structuralism; Feminism; Postcolonialism; Postmodernism; Poststructuralism. A further factor in the contribution to the development of modern critical theory was, in Britain, I. A. Richards' *Practical Criticism* (1929) and in America John C. Ransome's *The New Criticism* (1941). Their approach to literature was to read the text in isolation, divorced from historical, political or theoretical contexts, and to examine the 'literary artefact's' structural relationships, form and language in order to reveal its 'literariness' or aesthetic value.

In parallel with developments in Britain and America was the work of the Russian Formalists such as Viktor Shlovsky and Roman Jakobson, whose linguistic approach to literature was influenced by a series of lectures given by Ferdinand Saussure, later published as *Course in General Linguistics* (1913). In the lectures, Saussure argued that language was a system of signs, with each sign made up of a signifier—the physical representative, for example, a word, sound or image—and a signified—the concept or object that the signifier evokes. Perhaps most radically, Saussure declared that the link between the two elements was purely arbitrary, referring to the ways in which different languages have different words attached to the same objects or concepts: the word 'horse' in English becomes '*cheval*' in French, although the animal is the same, for example. This unpicking of meaning at the level of language enabled the Russian Formalists to apply similar logic to literature, particularly poetry, and to demonstrate how literary texts defamiliarised everyday language. This approach shared the close reading practices of the New Criticism in the West, but the Formalists, as their name suggests, took a more scientific approach to the formal workings of language. It was also in 1930s and 40s Russia that the critic Mikhail Bakhtin's theories concerning literature appeared; he moved away from the Formalists' insistence on the formal structures of texts—metre, rhyme, narrative—and considered that the socio-political context and content of texts were equally as important as their structures. Bakhtin's concept of the dialogic text, in which multiple voices interact and occasionally conflict and so disrupt meaning, is more fully developed in the later poststructuralist theory of the 1970s and 80s.

The 1960s saw radical changes in society generally and in culture and the arts specifically, most evidently in the gradual erosion of the hierarchical distinction between the categories of 'high' and 'popular' culture and its artefacts. This is an important moment for crime fiction; as popular literature, it now became, finally, a potentially suitable case for literary criticism. In terms of literary theory, it was the development of structuralism, beginning in France in the 1950s, that would make it possible for popular fiction to be accorded equal status with canonical literature. Structuralism was not concerned only with literature, but more broadly, and in similar fashion to Saussure's concept of language as a system, with what its practitioners perceived to be the structures of signs which constituted the human experience. Anthropologist Claude Lévi-Strauss explored the structures and role of myth and the evolution of tradition in societies and cultures while in his polemic text *Mythologies* (1957), Roland Barthes, another leading contributor to structuralism and later poststructuralism, focused on literature and the way it represents the sign systems that structure society and the individual's experience of the world. More practically, the literary theorist and philosopher Tzvetan Todorov applied structuralist theory to texts in *The Poetics of Prose* (1977), in which there is a chapter devoted to detective fiction, suggesting precisely how the conventions of the genre lend themselves to critical analysis.

All the different strands discussed above contribute to and are articulated in many-faceted poststructuralism. Perhaps the final blow to liberal humanism and the beginning of modern critical theory's concern with how texts of all kinds make meaning are inter-related at the level of language and are implicated in the production and maintenance of ideology and hence power in society came with Barthes' essay on 'The Death of the Author'(1968). Far from the author having authority over the text and thus limiting interpretation, Barthes suggested that meaning is instead located in the act of reading; that the reader is the point at which the multiplicity, polyphony and intertextuality of the text come into focus. For Barthes, 'the birth of the reader must be at the cost of the death of the author'. In 1969, Michel Foucault, another important contributor to poststructuralist theory, would resuscitate the author in 'What is an Author?', but not as the author of meaning. Rather, the author for Foucault is part of the proliferation of meaning and signification generated by a text and its contexts. Poststructuralism also owes much to the work of Jacques Derrida and his focus on the fragmentary nature of texts—Barthes refers to the text as 'a tissue of quotations drawn from the innumerable centres of culture' (1968)—and their multiplicity of meaning. Derrida's seminal work was *Of Grammatology* (1967), which challenged Saussure's semiotic system of an inseparable, although socially constructed, signifier and signified pairing, and instead posited a theory in which the signifier not only has no direct relation to that which it signifies but also where meaning is constructed in its difference from other signifiers—'dog' is 'dog' because it is not 'cog' or 'bog'. Derrida's approach to the text has become known as 'deconstruction', not in the sense of destruction but as a process of analysis that reveals the fluidity of language and the uncertainty of meaning. Without the possibility of fixing meaning, the text is open to multiple and potentially contradictory interpretations.

The notion of interpretation is also apparent in psychoanalytic criticism, which draws on Sigmund Freud's theorising of the human psyche. Freud claimed that the mind is composed of three elements: the conscious (superego), the preconscious (ego) and the unconscious (id). The superego and the ego are where accessible thoughts and memories are stored, but the unconscious is where unaccessible and repressed material is kept. These repressed ideas and thoughts, often concerned with sexuality and desire, are constantly seeking to escape the unconscious and are apparent in dreams and what Freud called 'parapraxes', linguistic slips of the tongue or the pen. Because they are repressed, such thoughts do not appear in literal but metaphorical or symbolic form, requiring interpretation if the individual is to understand them. In this way, psychoanalysis is analogous to literary criticism, and early proponents of psychoanalytic literary criticism in effect attempted to read the 'unconscious' of the text and often of its author. However, Freud's psychoanalytic theory was strongly based in patriarchy, focusing on masculine psychosexual development, with its Oedipus theory in which boys unconsciously wished to kill their fathers and sexually possess their mothers and where girls are aware of their inferiority, signified by their lack of a penis and hence suffer from penis envy, which can only be rectified when they fulfil their proper role and have a baby which substitutes for the penis.

The sexism inherent in Freud's work aroused the ire of feminists, while his supposedly scientific approach to interpreting the signs and symbols in dreams and slips of the tongue proves to be somewhat arbitrary and at times simplistic or even reductive. His example of a case of parapraxis in *The Psychopathology of Everyday Life* (1901) bears an uncanny similarity in its associative account and explanation to the apparent mind-reading performed by C. Auguste Dupin in Edgar Allan Poe's proto-detective fiction 'The Murders in the Rue Morgue' (1841) and is equally questionable.

The sexual focus of Freud's work is evident in *The Interpretation of Dreams* (1900), where he avers that dreams featuring sticks or snakes are clearly concerned with the penis in some way, while those about cupboards or empty rooms are about the vagina or womb. His interpretations are often convincing but perhaps say more about Freud than they do about his patients.

Significantly, though, psychoanalytic criticism has used crime fiction as a vehicle for its analysis. Marie Bonaparte, a disciple of Freud, wrote a psychoanalytic analysis of Edgar Allan Poe's short story, 'The Purloined Letter' in *The Life and Works of Edgar Allan Poe* (1949). Here, she declared the stolen letter at the centre of the narrative represented the maternal penis—or rather the absent penis of the mother. Bonaparte supported this reading with the location of the letter, which is hidden in full view in a letter rack hanging above the fireplace; the fireplace of course represents the female genitals and so the letter is the imagined absent penis. French psychoanalyst Jacques Lacan, whose work has been very influential in modern literary criticism, also drew on Poe's story in his 'Seminar on "The Purloined Letter" ', in *Ecrits* (1966). The importance of Lacan's ideas to literary theory is that he built on Freud's concept of the unconscious, but argued that the unconscious is produced by and structured like language; the unconscious does not therefore precede language but is in effect made possible by it.

Psychoanalytic theory is also associated with crime fiction by Geraldine Pederson-Krag in 'Detective Stories and the Primal Scene' (1949). The 'primal scene' is, in Freudian terms, the child's real or imagined observation of his or her parents' act of sexual intercourse. Pederson-Krag maps this onto the detective story: a secret between two people resulting in a murder (the sexual act and the parent perceived negatively by the child); a detective (the child), and a series of observations and events, or clues (what the child sees), which the observer-detective must put together in order to work out what has happened. Her essay references Arthur Conan Doyle and Sherlock Holmes in a similar context. More recently, Richard Raskin takes a psychoanalytic approach to crime fiction in 'The Pleasures and Politics of Detective Fiction' (1992); while philosopher/poststructuralist/cultural theorist Slavoj Zizek turns to detective fiction in *Looking Awry: An Introduction to Jacques Lacan Through Popular Culture* (1991), in which his chapter entitled 'Two Ways to Avoid the Real of Desire' is sub-titled 'The Sherlock Holmes Way' and 'The Philip Marlowe Way'.

Zizek's multi-disciplinary approach to reading culture draws upon the work of Karl Marx among many other philosophers, as has literary criticism. The formalist and structuralist theorists were focused on the text and how it made meaning, with social, historical and political contexts of lesser importance, but poststructuralism is particularly interested also in the ways in which language and texts are implicated in structures of power and ideology. Marx was not himself a literary theorist, but his concept of the economic basis of society and his perception of history as a class struggle implicitly raised interesting questions about the role of literature. In the Marxist model, there is an economic base to society—the material means of production, distribution and exchange—and a superstructure—the non-material aspects of society such as culture, art—including literature—religion and so on. In the 1970s and in the context of poststructuralism, the French Marxist philosopher Louis Althusser elaborated on this relationship in terms of ideology and power. Ideology here is the system of the values and assumptions that underpin a society, and in 'Ideology and Ideological State Apparatuses: Notes Towards an Investigation' (1970), Althusser explored the role of ideology in State power and State control. He made a distinction between State power in society, which he argued is maintained openly through 'repressive structures': the courts, prisons, the army, the police and State control, which is more subtly imposed, through ideological structures, or 'State ideological apparatuses': the family, schools, religion and art (including literature), which invisibly support the political and State status quo. The individual subject internalises the values and assumptions unquestioningly as the norm in a process that Althusser calls 'interpellation', in which the individual is persuaded to see him or herself as an independent agent with free choice. Literature is implicated in this process, popular literature particularly strongly as it is disseminated widely and represents mainstream values—and so ideologies.

Aspects of Marxism and its Althusserian and other variants have been appropriated by various strands of poststructuralism and postmodernism and indeed incorporated into literary criticism more widely. The best-known modern proponent of Marxist literary criticism is perhaps Terry Eagleton, although he has written widely on literary theory generally. Marxist literary analysis exposes the ideologies of a society that are, consciously or unconsciously, woven into the text. For Althusser, literature perpetuates these ideologies while for his erstwhile student, French Marxist theorist Pierre Macherey, it is the silences, the gaps and absences in a text that paradoxically speak of the ideologies that its narrative seeks to conceal. Marxist theory is particularly influential on the development of cultural materialism, which takes its name from a phrase coined by Raymond Williams in *Marxism and Literature* (1977) and which was first used to denote a particular approach to reading literature by Jonathan Dollimore and Alan Sinfield in *Political Shakespeare: Essays in Cultural*

Materialism (1985). Williams was influenced by the political and cultural values of the 'New Left' in 1950s Britain, and he insisted on the importance of the relationship between literature and society: cultural materialism reads texts in the contexts of their historical, social, cultural and perhaps most significantly, political moments. It is a peculiarly British critical practice; the American equivalent is New Historicism, pioneered by Stephen Greenblatt in 1982 (*The Power of Forms in the English Renaissance*). As its name suggests, New Historicism is more firmly focused on the historical moment; Greenblatt argues for what he calls the 'mutual permeability of the literary and the historical' whilst always recognising the subjectivity of the reader in the present and of the writer, whether of literature or historical document, in the past.

History and indeed Marxism have, though, been dismissed by postmodernism as representing what in *The Postmodern Condition* (1979) Jean-François Lyotard calls 'metanarratives' or 'grand narratives', that is narratives that claim to have authority over, objectively explain or interpret the truth or meaning of human behaviour. History can never be objectively recorded, if only because it tends to be produced by those in power who have a particular and therefore subjective perspective on events. Equally, postmodernism suggests that Marxism's focus on the power relations between social classes subsumes other sites of tension and oppression, especially in terms of gender and race. Drawing in part on poststructuralist theories concerning the instability of language and meaning and deconstructing metanarratives, including that of high or canonical literature, postmodern theory developed in tandem with and has contributed to a more liberal cultural climate. This in turn has made possible the articulation of what might loosely be called identity politics; postmodernism allows previously marginalised groups in society to construct their own narratives and to speak back to the centre. It is within the context of postmodernism that other 'isms' such as feminism and postcolonialism have also developed: postmodernism made it possible to question dominant discourses such as patriarchy or empire. It could be argued that in its theorisation of the world and in its insistence that all modes of thought are simply discursive constructs, postmodernism is itself in danger of becoming a metanarrative. But, as with all the theories discussed here, postmodernism is just one of many 'tools' that can be used to unravel a text and reveal how it makes meanings.

The metaphorical 'toolbox' of critical theory is very well equipped; there are too many 'isms' and other modes of literary analysis to include here. 'Tools' that might be considered more practical or scientific include narratology and stylistic criticism, which are both concerned with the technicalities of texts in terms not only of language but grammar, syntax and narrative structure. Narratology was heavily influenced by the Russian Formalists and its practitioners are less concerned with the meaning so texts than with revealing and explaining the general characteristics of narrative structure. Gérard Genette's seminal *Narrative Discourse* (1972) set in place a number of categories of narrative structure, such as *récit*, or the sequence in which events are related in a text, and *histoire*, which is how those events would have happened chronologically. Using these categories in combination with others—concerned with narrative perspective, narrator, language, action and settings—narratologists can explore the technical aspects of narrative, looking at how rather than perhaps why the narrative makes meaning. With its strong narrative conventions, crime or more specifically detective fiction, lends itself to narratological analysis.

Similarly, stylistics, which uses the methods of linguistics to analyse texts, finds crime fiction particularly suited to its demands, as Christiana Gregoriou's *Deviance in Contemporary Crime Fiction* (2007) demonstrates. Gregoriou draws upon both narratology and stylistics in her analysis of how and why crime fiction is textually deviant. However, in accord with other, more comprehensive guides to literary theory, stylistics does not have an entry in this text. As Peter Barry points out in *Beginning Theory: An Introduction to Literary and Cultural Theory* (1995; 2002), stylistics has resisted the postmodern indeterminacy that is central to much modern literary criticism and has maintained a positivist stance. Knowledge, in stylistics theory, can be accumulated through empirical investigation carried out by disinterested enquirers. Such an approach, while interesting and of practical use for the student wishing to gain a stronger understanding of the technicalities of texts, is out of alignment with the approaches and arguments articulated elsewhere in this book, where the emphasis is firmly on the history, politics, culture, themes, issues and concepts of crime fiction.

Cultural materialism

Andrew Bennett and Nicholas Royle's excellent *An Introduction to Literature: Criticism and Theory* 4th ed. (Harlow: Pearson Longman, 2009), succinctly sums up cultural materialism as an approach to literary criticism that 'focuses on the material conditions of the production and reception of literary texts' and describes its practitioners as being 'concerned to expose the ideological and political dimensions of such texts'. The immediacy with which crime fiction responds to its cultural moment and its concern with the deviant make it particularly suited to cultural materialist analysis. The genre deals with that which disrupts society, often in the process revealing that society's ideologies, while what constitutes crime can itself be determined by ideology and by politics. The concept of literature representing universal truths, unaffected by the historical moment and conditions of its production and of its consumption, can clearly be seen to be overturned in crime fiction, which precisely reveals the changing cultural constructions and perceptions of crime, criminality and even of the detective.

The school of cultural materialist criticism came into being in Britain, developing from the Marxist-inflected literary criticism of Welsh academic Raymond Williams, articulated in *Marxism and Literature* (1977); *Problems in Materialism and Culture* (1980); *Culture* (1981). Williams argued that literature is one social practice amongst many and is not something that can be separated or is disengaged from society. This concept has been further developed in the work of British academics Jonathan Dollimore and Alan Sinfield (*Political Shakespeare: Essays in Cultural Materialism*, 1985) and the practices of cultural materialism have underpinned much of the work of Catherine Belsey (e.g., *Shakespeare and the Loss of Eden: the Construction of Family Values in Early Modern Culture*, 1999). Cultural materialism developed at about the same time and shares some ideas and practices with the American school of thought called 'New Historicism' which, as its name suggests, is concerned with history in relation to literature and which endeavours to locate texts within their historical contexts. It does this by exploring a wide variety of historical sources other than accounts of history or literary texts themselves; legal, economic, anthropological, scientific, religious documents and indeed artefacts are all grist to the new historicist's or cultural theorist's mill as he or she rereads the literary text and reconsiders its meanings in a social and economic context. Of particular interest, particularly to the cultural materialist, are recovered histories of those who have been marginalised or excluded from society, and of course this includes the criminal or the criminalised.

The Marxist influence in cultural materialism is evident in its insistence on the subversive potential of literature, that is, the ways in which literature reveals the dominant ideas and ideals of society in any given moment and equally therefore exposes the ideologies that invisibly support that society and maintain the social, often class-inflected structures of power. Perhaps above all, it is cultural materialism's recognition of and emphasis upon social identity and its determinants—not only class but also often gender, race, ethnicity and so on—that distinguish it from new historicism. But both share an analytical practice that anthropologist Clifford Geertz called 'thick description' (*The Interpretation of Cultures*,

1973), in which culture is defined as comprising a web of signification that the analyst seeks to untangle.

Michel Foucault, a French philosopher and historian, has also been influential in the development of cultural materialism and new historicism, both in his insistence on drawing upon numerous and disparate historical sources and in his emphasis on and exploration of power and resistance in society. Foucault's theorisation of the historical development and construction of the discourses, which he describes as being 'groups of statements which provide a language for talking about [...] a particular topic at a particular historical moment', of sexuality, madness and, most importantly in terms of crime fiction, discipline (social control) in society, demonstrates how power is maintained through these discourses but also how, simultaneously, resistance is generated. As Foucault observes in *Discipline and Punish: the Birth of the Prison* (1975, trans. 1977), while sovereign or State power (discipline) is literally embodied in the eighteenth-century criminal whose execution converts him from an individual into the signifier of his crime, the condemned man's appearance on what is effectively a stage in front of a huge audience and his last dying words briefly but subversively construct him as the hero of his own narrative.

Cultural materialism, then, locates literary texts in the broad context of its historical moment; it takes into account its reception and consumption as well as its production; it is concerned with the recovered histories of the marginalised; it seeks to reveal the disruptive and the subversive aspects of society represented in literature; it relies not on metanarratives but on marginalia and overlooked cultural artefacts and sources; it recognises the subjectivity of the reader and of what has been written; it exposes and explores issues of power and ideology; it considers the past and its relationship to the present. Perhaps above all, as far as crime fiction is concerned, it reads history as a text and as comprised of texts; it rejects hierarchical distinctions between high and low literature, 'literary' texts and 'non-literary' texts, and it considers literature to be one form of text circulating among many others—political, scientific, legal, economic and so on. All these texts and all these categories are, for cultural materialists, produced and shaped by a society's dominant cultural and socioeconomic structures. Cultural materialism is above all political, particularly in its emphasis upon identity politics; here, feminism and postcolonialism have been influential.

Cultural materialists have tended to focus on literary texts from the past, particularly the Renaissance period, and crime narratives from history readily make themselves open to cultural materialist readings. It is illuminating to read the early fictional police anecdotes, *Recollections of a*

Detective Police Officer (1856), supposedly the autobiographical records of its protagonist, 'Waters', but in actuality written by William Russell, in the context of the ideology, politics and economics of the relatively recently formed Metropolitan Police Detective force (1842). Equally interesting is to consider the negative representation of the police in the early Sherlock Holmes stories in the context of the political row and major police reorganisation that occurred as a consequence of high-level corruption in the detective force in the late 1800s, as discussed by R. F. Stewart in *The Great Detective Case of 1877: A Study in Victorian Police Corruption* (2000). The *Newgate Calendars* are as much about economic control and class anxieties as they are about the containment of the criminal and, in their open support of State power may seem entirely to advocate the social status quo. But in fact, their representations of crime and criminality often function to subvert social certainties concerning crime, as in the case of Madame Churchill, hanged at Tyburn in 1708 for the crime of being present at the scene of a murder and so considered to be an accomplice. R. Sanders' *The Complete Newgate Calendar* (1760) implicitly acknowledges its anxiety about the verdict and sentence in its vilification of Deborah Churchill's character, especially in terms of her sexuality; in the climate of penal reform in the early 1800s, George Theodore Wilkinson's *Newgate Calendar Improved* (1816) is more open in its uncertainty that justice has been done, offering a more sympathetic depiction of Deborah and declaring there to be 'some hardship in her suffering the utmost rigour of the law'. Reading these accounts in combination with legal and penal documentation and with reference to accounts of the same crime in different media and in different moments reveals the ideological aspects of and political investment in the construction of crime and criminality.

Although Agatha Christie's texts may seem largely devoid of historical or political content, her first novel, *The Mysterious Affair at Styles* (1916), is set in the First World War but shows little concern with external events, while *The Murder of Roger Ackroyd* (1926) ignores the looming economic crisis that would result in the Great Depression (1929–32). Nonetheless, a cultural materialist reading that considers the historical, social, economic and political conditions in which the texts were produced and consumed reveals much: a predominantly female readership; evidence of eroding class barriers; a privileging of the feminine and the domestic; anxieties concerning social identity, all of which respond to the real conditions pertaining at the time, such as the diminution of the male population in Britain in the wake of the war and the migration of female domestic workers into industry. Simultaneously, the extent to which these texts represent the desire to retain pre-war values and support the prevailing ideologies also becomes apparent. Perhaps recognition of the impending economic crisis is after all visible in the foregrounding of money, property and inheritance: in both texts, these are the motives for the murders at the centre of the narratives. The dissemination of Christie's texts in the period is also culturally significant, as they circulated in the State-supported public libraries, a mark of approval that perhaps responds to the conservative values the texts espoused. As with the modern re-stagings of Shakespeare's plays, which are of particular interest to the cultural materialist, so too are the many dramatisations of Christie's detective fiction, whether on stage or the television. While many of the social and political issues contemporary to the novels' dates of publication remain, modern interpretations respond equally to modern social, economic and political conditions.

More recent crime fiction is equally open to cultural materialist readings. Val McDermid's early crime writing is noted for its concern with gender politics (the Lindsay Gordon series, 1987–2003), but her later series, loosely linked by detectives Carol Jordan and Tony Hill (1995–present), has wider social and historical interest for the cultural materialist. In *The Mermaids Singing* (1995), McDermid's focus on identity politics continues, but in a post-feminist context her text is less centred on women's rights and issues, although Carol Jordan is still shown to be a woman fighting to be treated equally in the chauvinistic world of the police. Rather, the narrative explores postmodern perspectives on gender and sexuality, particularly contemporary attitudes to homosexuality in the post-AIDS era, and issues surrounding transsexuality and transgender. The late twentieth-century discourses of science and medicine become important here, and *The Mermaids Singing* might be read against these but also other elements of cultural production—literature, film, autobiography and so on—that explore similar themes. There is another aspect of the text that is attractive to the cultural materialist; McDermid's text explores in fiction the possibility of a female serial sex killer. The historical context of this concept can be tracked back to the case of Fred and Rosemary West, arrested and tried in 1994 for the torture, rape and murder of twelve young women.

Rosemary West was charged with ten of these atrocities; she never confessed and the evidence against her was largely circumstantial. But after Fred West committed suicide while on remand, she became the target of public opprobrium and was declared to be a female serial sex killer. In 1996, Debbie Cameron discussed the case in two articles in *Trouble and Strife: the Radical Feminist Magazine*: 'Wanted: The Female Serial Killer' and 'Motives and Meanings', an attempted feminist analysis of Rosemary West. Reading *The Mermaids Singing* in the context of this case and the debates it aroused demonstrate the potential of popular literature to engage with and reveal social anxieties and tensions generated in part by feminism and by postmodern conceptions of the fluidity of gender and sexuality in the late twentieth century. Ultimately, McDermid's text refuses fully to represent the female serial sex killer; significantly, in the television series based loosely on the book (*The Wire in the Blood*, 2002–8), the serial killer survives and retains a female identity but is represented as insane, suggesting that society, at least in Britain, can accept transsexuality but is still unable to accept the female serial sex killer. *The Mermaids Singing* and other modern crime fiction offers much to the cultural materialist, as does criminography of the past. The criminal is marginal to and marginalised by society; criminality is itself socially and politically as well as legally constructed and the discourses surrounding crime intersect with many others. The popularity of crime narratives makes it particularly useful to the cultural materialist as its consumption occurs across society and increasingly across nations in an increasingly globalised community.

See also   *Contexts*: Crime and Criminality, Gender and Sexuality, Police and Policing; *Texts*: Early Criminography, Feminist Crime Fiction, Historical Crime Fiction.

Further reading

Barry, Peter, *Beginning Theory: An Introduction to Literary and Cultural Theory*, 2nd ed. (Manchester: Manchester University Press, 2002).

Milner, Andrew, *Re-imagining Cultural Studies: The Promise of Cultural Materialism* (London: Sage, 2002).

Wilson, Scott, *Cultural Materialism: Theory and Practice* (Oxford: Blackwell, 1995).

Feminism

Feminism is, broadly, both a philosophical and political movement concerned with challenging and changing the treatment and representation of women in society. What became known as 'the woman question' (the term 'feminism' only came into common use in the 1890s in Britain) had been the subject of debate from at least the late eighteenth century with the publication of Mary Wollstonecraft's *Vindication of the Rights of Women* (1792), which observed that marriage, for women, could be equated to slavery. Feminism has always worked to expose patriarchal bias in society and in the media in which society is represented back to itself and to suggest how women might escape the constraints imposed upon them as a consequence of their sex. Action in support of feminism ranges from acquiring legal and political rights to achieving recognition for women's writing and the search for a feminine mode of writing, as discussed by, amongst others, French theorist Hélène Cixous, whose '*écriture féminine*' (women's writing) is formulated in *The Newly Born Woman* (1975).

Literature has played an important role in the development of feminism. Seminal and polemical works include Wollstonecraft's *Vindication*; Virginia Woolf's *A Room of One's Own* (1929); Simone de Beauvoir's *Le deuxième sexe* (1949), translated into English as *The Second Sex* (1953). In the 1960s and 70s, literature itself came under scrutiny in feminism's exploration of the cultural and ideological construction of women: Kate Millet's *Sexual Politics* (1970) looked at the sexual power-politics of canonical texts by male authors such as Henry Miller and D. H. Lawrence; Germaine Greer's *The Female Eunuch* (1970) argued that romantic novels contributed to the disempowerment of women in the genre's representations of a false female experience. From the analysis of the sexist ideologies inherent in representation of women in the male-authored literary canon, in the 1970s there was a move to the exploration of women's writing and the woman writer. Elaine Showalter coined the word 'gynocriticism' to describe this female-centred approach and it was the subject of Showalter's *A Literature of Their Own: British Women Novelists from Brontë to Lessing* (1977) and of Sandra Gilbert and Susan Gubar's *The Madwoman in the Attic: The Woman Writer and the Nineteenth-Century Literary Imagination* (1979). Showalter and Gilbert and Gubar's texts made revisionist readings of the work of women writers with established literary reputations and that of lesser-known and marginalised female authors.

Early feminist literary criticism focused on the white, Western tradition of writing and was open to the criticism that in attempting to speak for all women it ignored the experiences of some. The concentration on gender issues was at the expense of other issues such as class, race, sexuality, nationality and so on. From the 1980s onwards, the drive of feminism has been to incorporate these other issues, with the work of black writers such as bell hooks (*Ain't I a Woman: Black Women and Feminism*, 1982; *Feminist Theory: From Margin to Centre*, 1984) drawing attention to and redressing the implicit association of woman with *white* woman. Nationality and sexuality have also been foregrounded, especially in Third World feminism and lesbian feminism. A key text focused on issues of gender and sexuality is Judith Butler's *Gender Trouble: Feminism and the Subversion of Identity* (1990), which makes the case that gender and sexuality are culturally constructed and as such are performed rather than innate biological givens.

Feminism is now generally considered in terms of three movements, or waves. The first 'wave' is concerned with legal and political rights for women and covers the period from the late eighteenth century to the first quarter of the twentieth century and the enfranchisement of women (partial in 1918 and full in 1928 in Britain). Second-wave feminism takes off in the 1960s and is broadly concerned with more personal issues such as domestic abuse, pornography, contraception and abortion and gender discrimination in the work-place. The emphasis on the personal and its association with politics led to the feminist rallying-cry of 'the personal is the political'. Third-wave feminism is the current phase and has a global and plural approach to women in the context of gender, sexuality, race, nationality and the relationship between power and gendered subjectivity.

Crime fiction has interesting and important discursive exchanges with feminism; the genre developed over the same period as the movement and there are particular resonances between second-wave feminism and criminography from the 1970s and 80s. It is in this period that the female detective provides a space in which to express many of the political concerns of the feminist movement. Writers such as Sara Paretsky and Sue Grafton in America and, in more muted fashion in Britain, Val McDermid, Liza Cody, Sarah Dunant and P. D. James, with her attenuated feminist detective Cordelia Gray, appropriated the strongly masculine hard-boiled genre of crime fiction in order to demonstrate that the female detective could be equally as effective, that a woman could successfully do what the hard-boiled texts suggested was a man's job. At the same time, the behaviour of these female detectives suggested equality in other spheres, such as sexuality, with the various protagonists often enjoying an active, and not always heterosexual, sex life outside marriage. Woven into these feminist crime narratives is a critique of patriarchy, apparent in the claim to female autonomy and the implicit demands for parity with men in all spheres of life.

By the end of the 1980s, the feisty, feminist detective was beginning to develop in other, interesting directions in response to feminist-engendered changes in society. Crime fiction offered a space in which to represent other, doubly marginalised groups of women and texts featuring black female detectives, other racial and ethnic minority women sleuths and lesbian investigators began to appear. An early example of a black female detective narrative is Dolores Komo's *Clio Brown, Private Investigator* (1988). As the title perhaps suggests, the middle-aged, plump protagonist's colour is of more significance than her gender. Black lesbian investigators appeared throughout the 1990s in America, including a police officer (Eleanor Taylor Bland's Marti MacAllister in *Dead*

Time, 1992) and the college-educated Virginia Keely in Nikki Baker's *In the Game*, 1991; *The Lavender House Murder*, 1992 and *Long Good-byes*, 1993. Texts such as these represented empowered black women and so carried a muted political message as well as explored issues around female identity. However, the four (1992–2000) Blanche White novels of BarbaraNeely combine feminist, social and racial politics with crime fiction in the representation of their ironically named, very and defiantly black African-American working class protagonist. In Britain the emphasis perhaps remained more strongly on gender issues, often articulated through a lesbian protagonist as in Val McDermid's Lindsay Gordon series (1996–2003; six novels), or Stella Duffy's Saz Martin series (1994–2005; five novels).

Nineteenth-century crime narratives, however, offer a rich source of material concerned with women and their representation in the fiction of the period which resonates with the concerns of first-wave feminism. The nineteenth-century feminine ideal of 'the angel in the house' articulated in Coventry Patmore's verse sequence of the same name (1854–6), in which woman is shown to be happiest when in her proper position, that is in the domestic sphere as sexually contained, dependent wife and nurturing mother, implicitly sets up its opposite. Those women who would or could not conform to the ideal were, in effect, demonised or, in crime-focused narratives, criminalised literally and/or morally, and punished for their improper femininity. In this context, the case against the eponymous heroine of Mary E. Braddon's *Lady Audley's Secret* (1862) seems clear: she is a bigamist who twice attempts to commit murder. Superficially, Lady Audley (wife of Sir Michael Audley and also of Mr George Talboys) epitomises the perfect Victorian wife and seems a suitable heroine for a novel. Blonde, beautiful and devoted to her husband, she fully conforms to the 'angel in the house' model of womanhood. But the text reveals that she has deserted her child, faked her own death, entered into a bigamous marriage and tried to murder both her first husband George and Robert Audley, the detective in the story, in an effort to retain her status as Lady Audley. It seems that Lady Audley is doubly criminal—literally, but also morally, as implied by the desertion of her child, her deceitfulness, and above all by her independence of action.

But again a feminist reading alters the perspective. The context for *Lady Audley's Secret* is the contemporary debate about the divorce laws which at the time were heavily in favour of men (the 1857 Matrimonial Causes Act made it possible for men to divorce their wives on the grounds of adultery while wives had to prove adultery *and* desertion or cruelty or bigamy or incest). Braddon was herself a victim of these laws as her life partner, John Maxwell, was married, but his wife had been declared insane and committed to an asylum and divorce was not an option. Seen in this light, Lady Audley's actions can be read differently. Encouraged by social values and internalised gender ideology to believe that her beauty will ensure a good marriage and social position, she discovers that her husband, George Talboys, has been disinherited for making what his father considers to be an unsuitable match. Subsequently George disappears, going to Australia to seek his fortune but leaving his wife without financial support and with a child. With no knowledge of her husband's fate, Helen Talboys strives to make her way in a world where the only roles suitable for one of her class are wife or governess. Working as the latter, she barely hesitates when the opportunity comes to exchange her role for that of Sir Michael Audley's wife, convincing herself that George must be dead. Her subsequent attempt to murder George on his sudden return is made in order to preserve her position as Lady Audley, as is her later attack on Robert Audley, who is close to revealing her true identity and consequently her bigamy.

Finally confronted with her guilt, Lady Audley and the text collude in declaring her to be mad rather than bad, but it is significant that the doctor, called to confirm her insanity, on listening to her story declares that he can find 'no madness [...]. When she found herself in a desperate position [...] she employed intelligent means, and she carried out a conspiracy which required coolness and deliberation [...]. There is no madness in that.' But there is deviance in her independence and her intelligence and in the exposure of the ease with which she recognises and uses the masculine idealisation of femininity. Fortunately for the men in the narrative, Lady Audley admits that her mother had fallen into madness after the birth of her child and that Lady Audley fears she too will become insane: with relief, the doctor has her committed to an asylum. The text closes with order restored, represented by the marriage of Robert Audley and Clara Talboys, the birth of their child and the reconciliation of George and his son. The picture painted is one of domestic bliss and proper, orderly femininity but, as Lady Audley herself has amply demonstrated, it is precisely a picture, a construct. The real secret in *Lady Audley's Secret* is that the 'angel in the house' is a cultural construct and not woman's natural mode of being.

See also *Contexts*: Crime and Criminality, Detectives and Detection, Gender and Sexuality, Race, Colour and Creed; *Texts*: American Crime Fiction, Early Criminography, Feminist Crime Fiction.

Further reading

Belsey, Catherine and Jane Moore (eds), *The Feminist Reader: Essays in Gender and the Politics of Literary Criticism*, 2nd ed. (Basingstoke: Macmillan, 1997).
Eagleton, Mary (ed.), *Feminist Literary Theory: A Reader*, 3rd ed. (Oxford: Blackwell, 2011).
Moi, Tori, *Sexual/Textual Politics*, 2nd ed. (London: Routledge, 2002).
Robbins, Ruth, *Literary Feminisms* (Basingstoke: Macmillan, 2000).

Postcolonialism

The alphabetical sequence of these entries necessarily places postcolonialism after feminism, but there is in fact a relationship, a synchronicity, between the two 'isms'. As with other 'isms'—cultural materialism, feminism, poststructuralism and postmodernism—postcolonialism developed partly in reaction to the tenets of liberal humanism, with its insistence on universal human values that were, mysteriously, white, Western and male. Liberal humanism ignored, elided and/or silenced the 'other' in all its many forms, including women in the Western world and the male and female inhabitants of much of the rest of the globe, and denied other races and ethnicities individual identity, subsuming them into often Anglo- or Eurocentric linguistically and culturally constructed conglomerates of nation or country. This is particularly significant when considered in the context of colonialism, in which Britain and other mainly European countries annexed vast swathes of the world and, in colonising these other nations imposed not only the rule but also the culture and values of the coloniser upon them.

Broadly speaking, postcolonialism is a catholic collection of theories and interdisciplinary approaches and practices, from Marxism to feminism, psychoanalytic theory to poststructuralism, and from sociology to anthropology, philosophy to literature, all concerned with colonialism, its effects and its aftermath, hence the umbrella term 'postcolonialism'. In actuality, the term incorporates three separate elements: colonialism, postcolonialism and neocolonialism. Colonialism is self-evidently focused on the historical moment, process and effects of colonisation; postcolonialism deals with what happens after colonialism, while neocolonialism looks at the continuing effects of colonialism once colonial rule has ended. From its relatively narrow initial focus on the mainly nineteenth and early twentieth-century colonisation associated with imperial expansion, postcolonialism now includes the discourses of displacement and multiculturalism consequent upon slavery and migration. Central to postcolonialism are issues of race, identity, hybridity and Diaspora. More importantly as far as literature is concerned, is voice; that is, the ability of the colonised to speak back to the coloniser and so lay claim to and assert a non-colonial identity. The significance of this in terms of literature is evident in the title of one of the first major theoretical accounts of postcolonial texts: *The Empire Writes Back* (Bill Ashcroft, Gareth Griffiths and Helen Tiffin, 2nd ed., London: Routledge, 2002 (1989)).

Postcolonialism shares with cultural materialism an interest in the histories of silenced and marginalised minorities, while one of the founding figures of postcolonial criticism, cultural theorist Edward Said, published his ground-breaking reappraisal of English literature, *Orientalism*, in 1978, just one year after Raymond Williams first articulated his ideas on cultural materialism. Said explored the role of literature in representing the East—the Orient—and implicitly British colonial attitudes and beliefs. Such literature, he suggested, effectively created an Anglocentric version of the Orient, a version often at odds with the reality, sometimes romanticised, sometimes demonised, but always with an implicit political agenda. In representations of the colonies/colonised in English literature of the nineteenth century, there is always a hierarchical binary opposition which locates the foreign as 'other', inferior and potentially threatening, thus fostering a sense of British national identity, establishing Britain as superior and implicitly justifying its colonial expansion. Literature also contributes to cultural imperialism, or the influence or domination of one nation's culture over others: canonical English literature—Shakespeare, the Romantic poets, the nineteenth-century novel and so on—becomes the reading material of the colonised people, often via the educational system of the colonial possession, and transmits the colonising nation's history, ideologies and values.

The effect of this cultural imposition, of the overlaying of the colonised country's own value system and the colonised subject's internalisation of the new ideologies and values, results, according to Frantz Fanon, another of postcolonialism's founding fathers, in the implicit devaluation of the colonised country's past as a time of pre-civilisation. For the colonised to assert their identity, to be able to speak back as equals to the colonial master, they must first reclaim their own past and history (Fanon, *The Wretched of the Earth*, 1961). In his later text, *Black Skin/White Masks* (1967), a psychoanalytic analysis of colonialism's impact on colonised and coloniser in the context of France's colonisation of Martinque, Fanon begins by stating that 'For the black man there is only one destiny. And it is white.' He goes on to say that 'the colonised is elevated above his jungle status in proportion to his adoption of the mother country's cultural standards'. Literature clearly plays a key role in cultural imperialism, and it becomes a potential site of cultural resistance as, in the aftermath of colonialism, the Empire indeed begins to write back. An important concept in postcolonialism is the doubling or instability of identity consequent on colonisation. The colonised subject is an inhabitant both of the pre-colonial nation and of the colonised country and the consequences of this double consciousness can be tracked through the literature produced in the colonial and postcolonial periods.

Initially, accepting of the superiority of the colonising culture, the colonial writer adopts (the usually European) literary style, structure and even substance; there is then a transition in which while the style and structure may still be European, the writer adapts the form to his or her own country's subject matter, beginning the process of cultural reclamation. Finally, the postcolonial writer becomes an adept and creates his or her own forms as well as asserting rights over content and implicitly over identity. The perception of fluidity, of doubling, of divided identity in colonial and postcolonial writing; its recognition of the instability of signification and its representation of often oppositional ideologies have encouraged postcolonial critics to adopt many of the theoretical approaches of poststructuralism and postmodernism. Perhaps the best-known early exponents of postcolonial criticism are Homi K. Bhabha, Gayatri Spivak and Henry Louis Gates Jr. While Bhabha and Spivak have tended to focus their interest on India and South Asia and Africa, Gates turned his attention to African-American literature, insisting that this always already-hybrid writing should be considered in the context of its culture of origin, not judged by imported or imposed cultural traditions. His theory is particularly relevant here, as there is a large body of African-American crime fiction, much of which, as Stephen Soitos has shown in *The Blues Detective* (1996), reveals African-American writers' conscious adoption, adaptation and finally adept subversion of the formulas of detective fiction.

While Soitos focuses on the early development of the African-American detective genre, he acknowledges its continuing existence in modern crime fiction. For example, African-American Walter Mosley's eleven novels featuring black detective Easy Rawlins (1990–2007) are consciously, as Soitos notes, set against the backdrop of black development in America, often referencing a particular and significant moment in that development: *A Little Yellow Dog* (1995) is set in 1964 and ends with the November assassination of President Kennedy that year; the action in *Little Scarlet* (2004) takes place during the Watts riots of 1965. Soitos draws attention to Mosley's reinterpretation of black double-consciousness and his representation of the black culture and spaces of Los Angeles and their place in African-American notions of identity. Crime fiction elsewhere has, as a genre, seems to have attracted relatively little attention from postcolonial criticism until recently; as the genre has spread across nations and cultures—colonising countries in which there have been no tradition of crime or detective fiction—so it has become a vehicle for writers to explore their own cultures' responses to this literary intruder. The notion of crime fiction as a colonising force works on two levels; the straightforward importation of the white, Western genre into colonial possessions as part of cultural imperialism—Arthur Conan Doyle's Sherlock Holmes stories were and are enormously popular in India—and the literary appropriation of a country and its inhabitants in crime fiction by writers from the colonising nations.

Examples of the latter kind of colonisation are, I suggest, H. R. F. Keating's Inspector Ghote series (26 novels, 1964–present). Inspector Ghote is a detective in the Mumbai police; Keating is white, British and did not even visit India until ten years after he began writing the novels. A similar approach is taken by Alexander McCall Smith, who enacts a double colonisation in setting his No. 1 Ladies' Detective Agency series in Botswana and by writing an African female detective, Precious Ramotswe (12 novels, 1998–present). By contrast to Keating, McCall was at least born and spent his early life in Rhodesia and worked briefly in Botswana, but has spent most of his adult life in Scotland. Doyle's Sherlock Holmes stories initially contributed to the wider imperative of cultural imperialism in India, but latterly they offer an insight into the 'adopt, adapt, adept' patterns of postcolonial literature, as Suchitra Mathur discusses in 'Holmes's Indian Reincarnation: A Study in Postcolonial Transposition' (in *Postcolonial Postmortems*, eds Christine Matzke and Susanne Mühleisen, 2006). Mathur's analysis of what she calls 'a Bengali avatar of Sherlock Holmes' in the 'Feluda' detective stories of Satyajit Ray shows how, despite Ray's open declaration of Holmes and his cases as the inspiration for the series and its detective, nicknamed 'Feluda', who 'frequently invokes Holmes as his model', the series is, finally, wholly Indian. The stories are, she asserts, not in the mimicry mode represented in V. S. Naipaul's *The Mimic Men* (1967), where the postcolonial subject simply—and disastrously—mimics his or her colonial masters. Rather, the 'Feluda' stories seem to respond to Bhabha's notion of mimicry, with its potential for subversion ('Of Mimicry and Man', in *The Location of Culture*, 1994) and finally, Mathur argues, the stories are in the 'writing back' mode discussed by Ashcroft *et al.*

As Priya Joshi has noted in *In Another Country: Colonialism, Culture and the English Novel in India* (2003), it was not only Doyle's Holmes stories that were imported into India as part of the colonial project, but other literature, including the sensation and detective fiction of Wilkie Collins. In Collins's *The Moonstone* (1868), called by T. S. Eliot the 'first, the longest and the best of modern English detective novels', the nineteenth-century Indian reader could see him or herself reflected back through the lens of the British perception of Indianness. Collins's text introduces the colonial into its narrative via the Indian diamond that gives the text its name, through the three Brahmin priests who are charged with its recovery, and in its representation of Mr Murthwaite, the traveller and expert on all things Indian. It also obliquely addresses issues of hybridity in the figure of Ezra Jennings, product of what the text implies is a misalliance between East and West, a racial mix evident in his physical description: 'His complexion was of a gypsy darkness [...]. His nose presented the fine shape and modelling so often found among the ancient people of the East,' while his 'thick, closely curling hair' is a magpie black and white. Jennings's mixed race—his hybridity—has rendered him weak and sickly; his recourse to opium, a drug produced in the East, contributes to his early death. Hybridity is also explored in the dispute between police detective Sergeant Cuff and the Verinder's gardener over the benefits or otherwise of propagating roses by grafting.

The Moonstone is, however, complex and conflicted in its representation and use of the colonial motif. In the wake of the Indian Mutiny of 1857, public opinion supported the colonial regime in India and demonised the Indian population, as did much of the literature produced at the time, including Collins's collaborative article, 'The Perils of Certain English Prisoners' written with Charles Dickens and published in his journal, *Household Words*, in 1857. Collins's stance, eleven years later in *The Moonstone*, seems very different. Opening his narrative with a critical account of the British army's attack and capture of Seringapatam in 1799 and the murderous theft of the Indian diamond by Colonel John Herncastle, and closing it with the return of the jewel to its rightful place in India, can be read as Collins's negative commentary on the colonial enterprise and the plundering of colonial possessions. The theft, by a man, of the diamond from the Indian cabinet in Rachel's orientalised boudoir and the clue of the stain on the nightgown have been read, by Tamar Heller amongst others, as a coded reference to the theft of Rachel's virginity and hence as an allegory of imperial despoilment and domination (see Heller, *Dead Secrets: Wilkie Collins and the Female Gothic*, 1972). Equally, the narrative's emphasis on the English characters' financially motivated appreciation of and desire for the diamond can be read in postcolonial terms as questioning the imperial ethics which implied that colonisation was altruistic and offered nothing but benefits to the colonised.

The Brahmin priests are rendered positively and sympathetically throughout the narrative, but aspects of their racial stereotyping reveals the impossibility of a wholly positive representation of the other in a colonial culture. Finally, Collins's critique of colonialism is subverted rather than being subversive. In positive mode, the Indians' murder of the perpetrator of the diamond's theft, Godfrey Ablewhite, is made to seem justified. They are shown being kind to a small English boy that they have rescued from the streets, and their religious devotion is clear; in crossing the oceans to rescue the diamond they have knowingly forfeited their caste in the service of their god. Conversely, the diamond brings out the worst in the English characters, leading to the disruption of the Verinder household, the falling-out of Rachel and Franklin Blake, contributing to the deaths of Lady Verinder and Rosanna and causing the murder of Godfrey Ablewhite. Peace and stability is only restored once the Moonstone has returned to its rightful home, suggesting that India too should be restored to its rightful, pre-colonial independent status in order to ensure in turn the stability of Britain itself.

But the text ultimately cannot escape the taint of racism and the hierarchical binaries of Said's *Orientalism*: the fear of reverse colonisation is all too apparent in the way the Indian jewel is shown negatively to 'infect' the English individuals with whom it comes into contact. On a more literal level, Mr Murthwaite articulates the coloniser's fear of the colonised in his description of the Indians as valuing the diamond that decorates their implicitly pagan idol above human life; they are, he says, possessed of 'the ferocity of tigers'. Betteredge's fear and suspicion of the Indians, despite his disclaimers, perhaps represent the anxieties and opinions of the ordinary Englishman. He describes them as 'snakey', is disturbed by the 'hocus pocus' of their use of clairvoyance and is quick to blame them for the theft of the diamond, even in the absence of any evidence to that effect. The Indians, the text seems to suggest, may be noble in some aspects, but it is a nobility founded in heathenish, potentially violent and barbarous characteristics that are entirely alien to and lesser than sound English values. The struggle between the two discourses—colonial critique and colonial stereotyping and hence validation of imperialism—is acted out on the pages of Collins's text.

The nineteenth-century novel is a rich source for what might be called an empirical approach to postcolonial criticism, in which the texts discussed are produced by the coloniser in the moment of imperial colonial expansion and so enact its actuality. In terms of the literature of the twentieth and twenty-first centuries, postcolonialism has been more concerned with the 'writing back' of the colonised countries themselves, whether from a historical or a contemporary perspective, and tends to take a more theoretical approach, informed by poststructuralism and postmodernism. Crime fiction's engagement with and *exposé* of colonialism in the nineteenth century—Sherlock Holmes's cases often feature an aspect of evil emanating from the Orient—has evolved into a postcolonial concern with colonialism's effects on present nations and nationalities: as with cultural materialism and feminism, postcolonialism engages with the politics of identity.

See also   *Contexts*: Crime and Criminality, Race, Colour, Creed; *Texts*: Hard-Boiled Crime Fiction, Historical Crime Fiction.

Further reading

Ashcroft, Bill, Gareth Griffiths and Helen Tiffin, *The Empire Writes Back: Theory and Practice in Postcolonial Literatures* (London: Routledge, 2002).

Matzke, Christine and Susanne Mühleisen (eds), *Postcolonial Postmortems: Crime Fiction from a Transcultural Perspective* (Amsterdam: Rodopi, 2006).

Mukherjee, Upamanyu Pablo, *Crime and Empire: The Colony in Nineteenth-Century Fictions of Crime* (Oxford: Oxford University Press, 2003).

Pearson, Nels and Marc Singer (eds), *Detective Fiction in a Postcolonial and Transnational World* (Farnham: Ashgate, 2009).

Said, Edward, *Culture and Imperialism* (London: Vintage, 1994).

Said, Edward, *Orientalism: Western Conceptions of the Orient* (Harmondsworth: Penguin, 1995).

Soitos, Stephen F., *The Blues Detective: A Study of African American Detective Fiction* (Amherst: University of Massachusetts Press, 1996).

Postmodernism

Identity politics are in some ways made possible by and are allied with postmodernism, while crime and detective fiction, with its focus on the deviant and the marginalised, has long been a locus of identity politics—feminist detectives, gay detectives, lesbian detectives, black detectives, ethnic detectives or disabled detectives—and the genre offers a discursive space in which these various marginal identities can speak back to the centre. But what is postmodernism and how does it make this possible? Heavily influenced by poststructuralism, postmodernism is notoriously hard to define, the very notions of 'concepts' or 'vocabulary' or indeed 'definition' all being reliant on language, which postmodernism declares to be undecidable, unstable and fluid. Initially, the term (possibly first coined in this sense by Arnold Toynbee in 1947) was used historically to suggest a moment when the certainties of modernity gave way to the twentieth century's sense of confusion and crisis in the aftermath of two world wars and mass genocide. Postmodernism called into question existing moral values and belief systems and this is still a concern of the postmodernism of the twenty-first century.

But postmodernism also has a relationship with modernism, that is, the artistic, literary and cultural movements developed between the late 1800s and early- to-mid 1900s—circa 1890–1939. As the 'post' suggests, postmodernism comes after modernism, although it shares with it some of the concepts and approaches of modernism. Postmodernism, though, resists this historical positioning. Rather, it sees itself as a critical apparatus through which cultures and societies can be explored, a stance that permits a level of ahistoricism and reveals the possibility of the postmodern in the past. However, it is the past that the postmodern also rejects, specifically the Enlightenment valorisation of reason and rationality as the keys to knowledge and progress. The mass conflicts of the first part of the twentieth century and particularly the Holocaust seemed beyond the power of Enlightenment reason to explain, and various movements and modes of thought, such as politics, philosophy and cultural theory, sought alternative ways of explaining what was an increasingly complex and fragmented world.

Postmodernism has evolved in the context of this complexity and fragmentation, and against and in response to the perceived decline in social, moral and political values and the concomitant erosion of belief in such values. Crucial to the perceived decline of (Western) Enlightenment values was the rise and rise of mass culture and of mass communication in the capitalist and consumerist West. Mass culture in particular, aided and abetted by mass communications, denies individualism and postmodernism seeks way of recognising individuality, albeit in fluid and unfixed forms. Many of the key concepts of postmodernism in its modern sense were articulated by Jean-François Lyotard in *The Postmodern Condition* (1979). Central to Lyotard's argument was what he called an 'incredulity toward metanarratives', where 'metanarrative' means the overarching or grand narratives of thought systems or theories: religion, philosophy, liberal humanism, Marxism, even history itself. Such thought systems suggested that it was possible objectively and rationally to observe and interpret and order human behaviour: postmodernism not only denies this is possible but also suggests that it is positively dangerous. Reliance on grand narratives, or what Andrew Bennett and Nicholas Royle call 'the belief in a transcendent explanatory system' (*An Introduction to Literature, Criticism and Theory*, 2009), for example religion, makes possible terror, oppression and persecution. Even a grand narrative such as Marxism, which focuses its attention on the class struggle in a way that seems positive, fails in that by looking only at class differences, it ignores or subsumes into itself other forms of social oppression—racial, sexual and gendered.

The alternative to grand narratives, for Lyotard, and a way of explaining and existing in the (post)modern world, is little narratives; local and independent explanations of individual events, explanations that are plural, local and contingent and which respond to a fragmented, unstable, dispersed world. Literature too is a grand narrative, one that is laden with value judgements and which traditionally distinguished between high and low (or popular) forms such as crime fiction. Postmodernism rejects such value judgements and indeed celebrates and draws upon the creative possibilities of genre fiction. Crime fiction can incorporate or represent small narratives and also is a vehicle for literary postmodernism. Notions of fragmentation and instability are central to poststructuralist thought, and postmodernism draws on poststructuralism's theorising of linguistic and discursive instability. Admitting that language lacks stable referentiality, that it is arbitrary in its relationship to what it represents or describes, means that thought systems, which are articulated in language, cannot possibly claim to represent reality—even reality, in poststructuralism and postmodernism, is brought into question.

What has been called the 'crisis of representation', the lack of connection between the reality and its representation, has, according to postmodernist critic Frederic Jameson, been exacerbated by the mass media that is very much part of the modern, or postmodern, world. Mass media give credibility and potentially authority to representations of different versions of reality. Jean Baudrillard developed this concept further, suggesting in *The Gulf War Did Not Take Place* (1991, trans. 1995) not that the war did not happen but that what the world saw was the media representation of it and that this was not necessarily, or could not objectively be, the reality. Theorising of this kind seems to take postmodernism into a bleak world of surface with no depth, of simulation without reality, where social, moral and cultural values are emptied of meaning. Jameson, though, argues positively for postmodernism as being perfectly fitted to the postmodern world in terms of culture, and as suggested above, the rejection of grand narratives has made possible a more open and liberal social and cultural climate, both for marginalised social constituencies and for non-canonical literature.

Postmodernism in crime fiction seems to take two forms. It either works ontologically, as in Brian McHale's definition (*Constructing Postmodernism*, 2001 (1992)), that is, the crime or detective narrative enacts postmodernism and foregrounds its mode of being, incorporating the tenets and concepts of postmodernism into its structure. Or, crime fiction draws on aspects of postmodernism such as the fluidity and fragmentation of identity, intertextuality, instability, deconstruction of grand narratives, and uses them in the interests of, for example, gender politics. Detective fiction is of particular interest to postmodern writers who follow the ontological route because, as McHale notes, conventional detective fiction's epistemological format—the plot of a detective story is organised as a search for knowledge as in 'whodunnit'—makes it ideal for revealing the instabilities inherent in the very notion that there is a who—or epistomologically a what, a reality—to be found. In creating his definition of 'postmodernism', McHale refers to Dick Higgins's term 'postcognitive art' which defines itself though 'postcognitive questions': 'Which world is this? What is to be done in it? Which of my selves will do it?' (cited in *Constructing Postmodernism*); for 'postcognitive', substitute 'postmodern'. McHale goes on to offer an analysis of Umberto Eco's *The Name of the Rose* (1983) in the context of postmodernism. By contrast to critics such as John Scaggs or Charles Rzepka, who class *The Name of the Rose* as postmodern detective fiction, McHale concludes that Eco's novel is instead a challenge to the enterprise of distinguishing between postmodernism and modernism.

Postmodern aspects of *The Name of the Rose* include its playful intertextual references to and parody of Arthur Conan Doyle's Sherlock Holmes and Watson in *The Hound of the Baskervilles* (1901); Eco's 'detective' is William Baskerville, while the detective assistant/Watson figure is Adso, the narrator of the text. But where Sherlock Holmes's rational detection leads inevitably to its epistemological conclusion, Baskerville's 'detection' is rational, but clues and evidence are misinterpreted and the solution achieved by accident rather that intent. Eco's work is also an example of postmodern historical fiction, or what Linda Hutcheon calls historiographic metafiction (*The Poetics of Postmodernism: History, Theory, Fiction*, 1988), that is, fiction which draws attention to its incorporation of history into its imagined world. *The Name of the Rose* shares similarities with other postmodern writing that uses the crime or more usually the detective fiction format: as Rzepka notes, postmodern detective fiction subverts the normative patterns of the genre, replacing certainty, rationality and comforting closure with 'open-ended plot, undecidable conflicts in testimony, indecipherable clues and impenetrable motives'. These tropes can be seen in the crime-inflected writing of Jorge Luis Borges, Alain Robbe-Grillet, Vladimir Nabokov, Friedrich Dürrenmatt and Thomas Pynchon. The fiction of Edgar Allan Poe, whose three Dupin tales are widely considered to be the first detective stories proper, inspired Borges and is central to the deliberately postmodern detective novels of Paul Auster's *New York Trilogy* (1985–6).

The other way that postmodernism subversively utilises the structures and conventions of crime fiction is allied to identity politics in order to destabilise those grand narratives that lead to marginalisation and oppression. Feminism has found this approach useful as in Barbara Wilson's *Gaudi Afternoon* (1990). The title pays homage to Dorothy L. Sayers's conventional detective novel, *Gaudy Night* (1935), but in Wilson's text conventions are cast aside, particularly in terms of gender, as characters fluidly move across and between genders in what the cover 'blurb' calls 'cross-dressing confusion' but which responds to the postmodern theory that gender is performative, as discussed by Judith Butler among others. Where the 'ontological' postmodern detective novel has not generally been attractive to the huge mainstream audience for crime fiction, with the exceptions of Eco's *The Name of the Rose* and Auster's *Trilogy* perhaps, Wilson's lighter, if politically aware text, was sufficiently popular for her to write a further three novels in the series (*Trouble in Transylvania*, 1993; *Death of a Much-Travelled Woman*, 1998 and *The Case of the Orphaned Bassoonists*, 2000). More forceful in its destabilisation of gender roles and expectations is Helen Zahavi's *Dirty Weekend* (1991). Here, the heroine, Bella, whose very name signifies not only beauty but war, turns the tables on the men who have been oppressing and sexually abusing her and embarks on a series of murders. The parodic yet often poetic style marks the narrative as postmodern, as does the text's self-referentiality. Bella kills her victims in a number of ways, all of which see her appropriating what might more usually be seen as masculine methods of murder, represented with graphic violence but written in a light, humorous tone. In the final murder, where she kills a serial sex killer, Bella stabs her victim in a scene that is deliberately described in sexualised terms: 'They sounded like a courting couple, grunting in the shadows of the pier.'

Parody and pastiche are evident in the humorous quasi-postmodern detective novels of Douglas Adams (*Dirk Gently's Holistic Detective Agency*, 1987 and *The Long Dark Teatime of the Soul*, 1988). With detective methods that draw on chaos theory, the Dirk Gently narratives destabilise the normative detective fiction model, but keep the comforting closure; if they have a political message it is very modest, but perhaps speaks to alternate therapies and points to ecological issues. Welsh-born Malcolm Pryce's crime series, set in Aberystwyth, Wales (six to date, 2001–11), and featuring private detective Louie Knight, is a deliberate parody of Raymond Chandler's crime fiction. Nonetheless, woven into the pastiche of hard-boiled detection and concealed by the humour are identity politics, as Pryce mercilessly exposes past and present constructions of Welshness and implicitly interrogates Welsh identity. Despite the apparent complexities of postmodernism and the potential it seems to offer for disengagement with the world and lived experience, its use in relation to crime fiction seems rather to draw it back into engagement if not with the real, with real issues.

See also   *Contexts*: Detectives and Detection, Race, Colour and Creed; *Texts*: Feminist Crime Fiction, Hard-boiled Crime Fiction, Historical Crime Fiction.

Further reading

Appignanesi, Richard and Chris Garratt, *Postmodernism for Beginners* (London: Icon Books, 1995).

Butler, Judith, *Gender Trouble: Feminism and the Subversion of Identity* (New York: Routledge, 1999 (1990)).

Docherty, Thomas (ed.), *Postmodernism: A Reader* (New York: Columbia University, 1993).

Hutcheon, Linda, *A Poetics of Postmodernism: History, Theory, Fiction* (New York: Routledge, 1988).

Jameson, Fredric, *Postmodernism, or, the Cultural Logic of Late Capitalism* (London: Verso, 1991).

Lyotard, Jean-François, *The Postmodern Condition: A Report on Knowledge*, Trans. Geoff Bennington and Brian Massumi (Manchester: Manchester University Press, 1984).

McHale, Brian, *Constructing Postmodernisim* (London and New York: Routledge, 2001 (1992)).

Chronology

1829	Sir Robert Peel founds the Metropolitan Police Force in London; first fully funded official police force in England
1830	Edward Bulwer Lytton, *Paul Clifford*
1832	First Reform Act
1834	Poor Law Amendment Act
1837–9	Charles Dickens, *Oliver Twist*
1838	Boston Police Department established (USA)
1841	Edgar Allan Poe, 'The Murders in the Rue Morgue'
1841	Catherine Crowe, *Susan Hopley, or, the Adventures of a Maid-Servant*
1842	Metropolitan Police Detective force established in London
1845	New York City Police established
1849	'Waters', 'Recollections of a Police Officer' series begins in *Chambers's Edinburgh Journal*
1850	Charles Dickens, 'A Detective Police Party' appears in *Household Words*
1850	National Detective Agency established by Allan Pinkerton in USA
1852–3	Charles Dickens, *Bleak House*
1856	Police forces now established across Britain
1857	Married Women's Property and Matrimonial Causes Act
1857	Indian Mutiny
1859	Charles Darwin, *On the Origin of Species*
1860	Wilkie Collins, *The Woman in White*
1861	Series of Acts sees the death penalty in England limited to murder, treason, espionage, arson in Royal dockyards and piracy with violence
1861	Ellen Wood, *East Lynne*
1861–5	American Civil War

1862	Mary Elizabeth Braddon, *Lady Audley's Secret*
1864	'Andrew Forrester Jnr', *The Female Detective*
1864	W. S. Hayward, *Revelations of a Female Detective*
1865	'Charles Felix', *The Notting Hill Mystery*
1865	'John B. Williams', ed., *Leaves from the Note-Book of a New York Detective*
1866	Émile Gaboriau, *L'Affaire Lerouge*
1867	'Seely Regester', *The Dead Letter* (USA)
1868	Capital Punishment Amendment Act ends public executions
1868	Wilkie Collins, *The Moonstone*
1870	Charles Dickens, *The Mystery of Edwin Drood* (unfinished)
1872	National Society for Women's Suffrage established (UK)
1874	Allan Pinkerton, *The Expressman and the Detective* (USA)
1878	Criminal Investigation Department (C.I.D) established in London
1878	Anna Katharine Green, *The Leavenworth Case* (USA)
1886	Fergus Hume, *The Mystery of a Hansom Cab* (Australia)
1886	Arthur Conan Doyle, *A Study in Scarlet* (published Christmas 1887)
1888	'Jack the Ripper' murders in London
1891	Arthur Conan Doyle, 'A Scandal in Bohemia', first Sherlock Holmes short story, published in *Strand Magazine*
1892	Arthur Conan Doyle, *The Adventures of Sherlock Holmes*
1894	Arthur Conan Doyle, *The Memoirs of Sherlock Holmes*
1894	Catherine Louisa Pirkis, *The Experiences of Loveday Brooke, Lady Detective*
1894	Arthur Morrison, *Martin Hewitt, Investigator*
1901	Death of Queen Victoria
1901	Arthur Conan Doyle, *The Hound of the Baskervilles*

1907	Maurice Leblanc, *Arsène Lupin: Gentleman-Cambrioleur* (trans. in 1909 as *The Exploits of Arsène Lupin*)
1907	Jacques Futrelle, *The Thinking Machine* (USA)
1907	R. Austin Freeman, *The Red Thumb-Mark* (Dr Thorndyke)
1908	Mary Roberts Rinehart, *The Circular Staircase* (USA)
1909	Carolyn Wells, *The Clue* (USA)
1910	Alice Wells appointed as the first woman police officer, Los Angeles
1910	Raymond Chandler becomes naturalised British subject
1911	G. K. Chesterton, *The Innocence of Father Brown*
1913	E. C. Bentley, *Trent's Last Case*
1914–18	World War I
1915	Edith Smith appointed as first woman police officer, London
1918	Women over thirty get the vote (UK)
1920	Agatha Christie, *The Mysterious Affair at Styles* (first appearance of Poirot)
1920	Prohibition Act bans alcohol (USA)
1920	Freeman Wills Crofts, *The Cask*
1920	H. C. Bailey, *Call Mr Fortune*
1923	Dorothy L. Sayers, *Whose Body?* (introduces Lord Peter Wimsey)
1925	Earl Derr Biggers, *The House without a Key* (first appearance of Charlie Chan)
1926	General Strike (UK)
1926	Agatha Christie, *The Murder of Roger Ackroyd*
1926	Agatha Christie's brief disappearance
1926	'S. S. Van Dine', *The Benson Murder Case* (first appearance of Philo Vance)
1928	Arthur Upfield, *The House of Cain* (first appearance of 'Boney', Australian indigenous detective)
1928	Patricia Wentworth, *Grey Mask* (first appearance of Miss Silver)
1928	All women over twenty-one get the vote (UK)

1929	The Wall Street Crash and the beginning of Great Depression
1929	Dashiell Hammett, *Red Harvest*
1929	'Ellery Queen', *The Roman Hat Mystery* (USA)
1929	W. R. Burnett, *Little Caesar* (USA)
1929	Margery Allingham, *The Crime at Black Dudley* (introduces Albert Campion)
1929	Gladys Mitchell, *Speedy Death* (introduces Beatrice Adela Lestrange Bradley, psychoanalyst detective)
1929	Josephine Tey (writing under the name Gordon Daviot), *The Man in the Queue* (first appearance of police detective Alan Grant)
1930	Agatha Christie, *Murder at the Vicarage* (first appearance of Miss Marple)
1931	'Francis Iles', *Malice Aforethought*
1931	Georges Simenon, *Pietr-le-Letton* (first police detective Maigret novel)
1932	Rudolph Fisher, *The Conjure Man Dies* (first black detective, USA)
1933	Prohibition repealed (USA)
1933	John Dickson Carr, *Hag's Nook* (introduces Dr Gideon Fell)
1933	Erle Stanley Garner, *The Case of the Velvet Claws* (introduces Perry Mason)
1934	James M. Cain, *The Postman Always Rings Twice*
1934	Ngaio Marsh, *A Man Lay Dead* (introduces Inspector Alleyn)
1939–45	World War II
1939	Raymond Chandler, *The Big Sleep* (first Philip Marlowe novel)
1939	'James Hadley Chase', *No Orchids for Miss Blandish*
1941	USA enters World War II
1942	Jorge Luis Borges, 'Death and the Compass'
1943	Margaret Millar, *Wall of Eyes* (USA)

1945	Atom bombs dropped on Nagasaki and Hiroshima
1945	Lawrence Treat, *V as in Victim* (first police procedural, USA)
1946	National Health Service Act passed (UK)
1947	Mickey Spillane, *I, the Jury* (introduces Mike Hammer, USA)
1947	India gain Independence
1949	'Ross Macdonald', *Moving Target* (introduces Lew Archer, USA)
1949	Patricia Highsmith, *Strangers on a Train* (USA)
1950	Joseph McCarthy begins anti-Communist movement, USA
1950	Julian Symons, *The Thirty-First of February*
1950–53	Korean War
1951	Maurice Procter, *The Chief Inspector's Statement* (first British police procedural)
1952	Hillary Waugh, *Last Seen Wearing...* (USA)
1952	Jim Thompson, *The Killer Inside Me* (USA)
1953	Coronation of Queen Elizabeth II
1955	'J. J. Marric', *Gideon's Day* (introduces Commander George Gideon of Scotland Yard)
1955	Patricia Highsmith, *The Talented Mr Ripley* (introduces Tom Ripley)
1955–75	Vietnam War
1956	'Ed McBain', *Cop Hater* (first 87th Precinct novel, USA)
1959	Chester Himes, *For the Love of Imabelle* (black police detective series, USA)
1961	Berlin Wall built
1962	P. D. James, *Cover Her Face* (introduces Inspector Adam Dalgleish)
1962	Cuban Missile Crisis
1963	Assassination of President John F. Kennedy (USA)
1964	'Amanda Cross', *In the Last Analysis* (first Kate Fansler novel)

1964	Civil Rights Acts outlaw racial and sexual discrimination in USA
1964	H. R. F. Keating, *The Perfect Murder* (introduces Mumbai police Inspector Ghote)
1964	Ruth Rendell, *From Doon with Death* (introduces police Inspector Wexford)
1964	Harry Kemelman, *Friday the Rabbi Slept Late* (Jewish-American detection)
1965	Anti-police riots in Watts, Los Angeles
1965	John Ball, *In the Heat of the Night* (first modern black detective novel)
1965	Murder (Abolition of Death Penalty) Act suspends death sentence for murder (UK)
1966	'Don Holliday', *The Man from C. A. M. P.* (early gay crime fiction)
1967	Decriminalisation of homosexuality (UK)
1968	Dorothy Uhnak, *The Bait* (begins female police detective series, USA)
1968	Martin Luther King assassinated (USA)
1969	Abolition of death penalty for murder confirmed (UK)
1970	Joseph Hansen, *Fadeout* (introduces gay serial detective Dave Brandstetter, USA)
1970	Reginald Hill, *A Clubbable Woman* (first in the Dalziel and Pascoe series, UK)
1970	Tony Hillerman, *The Blessing Way* (first in Native American Navajo detective series)
1971	James McLure, *The Steam Pig* (first in series of South African detective series)
1972	Capital Punishment suspended in USA
1972	P. D. James, *An Unsuitable Job for a Woman*
1972	'Bloody Sunday', Northern Ireland Troubles
1974	'Watergate Scandal' in USA forces resignation of President Nixon

1975   Sex Discrimination and Equal Pay Acts (UK)

1976   Capital punishment restored in some states (USA)

1976   Race Relation Act (UK)

1977   Ellis Peters, *A Morbid Taste for Bones* (introduces medieval detective Brother Cadfael)

1977   Marcia Muller, *Edwin of the Iron Shoes* (introduces feminist detective Sharon McCone, USA)

1980   Liza Cody, *Dupe* (introduces feminist detective Anna Lee, UK)

1981   Beginning of the 'AIDS Crisis'

1982   Falkland War

1982   Sara Paretsky, *Indemnity Only* (introduces feminist detective V. I. Warshawski, USA)

1983   Umberto Eco, *The Name of the Rose* (originally published in Italian, 1980)

1984   Barbara Wilson, *Murder in the Collective* (first mainstream lesbian crime novel, USA)

1984   Katherine V. Forrest, *Amateur City* (introduces lesbian police detective Kate Delafield, USA)

1985   Paul Auster, *City of Glass* (USA)

1985   Sue Grafton, *A is for Alibi* (introduces feminist detective Kinsey Millhone, USA)

1986   Michael Nava, *The Little Death* (introduces Hispanic gay serial detective Henry Rios, USA)

1987   Val McDermid, *Report for Murder* (introduces lesbian amateur serial detective Lindsay Gordon, UK)

1987   Ian Rankin, *Knots and Crosses* (introduces serial police detective John Rebus, Scotland)

1988   Thomas Harris, *The Silence of the Lambs*

1989   End of Cold War

1989   Mike Philips, *Blood Rights* (introduces black British detective Sam Dean)

1989   Fall of Berlin Wall

1990	Patricia Cornwell, *Post-Mortem* (introduces forensic investigator Kay Scarpetta, USA)
1990	Reunification of Germany
1990	Walter Mosley, *Devil in a Blue Dress* (introduces African-American detective Easy Rawlins)
1991	Gulf War
1991	End of Soviet Union
1991	End of apartheid in South Africa
1992	BarbaraNeely, *Blanche on the Lam* (introduces African-American female detective)
1992	Dana Stabenow, *A Cold Day for Murder* (features a Native American Alaskan police detective)
1993	Maastricht Treaty and establishment of European Union
1995	Val McDermid, *The Mermaids Singing* (introduces serial detectives forensic psychologist Tony Hill and Inspector Carol Jordan, UK)
1997	Henning Mankell, *Faceless Killers* (introduces depressive Swedish police detective Kurt Wallander)
1999	Deon Meyer, *Dead Before Dying* (first in series of Afrikaans police detective fiction)
1999	David Peace, *Nineteen Seventy-Four* (first novel in the Red Riding Quartet, based on the Yorkshire Ripper Murders of 1975-82)
2001	11th September terrorist attack on World Trade Centre, New York
2001	American and British forces embark on Afghan War
2003	Military invasion of Iraq
2005	Hurricane causes massive floods in New Orleans
2007	James Lee Burke, *The Tin Roof Blowdown* (USA crime fiction as a vehicle for a response to New Orleans Flood disaster)

2007   Minette Walters, *The Chameleon's Shadow* (UK crime fiction as a vehicle for exploring the after effects of the Iraq War)

2007   David Peace, *Tokyo Year Zero* (first novel in Tokyo Trilogy, based on Japanese serial killer Yoshio Kodaira)

2007   Ian Rankin, *Exit Music* (final Inspector Rebus novel)

2008   Stieg Larsson, *The Girl with the Dragon Tattoo* (first volume in the Millenium Trilogy)

2011   Henning Mankell, *The Troubled Man* (final Wallander novel, in which the detective appears to be losing his memory)

Index